KB055009

주한미군지위협정(SOFA)

노무 · 시설 분과위원회 1

주한미군지위협정(SOFA)

노무 · 시설 분과위원회 1

한국학술정보

| 머리말

미국은 오래전부터 우리나라 외교에 있어서 가장 긴밀하고 실질적인 우호 · 협력관계를 맺어 온 나라다. 6 · 25전쟁 정전 협정이 체결된 후 북한의 재침을 막기 위한 대책으로서 1953년 11월 한미 상호방위조약이 체결되었다. 이는 미군이 한국에 주둔하는 법적 근거였고, 그렇게 주둔하게 된 미군의 시설, 구역, 사업, 용역, 출입국, 통관과 관세, 재판권 등 포괄적인 법적 지위를 규정하는 것이 바로 주한미군지위협정(SOFA)이다. 그러나 이와 관련한 협상은 계속된 난항을 겪으며 한미 상호방위조약이 체결로부터 10년이 훌쩍 넘은 1967년이 돼서야 정식 발효에 이를 수 있었다. 그럼에도 당시 미군 범죄에 대한 한국의 재판권은 심한 제약을 받았으며, 1980년대 후반 민주화 운동과 함께 미군 범죄 문제가 사회적 이슈로 떠오르자 협정을 개정해야 한다는 목소리가 커지게 되었다. 이에 1991년 2월 주한미군지위협정 1차 개정이 진행되었고, 이후에도 여러 사건이 발생하며 2001년 4월 2차 개정이 진행되어 현재에 이르고 있다.

본 총서는 외교부에서 작성하여 최근 공개한 주한미군지위협정(SOFA) 관련 자료를 담고 있다. 1953년 한미 상호방위조약 체결 이후부터 1967년 발효가 이뤄지기까지의 자료와 더불어, 이후 한미 합동위원회을 비롯해 민 · 형사재판권, 시설, 노무, 교통 등 각 분과위원회의 회의록과 운영 자료, 한국인 고용인 문제와 관련한 자료, 기타 관련 분쟁 자료 등을 포함해 총 42권으로 구성되었다. 전체 분량은 약 2만 2천여 쪽에 이른다.

2024년 3월

한국학술정보(주)

| 일러두기

· 본 총서에 실린 자료는 2022년 4월과 2023년 4월에 각각 공개한 외교문서 4,827권, 76만 여 쪽 가운데 일부를 발췌한 것이다.

· 각 권의 제목과 순서는 공개된 원본을 최대한 반영하였으나, 주제에 따라 일부는 적절히 변경하였다.

· 원본 자료는 A4 판형에 맞게 축소하거나 원본 비율을 유지한 채 A4 페이지 안에 삽입하였다. 또한 현재 시점에선 공개되지 않아 '공란'이란 표기만 있는 페이지 역시 그대로 실었다.

· 외교부가 공개한 문서 각 권의 첫 페이지에는 '정리 보존 문서 목록'이란 이름으로 기록물 종류, 일자, 명칭, 간단한 내용 등의 정보가 수록되어 있으며, 이를 기준으로 0001번부터 번호가 매겨져 있다. 이는 삭제하지 않고 총서에 그대로 수록하였다.

· 보고서 내용에 관한 더 자세한 정보가 필요하다면, 외교부가 온라인상에 제공하는 『대한민국 외교사료요약집』 1991년과 1992년 자료를 참조할 수 있다.

| 차례

정/리/보/존/문/서/목/록					
기록물종류	문서-일반공문서철	등록번호	15655 3651	등록일자	2000-02-18
분류번호	729.414	국가코드		주제	
문서철명	SOFA - 한. 미국 합동위원회 노무분과 위원회, 1969-71				
생산과	북미2과	생산년도	1969 - 1971	보존기간	영구
담당과(그룹)	미주	안보	서가번호	--	
참조분류					
권차명					
내용목차	1. 1969년도 2. 1970년도 3. 1971년도				

마/이/크/로/필/름/사/항				
촬영연도	*롤 번호	화일 번호	후레임 번호	보관함 번호
2007-09-17	Re-07-08	8	1-182	

결 번

넘버링 오류

결 번

넘버링 오류

1. 1969

4

These minutes are considered as official documents pertaining to both Governments and will not be released without mutual agreement.

JOINT COMMITTEE
UNDER
THE REPUBLIC OF KOREA AND THE UNITED STATES
STATUS OF FORCES AGREEMENT

16 October 1969

MEMORANDUM FOR: Chairmen, Labor Subcommittee

SUBJECT: Procedures for Implementation of Paragraph 4(b) of SOFA Article XVII

1. The first sentence of paragraph 4(b) of Article XVII provides as follows:

"Employees or any employee organization shall have the right of further collective action in the event a labor dispute is not resolved by the foregoing procedures except in cases where the Joint Committee determines such action seriously hampers military operations of the United States armed forces for the joint defense of the Republic of Korea."

2. The foregoing provisions of the Status of Forces Agreement were designed to insure the continued availability of essential categories of Korean employees of the United States armed forces in the mutual defense of the Republic of Korea.

3. Your recommendations on the procedures to implement the above provisions of paragraph 4(b) of SOFA Article XVII are to be transmitted to the Joint Committee as soon as possible.

ROBERT N. SMITH
Lieutenant General
United States Air Force
United States Representative

YOON HA JONG
Republic of Korea
Representative

2246

43rd JC (Incl 13)
23 Oct 69

5

한 미 합 동 위 원 회

1969. 10. 16.

수 신 노무분과위원회 위원장

제 목 한미협정 제17조 4항(나)에 대한 시행절차

1. 한미협정 제17조 4항(나) 첫문장은 다음과 같다.
(고용원 또는 고용원 단체는 노동쟁의가 전기 절차에 의하여 해결되지 아니하는 경우에는 계속 단체행동권을 가진다.
다만, 합동위원회가 이러한 행동이 대한민국의 공동방위를 위한 합중국 군대의 군사작전을 심히 방해한다고 결정하는 경우에는 제외한다.)

2. 상기조항은 대한민국의 공동방위를 위하여 주한미군 한국인 종업원중 중요직책에 있는 자의 계속 근무를 확실히 함을 뜻한다.

3. 한미협정 제17조 4항(나)중 상기조문에 대한 시행절차에 관한 건의를 조속한 시일내에 한미합동위원회에 상전하시기 바랍니다. 끝.

서 명	서 명
미측 대표	한국측 대표

6

기 안 용 지

분류기호 문서번호		(전화번호 :		전결규정 조 항 전결사항
처리기한		기 안 자	결 재 자	
시행일자				
보존년한				

보 조 기 관	

협 조	

경 유 수 신 참 조	시행	통 제		발 송		정 서	

제 목 SOFA 노무분과 회의 개최

제 43차 SOFA 회의 (69. 10. 23.) 에서 하달된 과제 " SOFA 제 17조 4항 (b)에 대한 시행절차에 관한 건의" 에 관하여 한미 합동 노무분과위원회 회의를 가까운 시일내에 개최코자 하오니 귀견을 회시하여 주시기 바랍니다. 끝

공통서식 1-2-1 (갑)
1967. 4. 4. 승인

(18절지 2급인쇄용지 70g/m²)
(조 달 청 50,000매 인쇄)

한미협정 제17조

1. 본조에 있어서

가. "고용주"라 함은 합중국군대(비세출자금기관을 포함한다) 및 제15조 1항에 규정된 자를 말한다.

나. "고용원"이라 함은 고용주가 고용한 군속이나 제15조에 규정된 계약자의 고용원(미합중국에 거주하는 자)이 아닌 민간인을 말한다. 다만 (1) 한국노무단("케이. 에스. 씨")의 구성원 및 (2) 합중국군대의 구성원 군속 또는 그들의 가족의 개인이 고용한 가사사용인은 제외된다. 이러한 고용원은 대한민국국민이어야 한다.

2. 고용주는 그들의 인원을 모집하고 고용하며 관리할 수 있다. 대한민국 정부의 모집사무기관은 가능한 한 이용된다.

고용주가 고용원을 직접 모집하는 경우에는 고용주는 노동행정상 필요한 적절한 정보를 대한민국 노동청에 제공한다.

3. 본조의 규정과 합중국군대의 군사상 필요에 배치되지 아니하는 한도 내에서 합중국군대가 그들의 고용원을 위하여 설정한 고용조건, 보상 및 노사관계는 대한민국의 노동법령의 제규정에 따라야 한다.

4. 가. 고용주와 고용원이나 승인된 고용원단체간의 쟁의로서 합중국군대의 불평처리 또는 노동관계 절차를 통하여 해결될 수 없는 것은 대한민국 노동법령중 단체행동에 관한 규정을 고려하여 다음과 같이 해결되어야 한다.

1) 쟁의는 조정을 위하여 대한민국 노동청에 회부되어야 한다.

2) 그 쟁의가 전기(1)에 규정된 절차에 의하여 해결되지 아니하는 경우에는 그 문제는 합동위원회에 회부되며 또한 합동위원회는 새로운 조정에 노력하고저 그가 지정하는 특별위원회에 그 문제을 회부할 수 있다.

8

3) 그 쟁의가 전기에 절차에 의하여 해결되지 아니한 경우에는 합동위원회는 신속한 절차가 뒤따를 것이라는 확증하에 그 쟁의를 해결한다. 합동위원회의 결정은 구속을 가진다.

4) 어느 승인된 고용원단체 또는 고용원이 어느 쟁의에 대한 합동위원회의 결정에 불복하거나 또는 해결절차의 진행중 정상적인 업무요건을 방해하는 행동에 종사함은 전기 단체의 승인철회 및 그 고용원의 해고에 대한 정당한 사유로 간주한다.

5) 고용원단체나 고용원은 쟁의가 전기(2)에 규정된 합동위원회에 회부된 후 적어도 70일의 기간이 경과되지 아니하는 한 정상적인 업무요건을 해방하는 어떠한 행동에도 종사하여서는 아니된다.

나) 고용원 또는 고용원단체는 노동쟁의가 전기절차에 의하여 해결되지 아니하는 경우에는 계속 단체행동권을 가진다. 다만 합동위원회가 이러한 행동이 대한민국의 공동방위를 위한 합중국군대의 군사작전을 심히 방해한다고 결정하는 경우에는 제외된다. 합동위원회에서 이문제에 관하여 합의에 도달할 수 없을 경우에는 그문제는 대한민국정부의 관계관과 아메리카합중국외교사절간의 토의를 통한 재검토의 대상이 될 수 있다.

다) 본조의 적용은 전쟁적대행위 또는 전쟁이나 적대행위가 절박한 상태와 같은 국가비상시에는 합중국군당국과의 협의하에 대한민국 정부가 취하는 비상조치에 따라 제한된다.

5. 가) 대한민국이 노동력을 배정할 경우에는 합중국 군대는 대한민국 국군이 갖이는 것보다 불리하니 아니한 배정특권이 부여되어야 한다.

나) 전쟁, 적대행위 또는 전쟁이나 적대행위가 절박한 상태와 같은 국가 비상시에는 합중국군대의 임무에 긴요한 기술을 습득한 고용원은 합중국군대의 요청에따라 상호 협의를 통하여 대한민국 병력이나 또는 기타 강제복무가 연기되어야 한다.

9

합중국군대는 긴요하다고 인정되는 고용원의 명단을 대한민국에 사전에 제공하여야 한다.

6. 군속은 그들의 임용과 고용조건에 관하여 대한민국의 제법령에 따르지 아니한다.

10

주한 미군 전시 후방 필수요원 요청서

부 대 명	현재원	필수요원	경비요원	필수요원 계
미 8군 사령부	723	150 - 170		150 - 170
군사 고문단	308	50 - 60		50 - 60
미 8군 칙활대	431	75 - 90		75 - 90
미 4 유도탄 사령부	286	35 - 40		35 - 40
미 38 대공 포병여단	35	10 - 15		10 - 15
미 1 군단	939	100 - 115	80	180 - 195
미 2 사단	1,951	110 - 130	30	120 - 135
미 7 사단	1,435	90 - 105	30	120 - 135
미 8군 군수기지 사령부/ 미 8군 후방 사령부	6,463	1,800 - 2,050	410	2,210 - 2,460
군사 합동 보안 지역	65	5 - 10		5 - 10
미 8군 지원 사령부	8,270	2,450 - 2,800	500	2,950 - 3,300
미 65 의무단	368	60 - 70		60 - 70
8군외 육군 부대	1,206	260 - 300	50	310 - 350
주한 미 공군	3,573	500 - 580	100	600 - 680
주한 미 해군	249	55 - 65		55 - 65
고여처	2,914	350 - 400		350 - 400
초청 청부 기관	5,614	1,700 - 1,900	80	1,780 - 1,980
합계:	34,830	7,800 - 8,900	1,300	9,100 - 10,200

별첨 2

2. 1970

12

기 안 용 지

분류기호 문서번호	미이723-	(전화번호)	전결규정 조 항 전결사항
처리기한		기 안 자	결 재 자
시행일자		북미 2과 박양천	
보존년한	3 년	70.5.22.	국 장
보조기관	과 장		
협 조			
경 유 수 신 참 조	노동청장 노정국장	발송 434 1970. 5. 23	정 서
제 목	면담 요록 송부		

1. 70. 5. 22. 10:00 덱스탐 주한 미공사는 윤석헌 외무차관을 외무부로 방문하고 면담한바 아래와 같은 귀청 관련 사항이 있었기에 송부하오니 참고하시기 바랍니다.

덱스탐 공사 : "미국대사관은 현재 대사관과 대사관 직원 관사 지역의 경비를 위하여 봉신회사와 경비계약을 체결하고 있는바, 봉신의 서비스에 불만이 많으므로 금년 6.30. 계약이 만료되는 기회에 이를 해제하고 U.S. Mission Club (비영리 단체)와 계약을 하기로 결정하였다. 본건 계약에 의하여 고용되고 있는 사람은 98 명인데 그중 책임자격인 4명 (Area

공통서식 1—2—1 (갑)
1967. 4. 4. 승인

(18절지 2급인쇄용지 70g/m²)
(조 달 청) (500,000매 인쇄)

13

Commander 1명, Inspector 2명, Investigator 1명)을 제외한 94 명의 경비원은 그대로 U.S. Mission Club이 인수하여 계속 고용할 것이며, 보수는 종전보다 10 % 인상되고 또한 1개월 반의 급료에 해당되는 퇴직금을 지불하기로 되어 있다. 후 봉신회사 측에서 계약 해제에 대한 불만 때문에 어떠한 물의를 일으킬 가능성이 있으나 실정이 이러함으로 오해없기 바란다.

이정보가 봉신측에 사전에 알려지면 매우 곤난한 사태가 일어날수 있으므로 비밀을 지켜주기 바란다"

끝.

발번문서 로 재분류(70. 12. 31)

14

외 무 부

미이 723 - 70. 5. 23.

수신 : 노동청장

참조 : 노정국장

제목 : 면담 요록 송부.

1. 70. 5. 22. 10:00 데스땀 주한 미공사는 윤석헌 외무차관을 외무부로 방문하고 면담한바 아래와 같은 귀청 관련 사항이 있었기에 송부하오니 참고하시기 바랍니다.

데스땀 공사 : "미국대사관은 현재 대사관과 대사관 직원 관사 지역의 경비를 위하여 봉신회사와 경비 계약을 체결하고 있는바, 봉신의 서비스에 불만이 많으므로 금년 6. 30. 계약이 만료되는 기회에 이를 해제하고 U.S. Mission Club (비영리 단체)와 계약을 하기로 결정하였다. 본건 계약에 의하여 고용되고 있는 사람은 98 명인데 그중 책임자격인 4 명 (Area Commander 1명, Inspector 2명, Investigator 1명)을 제외한 94명의 경비원은 그대로 U.S. Mission Club 이 인수하여 계속 고용할 것이며, 보수는 종전보다 10 %

15

인상되고 또한 1개월 반의 급료에 해당되는 퇴직금을 지불하기로 되어 있다. 혹 봉신회사측에서 계약 해제에 대한 불만 때문에 어떠한 물의를 일으킬 가능성이 있으나 실정이 이러함으로 오해없기 바란다.

이정보가 봉신측에 사전에 알녀지면 매우 곤난한 사태가 일어날수 있으므로 비밀을 지켜주기 바란다.

끝.

외 구 부 장 관

16

Key SOFA Negotiations on Article XVII, Para 4 (b)

68th Meeting - Paragraph 5 - US Presentation

69th Meeting - Paragraph 7 - ROK Presentation

71st Meeting - Paragraph 18-20 - US Presentation

75th Meeting - Paragraph 6-9 - ROK Presentation

78th Meeting - Paragraph 1-9 - US Presentation

79th Meeting - Paragraphs 1-6 - ROK Presentation

80th Meeting - Paragraphs 1-3; 21-24 - US Presentation

81st Meeting - Paragraphs 28-29 - ROK Presentation

82nd Meeting - Paragraph 14, d - Agreement

117

that it was necessary to be specific because the Korean negotiators would have great difficulty in explaining to the National Assembly the meaning of the words "basic management needs of the United States armed forces." Mr. Habib reiterated that while the U.S. armed forces were prepared to commit themselves to conform to Korean laws and practices, it was necessary to include a qualification which provided for unforeseeable contingencies. Mr. Chang replied that the qualification suggested by the U.S. negotiators was much too general, for it could be applied to any situation. Mr. Habib replied that implementation of the Agreement must be left to the Joint Committee. If the ROK authorities believed that the U.S. armed forces were not carrying out their commitment, they retained the right to raise the question in the Joint Committee.

19. The meeting was adjourned after the U.S. negotiators indicated that they would give careful study to the Korean proposals.

- 75 -

18

68TH MEETING(December 23, 1964)

1. The discussion was begun by Mr. Habib, who stated that since the Labor Article was last discussed (at the 65th negotiating meeting), the U.S. authorities had carefully reviewed the status of this article, including the views expressed by the Korean negotiators at the formal and informal negotiating sessions during the past ten months. The U.S. negotiators were now prepared to table significant modifications of the U.S. draft, which were designed to be responsive to the views of the Korean authorities to the maximum extent consistent with the essential requirements of the U.S. armed forces in carrying out their important defense mission in Korea. For the convenience of the negotiators, the U.S. negotiators were tabling a fresh draft of the entire article, in which the modifications being proposed at this meeting were underlined. The U.S. negotiators hoped that early agreement could be reached on the article on the basis of the modified U.S. positions now being tabled. Mr. Habib then tabled the revised U.S. draft and said he would explain the modifications.

2. With regard to Paragraph 2, Mr. Habib explained, the U.S. negotiators propoe revision of the first sentence, divifing it into two seperate sentences. The first sentence of the revision is a simple and direct statement that the U.S. armed forces, as the employers of over 33,000 Korean personnel, may recruit, employ, and administer such personnel. The new second sentence had been included in response to Korean desires and explicitly states that the recruitment services of the Government of the Republic of Korea will be utilized insofar as is practicable. The third sentence in the revised paragraph was included earlier at the request of the ROK authorities. The U.S. negotiators believe that this revised Paragraph 2 fully takes into account the views of the ROK authorities, as expressed at both formal and informal negotiating meetings, and therefore should be acceptable to the Korean negotiators.

3. With regard to Paragraph 3, Mr. Habib said the U.S. negotiators were proposing a modification of this paragraph in response to the objections expressed by the Korean negotiators at the 65th meeting to the phrase "the basic management needs" in the earlier

19

U.S. draft. This phrase was to be to broad and ambiguous and therefore it has been replaced by the words "the military requirements." The U.S. armed forces, which are in Korea pursuant to the U.S.-ROK Mutual Defense Treaty of November 17, 1954, are here to assist in the defense of the Republic of Korea. The U.S. armed forces have tried to be good employers to their Korean employees and expect to continue to conform generally to ROK labor laws and practices. Under the present conditions of armistice, the U.S. armed forces must be prepared to meet any military contingencies, including developments which are unforeseeable. The U.S. negotiators believe that the ROK authorities, including the National Assembly, recognize the realities of the military situation in Korea and will be prepared, therefore, to agree that the words "the military requirements" are necessary in this context in Paragraph 3.

4. Mr. Habib recalled that the ROK negotiators had expressed a strong desire to append an Agreed Minute to the Labor Article which would establish procedures for the settlement of labor disputes which cannot be settled internally by the U.S. armed forces. In resp-

20

onse to this desire, the modified U.S. draft contained a new Agreed Minute 5, along the lines proposed by the Korean negotiators at the 65th negotiating meeting. This ne Agreed Minute would provide for a three-stage procedure for settling any labor dispute which cannot be settled internally by the U.S. armed forces. The first step would be to refer the dispute to the ROK Office of Labor Affairs, Ministry of Health and Social Affairs, for conciliation. If the dispute cannot be settled through the conciliation efforts of the Office of Labor Affairs, the Minute would provide that the dispute may then be referred to the Joint Committee. At that time, the Joint Committee might refer the matter to a labor sub-committee or to a specially designated committee for further fact-finding, review, and conciliation efforts. If the dispute cannot be settled by the procedures outlined above, the proposed Agreed Minute provides that the Joint Committee will resolve the dispute and its decisions shall be binding. The U.S. Government believes that the ROK and U.S. authorities should be able to resolve any labor dispute through these procedures.

5. Mr. Habib pointed out that if the disputes

- 79 -

21

machinery is to be effective, every settlement must be adhered to. Therefore, the proposed Agreed Minute stipulates that neither an employee organization nor employees shall engage in any practice disruptive of normal work requirements while the settlement procedures are in progress. This is a normal characteristic of conciliation procedures. The U.S. negotiators believed that agreement had already been reached that the decisions of the Joint Committee in the settlement of disputes must be binding. Therefore, failure of any recognized employee organization or employee to abide by decisions of the Joint Committee in the settlement of disputes should be considered to be just cause for withdrawal of recognition of that employee organization and/or the dischage of that employee. It is the firm view of the U.S. Government, Mr. Habib continued, that the Korean employees of the U.S. armed forces, like the American civilian employees of those forces and the civilian employees of the ROK armed forces, are a vital factor in the defense of the Republic of Korea. In this regard, such employees are considered to be in a comparable position to the civilian employees of the ROK armed forces and the American civilian employees of the U.S. armed forces. It is the intention of the U.S. armed forces to do everything possible to promote and maintain good employer-employee relations with their Korean employees and, in cooperation with the ROK Government, as provided in Agreed Minute 5, to resolve labor disputes which cannot be settled internally.

6. Mr. Habib pointed out that the revised draft also contained a revised Agreed Minute #2. The first sentence of the Minute, identical with that in the previous version, would make clear that the undertaking of the U.S. armed forces to conform to Korean labor laws, customs, and practices does not imply any waiver of the immunities of the U.S. Government under international law. ROK Government authorities have indicated agreement with this principle. The second sentence would stipulate that the U.S. Government may terminate employment at any time that the continuation of such employment is inconsistent with the military requirements of the U.S. armed forces. As the U.S. negotiators had previously explained, the military requirements of the U.S. armed forces make it necessary for them to have this authority in order to in-

sure that essential defense and security requirements can be met.

7. Mr. Habib concluded his presentation of the revised U.S. draft by saying that the U.S. negotiators believe the Korean negotiators will find the revisions generally responsive to their views and consistent with joint U.S.-ROK defense requirements. The U.S. negotiators believe that the revised U.S. draft of the Labor Article would aid materially in maintaining and enhancing the effective employer-employee relations which currently exist between the U.S. armed forces and their Korean employees. The U.S. negotiators have tabled this draft with the full understanding that the U.S. armed forces highly value their Korean employees and the existing relationship with them. The U.S. armed forces believe that they have established a good reputation as an employee and are determined to continue their efforts to promote the well-being and training of their employees.

8. Mr. Chang replied that the Korean negotiators would comment in detail on the revised U.S. draft at a subsequent meeting. However, he wished to make some preliminary comments. The U.S. negotiators had said

that their revised draft contained significant modifications. The Korean negotiators recognized this to be the case with respect to the substitution of "military requirements" for "basic management needs." However, the Korean negotiators expressed the view that the addition of a new sentence to Agreed Minute #2 would be unnecessary duplication of the revised Paragraph 3 and that the U.S. negotiators had retreated to a rigid position in the application of the phrase "military requirements". With regard to Agreed Minute #5, the revised draft appeared to be not significantly different from the views expressed by the U.S. negotiators at the 65th meeting.

9. Mr. Chang stated that even the phrase "military requirements" was still ambiguous and too broad. The Korean negotiators would like to have it defined or explained. Mr. Habib replied that "military requirements" were those requirements which contributed to the accomplishment of the military mission of the U.S. armed forces. The interpretation of the phrase in individual cases would be up to the Joint Committee, which therefore would have a very important role to play in this regard. Mr. Chang replied that the Korean negotiators believed interpretation of the

phrase should not be left to the Joint Committee. The phrase should be defined before reaching agreement on this Article.

10. Mr. Habib replied that if a specific case arose presumably it would be referred to the Joint Committee. Basically, the U.S. armed forces are in Korea to fulfil certain defense and security requirements. Whatever actions they perform should be consistent with those requirements. The same rule should apply to the Korean employees of thos forces. Paragraph 3 of the U.S. draf states "to the extent not inconsistent with...the military requirements."

11. Mr Chang replied that the Korean negotiators viewed the revision of Paragraph 3 as the only major change proposed by the U.S. negotiators. However, the phrase "military requirements" was ambiguous. If this revised draft were agreed to, the Korean employees of the U.S. armed forces would be denied rights which the now enjoy. The purpose of the Labor Article is to safguard their rights. Therefore, the Korean negotiators called on the U.S. negotiators to take into consideration the rights which the Korean employees presently enjoy and the comments of the Korean negotiators.

12. Mr. Habib replied that the U.S. negotiators

doubted very much that this language would deny the rights of the Korean employees. This was not the intent nor did the language have this meaning. The remarks of the Korean negotiators called into question the sincerity of the U.S. negotiators with regard to the other portions of the article. This paragraph had been carefully drafted with the military mission of the U.S. armed forces in mind. The Korean negotiators were raising unjustified questions and finding differences where they did not exist.

13. Mr. Chang replied that the Korean negotiators did not mean to question the sincerity of the U.S. negotiators. The introduction of the phrase "military requirements" was the major modification proposed by the U.S. negotiators. If the Korean negotiators accepted the U.S. revised draft, the privileges presently enjoyed by the Korean employees of the U.S. armed forces would diminished.

14. When asked to explain how the privileges would be diminished, Mr. Chang replied that subparagraph (d) of Agreed Minute #5 would eliminate the right of the employees to strike. Mr. Habib replied that the provisions of subparagraph (d) were normal procedures which

27

were provided for in ROK labor laws. Mr. Chang said that the ROK law provided that disruptive practices were not allowed for a specific number of days. However, argument concerning a labor dispute could drag on and on in the Joint Committee.

15. Mr. Reed stated that it was his understanding that the ROK law provided that during mediation and arbitration procedures, there was no right to strike, even after the 20-day and 30-day cooling-off periods. Mr. Chang replied that if conciliation failed, the righ to strike after a certain number of days existed. Mr. Reed pointed out that the concept of a limited period was not contained in the U.S. draft/ Article 7 of the ROK Labor Disputes Act provides that there shall be no disruptive action unless mediation or arbitration efforts fail. The procedures proposed by the U.S. negotiators were intended to lead to the settlement of disputes. The U.S. negotiators did not believe that any strike would be justified if these procedures were followed.

16. Mr. Chang replied that the Korean negotiators would study the U.S. proposals. The meeting was then adjourned with the understanding that the Korean negotiators would call the next meeting.

69TH MEETING(January 25, 1965)

1. Opening the meeting, Mr. Chang recalled that the Labor Article had been discussed during the past ten months at eight negotiating meetings. The Korean negotiators believe that considerable progress has been made toward agreement on certain points. The Korean negotiators appreciated the endeavors of the U.S. negotiators in contributing to that progress and particularly in proposing modifications at the previous meeting.

2. Mr. Chang stated that the Korean negotiators had reviewed the revised U.S. draft and had carefully considered the views expressed by the U.S. negotiators when they tabled that draft. As the Korean negotiators had clearly stated in the past, the Korean position is that the rights and privileges currently enjoyed by Korean employees of the U.S. armed forces should be improved through the conclusion of the Status of Forces Agreement. However, the Korean negotiators do not intend to be inflexible in negotiating this article. Rather, they are prepared to compromise, at least to the extent that the Korean employees can continue to have the rights and privileges which they are presently enjoying.

3. With this basic position and these requirements in mind, Mr. Chang continued, the Korean negotiators had made most significant modifications in the Korean draft. He then tabled a revision of the Korean draft, noting that the revised portions were underlined. Mr. Chang stated that he would explain the revisions, paragraph by paragraph, and at the same time would comment on the U.S. revised draft.

4. With regard to paragraph 1, Mr. Chang said the Korean position remains the same but the new draft had been designed to streamline the text. Excluded from the text were the phrase "the contractors", "the Korean Service Corps", and "a domestic employed by an individual member of the U.S. Armed Forces". As for the contractors, Mr. Chang pointed out that the standing position of the Korean negotiators, as had been clearly stated during discussion of the Contractors Article, is that the terms and conditions of employment of the Korean employees by invited contractors shall be governed by the applicable Korean labor legislation. As regards the Korean Service Corps, the U.S. negotiators would recall that the Korean negotiators had already proposed that this subject not be raised within the framework of the SOFA negotiations. The phrase relat-

ing to a domestic employed by an individual member of the U.S. armed forces, civilian component, or dependent thereof, had been deleted because a domestic is not covered by the Korean labor laws.

5. Mr. Chang stated that the Korean negotiators were now prepared to accept the language of Paragraph 2 of the revised U.S. draft, with a minor change of wording.

6. Turning to Paragraph 3, Mr. Chang noted that there had been no substantial difference of opinion with regard to the principle that the conditions of employment should conform with those laid down by Korean labor legislation. At previous negotiating sessions, the Korean negotiators had expressed the view that the implication of the phrase "military requirements", as well as that of the phrase "basic needs" which it replaced, was ambiguous and too broad. In that regard, Mr. Habib had stated that the interpretation of the phrase in individual cases would be referred to the Joint Committee. With these views in mind, the Korean negotiators were now proposing this revised draft of Paragraph 3 and a new Agreed Minute #4. The revised portion of Paragraph 3 reads "except as may otherwise

31

be mutually agreed" in place of the phrase "to the extent not inconsistent with the provisions of this Article or the military requirements of the United States Armed Forces." The proposed Agreed Minute #4, which meets the substance of the U.S. requirements in principle, reads as follows:

"4. In case where it is impossible for the employers to conform, on account of the military requirements of the United States Armed Forces, with the Korean labor legislation under the provisions of Paragraph 3, the matter shall in advance be referred to the Joint Committee for mutual agreement.

"The Republic of Korea will give due consideration to the military requirements of the United States Armed Forces."

Mr. Chang stated that the revised draft which he had just read had been designed to meet fully the requirements of the U.S. negotiators. In their sincere effort to reach agreement on this article, the Korean negotiators now accepted the phrase "the military requirements of the United States Armed Forces". Under the provisions of the revised draft, the Korean negotiators clearly recognize the possibility of deviation by the

U.S. authorities from Korean labor legislation on the grounds of "military requirements." The Korean negotiators were further proposing that such U.S. deviation should be referred to the Joint Committee for mutual agreement. They believed the U.S. negotiators would have no objection to this proposal.

7. With regard to Paragraph 4 of the U.S. draft, Mr. Chang said that the Korean negotiators were of the opinion that the provisions of subparagraph (a) relating to the right to strike, organization of labor unions, etc., were covered by Paragraph 3 of the revised Korean draft, which stipulates that employer-employee relations must conform with the existing Korean labor legislation. The Korean negotiators believed that subparagraph (a) was unnecessary duplication and therefore they proposed its deletion from this article. They were prepared to accept subparagraph (b) of the U.S. draft with a minor change of wording. This appeared as Paragraph 4 of the revised Korean draft.

8. With regard to Paragraph 5, Mr. Chang stated that the Korean negotiators accepted subparagraph (a) of the U.S. revised draft, substituting "allocation

privileges" for "employment privileges". They believed the change to be readily understandable from a logical point of view. With regard to subparagraph (b), Mr. Chang stated that no eligible Korean youth can be exempted from his military service, for it is the solemn duty of all youths under the provisions of the Constitution to serve in the armed forces. However, some may be granted deferment, not exemption, from their military service under very special circumstances in accordance with the Korean draft law. This law provide that "exemption" is granted only to those who are disabled or crippled. Therefore, the Korean negotiators propose the adoption of sub-paragraph (b), as amended in the revised Korean draft.

9. Mr. Chang said the Korean negotiators accept Paragraph 6 of the revised U.S. draft.

10. Turning to the Agreed Minutes, Mr. Chang noted that Agreed Minute #1 of the U.S. draft had been deleted from the Korean revised draft. The deletion was self-explanatory in the light of the Korean position regarding Paragraph 1.

11. Mr. Chang said tha Korean negotiators agreed to the first sentence of Agreed Minute #2 of the U.S.

draft, which appears as Agreed Minute #1 of the revised Korean draft. But, he continued, the Korean negotiators are firmly against inclusion of the second sentence. At the previous meeting, the Korean negotiators had expressed the view that this sentence constituted unnecessary duplication of Paragraph 3 of the revised U.S. draft. In this connection, they believed that Agreed Minute #4 of the revised Korean draft would provide proper procedures.

12. Mr. Chang noted that Agreed Minutes #2 and #3 were identical with Agreed Minutes #3 and #4 of the U.S. revised draft.

13. Mr. Chang stated that full explanation of Agreed Minute #4 had been included in the explanation given of Paragraph 3.

14. Turning to Agreed Minute #5, which would establish procedures for the settlement of labor disputes, which cannot be settled through the use of existing procedures of the U.S. armed forces, Mr. Chang stated that the Korean negotiators were now ready to agree in principle to the adoption of a three-stage procedure for the settlement of disputes, as proposed by the U.S. negotiators at the 68th meeting. However,

they thought subparagraph (b) of the revised U.S. draft was unnecessarily complicated in providing for reference of a dispute to the Joint Committee and then to a special committee designated by the Joint Committee, for subparagraph (c) provides for reference once again to the Joint Committee. In order to simplify those steps, the Korean negotiators were proposing that the Joint Committee designate a special committee to which a labor dispute would be referred before reference to the Joint Committee. They had modified subparagraph (b) in their revised draft and hoped that the U.S. negotiators would agree. With regard to the third step in the settlement process, the Korean negotiators had no objection to the revised U.S. draft.

15. With regard to subparagraph (d), relating to the prohibition of acts of dispute during the settlement procedures, Mr. Chang stated that the Korean negotiators maintained their position that the Korean employees may conduct acts of dispute in accordance with the spirit of the Korean laws while no practice disruptive of normal work requirements should be permitted in violation of the cooling-off period set forth in the relevant Korean labor legislation. The

Korean negotiators cannot accept any provision that precludes the exercise of fundamental rights of laborers for an indefinite period. However, the Korean negotiators do not maintain that the employees should be able to engage in disruptive practices at any time they feel like it. Therefore, the Korean negotiators proposed subparagraph (d) of their revised draft and subparagraph (e) which is almost identical with subparagraph (d) of the U.S. draft. The Korean negotiators hoped that the U.S. negotiators would find their proposals acceptable. They had tried their best to meet the U.S. requirements and urging the U.S. negotiators to study the revised Korean draft carefully and respond at an early date.

16. Mr. Habib replied that the U.S. negotiators would study the Korean draft and comment on it at a later meeting. At present, they would like to ask a few questions in order to clarify the Korean position.

17. With regard to Agreed Minute #1, the Korean negotiators had said that it was equivalent to Agreed Minute #2 of the U.S. draft. This was not the case, however, as the Korean draft contained the language

37

"to conform with those laid down by the legislation of the Republic of Korea" while the U.S. draft reads "to conform to Korean labor laws, customs, and practices." The U.S. negotiators failed to understand what the language of the Korean draft meant. Mr. Chang replied that the Korean negotiators understood that the basic intention of the U.S. negotiators is that the U.S. authorities will not conform with decisions of the Korean courts or labor committees. The Korean negotiators believed that customs and practices are not related to court decisions or to Korean law and therefore need not be mentioned. Mr. Habib remarked that the intent of the Korean negotiators appeared to be to exclude reference to customs and practice from the language of this Agreed Minute. Mr. Chang confirmed this and it was agreed to change the language of the Agreed Minute in the Korean draft to read: "to conform with the labor legislation of the Republic of Korea."

18. Mr. Reed inquired about the reference in Agreed Minute #5 subparagraph (d) of the revised Korean draft to Article 14 of the Korean Labor Dispute Law. Mr. Chang thereupon read Article 14, as

38

follows:

"Article 14. (Cooling Period). No act of dispute shall be conducted unless 20 days in the case of general enterprise and 30 days in the case of public utility after a lawful adjudication of the labor committee prescribed in Article 16 has been rendered."

There then followed a discussion as to whether subparagraph (d) of the Korean draft was consistent with Article 14 of the Labor Dispute Law. Mr. Chang confirmed that while Article 14 refers to a 30-day cooling off perid following adjudication by the labor committee, subparagraph (d) refers to a 30-day cooling off period following referral to the Office of Labor Affairs. Mr. Habib stated that the U.S. negotiators would study this question, as well as the rest of the revised Korean draft. The meeting was then adjourned.

71ST MEETING (February 26, 1965)

1. Mr. Habib stated that the U.S. negotiators would like to discuss the Labor Article, in order to exchange views on the recently tabled revised U.S. and ROK drafts and seek clarification and expression of the Korean positions on certain aspects of the new ROK draft. The U.S. negotiators propose to concentrate the discussion at this time mainly on questions of principle in which there appears to be a significant divergence of views between the two sides and to leave minor differences for later discussion and resolution.

2. Mr. Habib noted that Invited Contractors are included in the definition of "employers" in paragraph 1, while the ROK draft, by omission, excludes them from the definition of employers. Invited Contractors are American-based firms which are utilized to perform functions in Korea solely for the U.S. military forces. Although these functions could be performed directly by the U.S. military, the U.S. has found from experience that certain functions and work can be more effectively and efficiently performed under contract with Invited Contractors. American firms are utilized as Invited

Contractors only when technical or security considerations dictate, or when the materials or services required by United States standards are unavailable in Korea; otherwise, USFK utilizes Korean contractors. In the interests of uniformity and good labor relations, the U.S. negotiators consider it highly important that Invited Contractors are subject to the same obligations undertaken by the U.S. in the Labor Article. This can only be accomplished by including the "Invited Contractors" as employers by definition. The Invited Contractors-whose Korean employees are represented by the same union as other USFK employees - are thus obliged to adhere to wage scales, and grievance and disputes procedures established for employees working directly for an agency of the U.S. Government. This situation insures that every Korean, whether employed by a private American firm working for the USFK under contract or by an agency of the U.S. Government, receive similar rights and advantages. Such an arrangement is now in effect and is practical, since Invited Contractors are limited to working solely for the U.S. Government in Korea.

41

3. Mr. Chang stated that the ROK draft omitted Invited Contractors because the Koreans felt such employee should be differentiated from direct-hire employees of the U.S. military. The ROK negotiators felt Invited Contractors should be subject to Korean labor laws, just as Korean employees of other foreign business firms. Mr. Habib emphasized that the Invited Contractors operate in Korea for only one purpose - to assist in the defense of Korea - and therefore they are not like other foreign business firms. Mr. Chang agreed that this question deserves further consideration and he asked for information on the number of Invited Contractors and of their Korean employees. Mr. Habib replied that there are about 40 USFK Invited Contractors who employ about 5,000 Koreans. It was agreed that the U.S. negotiators would provide additional information about the role of the USFK Invited Contractors and their Korean employees, outside the meeting, and that the ROK negotiators would reconsider their position on this subject.

4. Mr. Habib also questioned the second sentence of the ROK para 1, which states: "Such civilian

personnel shall be nationals of Korea." Mr. Habib pointed out that the Labor Article provides the only authorization in the entire agreement for the U.S. to hire civilian employees. If this sentence in the ROK draft were accepted, it would render meaningless the definition of "Civilian Component" as being persons of U.S. nationality, agreed to on 19 March 1963 at the 17th meeting. Under this ROK language, all of USFK's civilian employees would have to be Korean. He indicated that he did not think this was their intention. The question of nationality of USFK employees is covered in previously agreed portions of the SOFA, i.e., Article 1, Definitions Article (paras (b) and the Agreed Minute) and in the Invited Contractors Article (para 1 and Agreed Minute 2). The reference to the nationality of USFK Korean employees in para 1 of the ROK draft appears to be in contradiction to these previously agreed portions of the SOFA. Mr. Chang indicated that the ROK negotiators understood the point being made by Mr. Habib, and indicated that they would reconsider the matter.

5. Mr. Habib pointed out that the U.S. draft

43

provides that the U.S. will conform to ROK labor laws, customs and practices "to the extent not inconsistent with the provisions of this Article or the military requirements of the USFK," while the ROK draft stipulates conformance to ROK labor legislation, "except as may otherwise be mutually agreed." With regard to the phrase in Para 3 of the U.S. draft, "To the extent not inconsistent with the provisions of this Article," the U.S. as a sovereign nation, cannot be subject to the jurisdiction of ROK labor courts. This fact had been recognized by the ROK negotiators, as reflected in Agreed Minute No. 1 of the revised ROK draft, which indicates the U.S. undertaking to conform with ROK labor laws "does not imply any waiver by the United States Government of its immunities under international law." This phrase in the U.S. draft of Para 3 is also directly related to the Agreed Minute No. 5, as proposed by both sides, which establishes joint ROK Government-U.S. Government procedures for resolving labor disputes between USFK and its Korean employees. These procedures were proposed by the U.S. to provide for fair and equitable ROK-US settlemen of such labor disputes, while not subjecting the U.S. Government to the ROK Labor Dispute Adjustment Law. On that basis, the phrase in Para 3 of the U.S. draft, "to the extent not inconsistent with the provisions of this Article," must be included in the Labor Article to be consistent with Agreed Minute No. 1 of the ROK draft, Agreed Minute No. 2 of the USFK draft, and Agreed Minute No. 5 of both the U.S. and ROK drafts. Mr. Chang indicated that the ROK negotiators would be prepared to reconsider the Korean position relating to inclusion of the phrase, "to the extent not inconsistent with the provisions of this Article."

6. Regarding the words, "military requirements" in para 3, Mr. Habib stated that both the U.S. and ROK sides agree to the propriety of Joint Committee review of any action contrary to ROK labor laws which is taken in connection with US-ROK defense requirements. However, the ROK draft which requires that non-conformance based on military requirements be mutually agreed upon in advance by the Joint Committee is too inflexible. As the ROK side knows, military requirements are not of such a nature as to always be foreseeable. The

fulfillment of the defense mission in Korea is made more difficult by the existing armistice situation, which requires the United States and the ROK Forces to be prepared at any time to meet any military contingency. In this uncertain environment, unforeseeab military requirements may necessitate immediate solution The provisions of the ROK draft could place the United States Forces in the untenable position of either delaying action until agreement was reached in the Joint Committee, possibly jeopardizing the mission, or taking immediate necessary action without approval of the Joint Committee, in violation of the agreement. Neither of these alternatives is acceptable. USFK must have authority to vary from the ROK labor laws when necessary to satisfy the military requirements, which are paramount. The failure to do so could seriously hamper military operations in an emergency.

7. Mr. Chang emphasized that the language of the U.S. draft would make it possible for the USFK to take any action in non-conformance with ROK labor laws without seeking agreement of ROK authorities. The ROK side considers this language too broad. The ROK

46

negotiators are not seeking an absolute commitment of U.S. conformity to ROK labor laws, but they desire the inclusion of the clause "except as may otherwise be mutually agreed." In any emergency situation short of hostilities, the ROK negotiators feel that there would be sufficient time for both sides to consult in the Joint Committee. In the event of hostilities, of course, such advance consultation may not be feasible or possible, and enforcement of the Article could be suspended.

8. Mr. Habib pointed out that this Article was being negotiated to cover all contingencies, to be effective in time of peace as well as at a time of national emergency. The ROK response has clarified the Korean position, and the U.S. negotiators will further consider this issue.

9. Mr. Habib pointed out that the U.S. draft of para 4 consists of two subparas, while the ROK draft includes only the second subpara, and that subpara is worded differently. Omitted from the ROK draft is the U.S. subpara which gives the USFK Korean employees the same right to strike as an employee

47

in a comparable position with the ROK Armed Forces, and which provides USFK employees the right to organize and join a Union "whose objectives are not inimical to the U.S. interests." Mr. Habib emphasized that the U.S. side considers this to be one of the most significant paragraphs in the Labor Article. Korean employees of USFK, like the ROK armed forces civilian employees, have a vital role in the effective defense of the Republic. ROK Ministry of National Defense and USFK Korean employees work in direct support of the same objective - the defense of the Republic. The Korean people, in developing their present constitutio wisely provided in Article 29 that public officials shall not be accorded the right to strike. This ROK Government position is the same as the U.S. Government position on the problem of the right of government workers to strike. We tabled the new Agreed Minute No. 5 on 23 December 1964 in order to provide effective machinery for full US-ROK cooperatio and close collaboration in equitably and fairly resolving labor disputes involving Korean employees. We believe it is in our mutual interests to provide effective means to resolve labor disputes without disruptive actions which could jeopardize the joint defense efforts.

10. Mr. Habib pointed out that the USFK currently maintains and will continue to "maintain procedures designed to assure the just and timely resolution of employee grievances." Such grievance procedures have been significantly refined and improved, and they are believed to be operating effectively to resolve employee grievances. Both sides understand that one party in a dispute cannot formally "insure" what the actions of the other party will be. Therefore, we believe that the U.S. language, i.e., "maintain procedures designed to assure" employees grievances is more realistic than the proposed ROK language that "Employers shall insure the just and timely resolution of employee grievances."

11. Mr. Chang indicated that the Korean negotiators would give further consideration to the point raised about variations in language regarding the resolution of employee grievances. With regard to the strike question, Mr. Chang emphasized that all laborers

are guaranteed the right of collective action under the ROK constitution and the ROK negotiators cannot agree to the proposed language of the U.S. draft.

12. Mr. Habib pointed out that the provisions of para 4(a) of the US draft are closely related to Agreed Minute No. 5. The fundamental difference in the two drafts of this Agreed Minute relates to whether or not USFK Korean employees or organized employee organizations can engage in practices disruptive of normal work requirements. The tabled U.S. draft of the Labor Article would conserve and expand the rights of the USFK employee, and provide the basis for sound employer-employee relationships as well as for joint ROK-US procedures for resolving labor disputes.

13. Mr. Habib emphasized that the procedures established by Agreed Minute No. 5 would insure that the interests and views of USFK Korean employees will be given full consideration and their rights protected. With regard to the reference in the ROK draft to utilizing procedures in Article 14 of the Labor Dispute Adjustment Law, it should be clearly understood that the US Government cannot be subject

to the provisions of this law. Every USFK Korean employee, at the time of employment signed an affidavit which states:

> "Any employee who engages in any strike against the Government of the United States or who is a member of an organization which asserts the right to strike against the Government shall be immediately removed from employment."

In addition, the labor union of the USFK Korean employees, the Foreign Organizations Korean Employees Union (FOKEU) pledged in 1961 as a basic requirement for USFK recognition that it "shall not assert the right of collective action (strike or slow down) of direct hire employees against the United States Government." This pledge was the basis on which the USFK agreed to recognize and cooperate with the union. The US Government is convinced that the best interests of both the ROK and US Government, as well as of USFK Korean employees, require that the SOFA provide for an equitably means of resolving labor disputes as provided in Agreed Minute No. 5. We firmly believe that granting USFK defense employees

- 109 -

51

the right to engage in disruptive activities would be contrary to joint US-ROK defense interests, as well as the best long-term interests of these employees. USFK employees are not ordinary employees, but are comparable in importance in the defense of the Republic to civilian defense employees working for the ROK Government, and we are not prepare to concede that they have the right to strike.

14. Mr.Chang reiterated the ROK objection to the no-strike provisions of the US draft, and indicate that the US side was misinterpreting Article 29 of the ROK Constitution. Both sides agreed they would review ROK legislation relating to this subject, and Mr. Chang indicated he would reply in more detail at an early meeting.

52

72ND MEETING(March 2, 1965)

1. Mr. Habib indicated that he would resume discussion of the Labor Article with paragraph 5, where the negotiators left off at the 71st meeting. He indicated that he would discuss only the most important points which required further explanation and elaboration.

2. Mr. Habib pointed out that Paragraph 5 of both drafts deals with important topic of the availability of the key USFK Korean employees for their assigned defense tasks in time of emergency. The U.S. draft of this paragraph states such employees "shall" be available to continue to perform their key roles in the Joint US-ROK defense effort. The ROK draft states only that essential USFK employees "may" be deferred.

3. Mr. Habib said that the comments of the ROK negotiators at our 71st negotiating session, as well as the proposed ROK draft of para. 5, indicate that ROK Government authorities apparently do not fully realize the important role that the Korean civilian employees of the United States Forces in

Korea play in the joint US-ROK defense of the Republic of Korea. It is true that during the years of the Korean War, the USFK Korean employees were used mainly in jobs requiring unskilled labor. But this situation has greatly changed in recent years and most USFK Korean employees are employed in important defense work essential to the security of the Republic of Korea. Less than 5 percent of the present USFK Korean employees are in the unskilled labor-pool category. The majority of USFK Korean employees are in responsible administrative, technical, industrial, or professional-type positions. Most USFK employees possess special training and a wide variety of skills and many of them hold vital position in the support and backup of the joint US-ROK defense effort.

4. Mr. Habib stated that both the U.S. and ROK drafts provide that lists of essential employees will be provided. The U.S. draft of this paragraph assures the U.S. and ROK defense planners that, in time of emergency, essential USFK employees shall be available to continue to perform their important roles in the

joint US-ROK defense effort. Effective defense planning requires that the USFK must be assured in advance that its essential Korean employees shall be available to continue their defense work in the event of a national emergency. If the ROK SOFA authorities can only agree that such essential employees "may" be deferred, the USFK cannot then make realistic plans that definitely count on the continued use of such employees in the joint US-ROK defense of Korea in an emergency.

5. The U.S. side emphasized that it is on the basis that such employees would be available in an emergency that the USFK has been promoting policies of upgrading its Korean employees into important defense positions and replacing third-state nationals and U.S. personnel with skilled Korean personnel. In view of the relative abundance of manpower in the ROK and the relatively modest demands on the ROK manpower pool by the USFK, we doubt the desire to deny USFK deferment of essential Korean workers in an emergency. If this should prove to be the case, however, the USFK might have to reconsider its policies of

- 113 -

55

expanding utilization of Korean nationals and of replacing third-state and U.S. nationals with Koreans in essential defense positions within the U.S. military establishment in Korea. Perhaps the explanation for the variation between the ROK and U.S. drafts can be found in the remarks of the Korean negotiators at the 71st meeting, that they felt in time of national emergency the provisions of the Labor Article might not be enforced. But Para. 5 is written to enable the US and ROK authorities to do sound, advanced planning for just such a national emergency. Therefore, USFK's employees must be available to continue to serve in their defense roles in any emergency which would threaten the security of the Republic of Korea.

6. At the 69th negotiating session, the Korean side stated that no eligible Korean youth can be exempted from his military service, for it is the solemn duty of all Korean youths to serve in the Armed forces. Mr. Habib emphasized that the US side agreed with these sentiments and does not intend to place on its list of essential employees to be

- 114 -

56

exempted or deferred, eligible Korean youths who have not yet served their basic term of military service. However, the USFK has many Korean employees who are veterans of the military service and who now occupy essential positions with the US forces. In a national emergency, the USFK must retain such essential Korean personnel. The USFK plans to give the Ministry of National Defense its lists of such personnel in advance, as indicated in the revised ROK draft. It is agreed that if the ROK military establishment, in reviewing the USFK lists against its own mobilization plans for an emergency, desires that individual reserve officers be subject to recall to key positions in the ROK military service, such arrangements can be worked out amicably by Korean and American authorities.

7. In summation, Mr. Habib indicated that both sides apparently were in agreement that lists of essential USFK employees should be prepared in adbance of an emergency. In addition, U.S side want assurances that once the lists are submitted, these essential employees will be available in times of

57

emergency. The US side would appreciate an explanation of the ROK position in light of the foregoing factors.

8. Mr. Chang noted that the US side indicated that less than five percent of the present USFK employees are in the unskilled labor-pool category. Therefore, almost 90 percent must be skilled or managerial. What is the approximate number who are considered essential and should be exempt from military service? The ROK draft clearly envisages the availability of these employees to the US forces in any emergency, even though the ROK draft uses the words "may be deferred." But the US draft clearly contradicts the spirit of the ROK Constitution The US-ROK differences are only differences in expression.

9. Mr. Chang continued that the ROK side cannot accept the word "exempt" as used in the US draft. Once the US list of essential Korean employees is submitted, there should be US-ROK consultations and agreement on the list, including the number, types, and skills of employees to be made available to the

US forces. Such agreement should be reached in advance, and then the ROK side would do its best to defer the required personnel.

10. Mr. Habib replied that Para. 5 provides the basis for effective advance planning for an emergency, and that the US must have assurances in advance that the US forces' essential Korean employees will be available in an emergency to continue in their important defense work. The US side will give the Korean side an estimate of the number of essential employees at a later meeting.

11. Turning to consideration of Agreed Minute No. 2, Mr. Habib noted that the first sentence of Agreed Minute No. 2 of the US draft, and Agreed Minute No. 1 of the ROK draft are essentially similar, with only minor differences in wording. The ROK draft does not include the second sentence of the US draft of this Agreed Minute, but the US negotiators consider it important to include the sentence which makes clear the right of the USFK to terminate employment of its employees. The USFK follows procedures to assure just and timely

- 117 -

59

resolution of employee grievances, and provides severance pay to terminated employees in accordance with Korean law, custom, and practice. We have every intention of continuing to be a good employer, but since the only reason for USFK being in Korea is to assist in the joint US-ROK defense effort, USFK must maintain its right to terminate employment in accordance with military requirements.

12. Mr. Habib pointed out that unless this sentence is included, the USFK has no clear-cut right anywhere in the agreement to terminate employment. We have a very carefully conceived labor program. We are going to continue to be a good employer. What is objectionable about this second sentence which the ROK draft omits?

13. Mr. Chang indicated that although we believ the USFK in principle may terminate employment whenever it wishes, we believe the USFK should conform to the relevant provisions of the ROK laws in such matters. This includes advance notification and showing due cause, etc. He pointed out that Article 27 of the ROK Labor Standards Law provides

that there can be no termination of employment without justifiable reason. The ROK side has provided - in paragraph 3 and the Agreed Minutes No. 4 - for cases in which it is impossible for the employers to conform to ROK laws because of military requirements.

14. Mr. Habib emphasized that paragraph 3 deals with conformity while Agreed Minute No. 2 deals with the right to terminate employment. The ROK negotiators were apparently confusing conditions of termination with the right to terminate. The former was covered in Para. 3, in which US armed forces pledged to conform with ROK labor laws, customs, and practices. It was emphasized that the right to terminate, as distinct from conditions of termination, should be spelled out in the agreement. Mr.Habib stated that the USFK will conform to ROK practices and customs relating to termination of employment, and if the ROK Government questions any USFK action in this regard, it can take it up with the Joint Committee.

15. Mr. Chang replied that the ROK Government is prepared to assure the US side of the right to

terminate for justifiable reasons. The ROK para. 3 gives the US enough authority to terminate. Mr. Chang indicated that the ROK side would study the US statements and reply at an early meeting.

73RD MEETING(April 20, 1965

1. Taking up the Labor Article, Mr. Habib tabled a revised draft draft of the entire article. He stated that the US negotiators were tabling this draft, in a spirit of compromise, in order to reach early full agreement on this article. As revised, the US draft would provide continued fair and equitable treatment for Korean employees of the US armed forces, as well as sound and just procedures for the resolution of labor grievances and disputes. Mr. Habib said he would discuss the changes in the draft on a paragraph by paragraph basis. The principal revisions related to Paragraphs 3,4,5 and their Agreed Minutes.

2. Paragraph 1 and related Agreed Minute #1 - In Paragraph 1, Mr. Habib said, the word "para-military" had been added to differentiate the paramilitary Korean Service Corps from the direct hire employees of the US armed forces covered by this article. The US armed forces plan to discuss the status of the Korean Service Corps, which is commanded by ROK Army officers on active duty and in reserve(and which has operated outside ROK labor

63

laws and courts) directly with authorities in the Ministry of National Defense. In order to expedite agreement regarding the language relative to domestic servants, the US negotiators had deleted the second sentence of the previous draft of Agreed Minute #1, subject to an understanding that the present situation with respect to domestics employed by individual members of the US armed forces and civilian component shall continue. As the Korean negotiators were aware, Mr. Habib continued, individual members of the United States armed forces, civilian component, and dependents hire and pay domestic servants directly, subject only to USFK security and health checks and general guidance. Applicable Korean laws would govern employment of such domestics.

3. Paragraph 2 - Mr. Habib noted that the US and Korean negotiators are in agreement regarding Paragraph 2, except for minor differences of wording. The US negotiators concurred in the Korean proposal to substitute the word "such" for the word "available in the second sentence, subject to Korean

understanding that we can not furnish information not available to us as part of our normal operating procedure. The US negotiators foresee no problems in supplying the information desired by the Korean authorities, as indicated in Paragraph 20 of the Agreed Joint Summary of the 46th negotiating meeting.

4. Paragraph 3 and related Agreed Minute #5 - Mr. Habib stated that the US negotiators believe that they are in essential agreement with the Korean negotiators regarding Paragraph 3, except for possible differences in interpretations of the phrase "military requirements". In order to be responsive to the Korean desire for review and consideration by the Joint Committee of situations in which the US armed forces cannot conform to the ROK labor legislation because of military requirements, the US negotiators were tabling a new Agreed Minute #5. The US negotiators believe, Mr. Habib continued, that the US armed forces only rarely, if ever, will not be able to conform to ROK labor legislation applicable under this Article,

65

except in emergency situations. The new Agreed Minute #5 would provide that when the US armed forces cannot conform to ROK labor legislation on account of military requirements, the matter shall be reported, in advance whenever possible, to the Joint Committee for its consideration and review. The US negotiators believe that the Agreed Minute demonstrates the good faith of the US armed forces, in pledging to conform to the ROK labor laws, customs, and practices, to the extent not inconsistent with the provisions of this article, and to agree to this type of Joint Committee consideration of possible situations in which military requirements may be at variance with ROK labor legislation. In this regard, the ROK negotiators had mentioned the possibility that in an emergency the provisions of the labor Article might be suspended. The US negotiators believe that the new US language is the best way to take care of unforeseeable situations in which military necessity may require non-conformance to ROK labor legislation.

5. Paragraph 4 - Mr. Habib stated that the

US negotiators were tabling a new Paragraph 4 which sets forth clearly the positive US commitments to be a good employer, pursuing enlightened policies and procedures relating to employer-employee relationships. Subparagraph (a) would provide that employers will maintain procedures designed to assure the just and timely resolution of employee grievances. Subparagraph (b) would provide the employees the right to organize and join a union. Under its terms, membership or non-membership in such groups would not be a factor in employment or in other actions affecting employees. Subparagraph (c) would assure recognized unions the right of consultation with US military authorities. Such labor-management consultations are currently an established part of the US armed forces' relations with the recognized union.

6. Subparagraph (d) of Paragraph 4, Mr. Habib continued, incorporates much of the previously tabled Agreed Minute #5, setting forth procedures for settling labor disputes which cannot be settled by use of established USFK procedures. These

- 125 -

67

procedures closely parallel the previously-tabled Korean proposals, and provide that disputes which cannot be settled by use of USFK procedures shall be referred to the ROK Office of Labor Affairs for conciliation. If a dispute cannot be settled by the Office of Labor Affairs, it would be referred to the Joint Committee, which might refer it to a Labor Sub-Committee or to a specially designated committee or take it under consideration directly. The Joint Committee would be the final arbiter of any such labor disputes. The US and Korean negotiators were in agreement that its decisions shall be binding upon employers, employees, and the union.

7. As stated in subparagraph (e) of Paragraph 4, Mr. Habib continued, the US negotiators firmly maintain that a Korean working for the US armed forces in the joint US-ROK defense effort shall be subject to the same legal provisions concerning strikes and other work stoppages as an employee in a comparable position in the employment of the armed forces of the Republic of Korea. Both

categories of Korean employees of our two governments are working directly in the defense of their country. The US negotiators believe firmly in the principle that our employees must be subject to the same ROK legal provisions with regard to strikes or work stoppages as comparable employees working for the ROK armed forces. This is a basic and unchanging US position, which is related directly to the effectiveness of the US armed forces in the defense of the Republic of Korea.

8. Paragraph 5 - Mr. Habib pointed out that Paragraph 5 of both drafts deals with the important topic of the availability of essential Korean employees of the US armed forces for their assigned defense tasks in time of emergency. The newly-tabled Paragraph 5 of the US draft had been patterned after the language of the Korean draft tabled at the 69th negotiating session. It is almost identical with the Korean Paragraph 5 except for the use of the word "shall" instead of "may" in subparagraph (b). The use of the word "shall" would assure US and Korean defense planners that in time of emergency,

essential employees of the US armed forces in Korea would be available to continue to perform their essential roles during the emergency. USFK requirements for Korean manpower, Mr. Habib continued, are very small in comparison to Korean manpower availabilities. On the other hand, the role of the US forces in a war emergency in the Republic of Korea would be of an extremely important and probably decisive nature. Their essential civilian employees are basic to the effectiveness of the US armed forces. Therefore, the US negotiators wished to emphasize that deferment of essential USFK personnel in advance must be provided for. This vital matter cannot be left to consideration and decision in time of emergency. There would be a great deal of paper work in listing and processing essential employees who would be deferred. This work must be accomplished to our mutual satisfaction before the emergency arises, if implementation is to be effective. The US negotiators believe that the details can be worked out in consultation between the US armed forces and officials of the Ministry of National Defense in advance, to the mutual satisfaction of both parties.

9. Mr. Habib noted that the Agreed Minutes in the new US draft had been renumbered so that they now appear in the same order as the paragraphs to which they refer.

10. Mr. Habib stated that the revised US draft was the result of many hours of discussion of this Article by both sides over the part 15 months. The US negotiators urged early acceptance of the revised draft by the Korean negotiators. The US negotiators believe that it fully protects the legitimate rights and interests of Korean employees of the US armed forces and, at the same time, is consistent with joint US-ROK defense requirements.

11. Mr. Chang replied that the Korean negotiators appreciated the compromising spirit in which the US negotiators had presented their revised draft in the hope for full agreement as soon as possible. The Korean negotiators would carefully consider the US draft and respond in a

- 129 -

71

few days. However, the Korean negotiators believed that considerable differences still existed between the positions of the two sides. They wished, therefore, to make some preliminary comments to indicate the basic Korean position.

12. With regard to Paragraph 1, Mr. Chang said the Korean negotiators still wished to settle the question of the Korean Service Corps outside the framework of the SOFA negotiations, since the US negotiators had insisted that the KSC is a semi-military or paramilitary organizations, while the Korean negotiators had maintained otherwise and agreement on the question was not foreseeable.

13. With regard to subparagraphs (a),(b), and (c) of Paragraph 4, Mr. Chang recalled that the US negotiators had stated that the US armed forces will conform to ROK labor laws to the maximum extent possible. The Korean negotiators believe, therefore, that the detailed provisions set forth in these subparagraphs were unnecessary. However, they had no objection if the US negotiators felt it necessary to include them, subject to

agreement on the other outstanding problems of the Labor Article.

14. Regarding Paragraph 4(e), which had to do with the right to strike, Mr. Chang said the Korean negotiators believed that if they accepted the US language, the Government of the Republic of Korea would be obliged to enact a law prohibiting the employees of the US armed forces from resorting to strikes. The Korean negotiators doubted that the language of the US draft was in accordance with ROK labor legislation.

15. Regarding Paragraph 5(b), Mr. Chang noted two main points. First, employees shall be deferred on the request of the US armed forces. Secondly, a list of essential employees is to be furnished in advance. The US proposal did not appear to provide for the mutual satisfaction desired by the Korean negotiators. If they accepted the US language, the ROK authorities would have to defer everyone whose name appeared on the list furnished in advance. They believed that the ROK authorities should have discretion, in consultation with the US armed forces,

to decide who would be deferred.

16. Mr. Habib pointed out that what the Korean negotiators wanted was implied in the US language. The US negotiators believed that there would be mutual satisfaction, since there must be agreement on the attainment of essential skills by the employees whose names would appear on the list furnished by the US armed forces. The Joint Committee would be the mechanism for attaining mutual satisfaction. If the Korean authorities questioned that any person named on the list had actually attained the required skills, they could raise the question in the Joint Committee.

17. Mr. Chang said the Korean negotiators still felt that the language regarding this question could be more specific. He said they would propose such language.

18. Mr. Chang noted that the US negotiators had modified the language of Agreed Minute #5, by providing for notification "in advance whenever possible". The phrase "whenever possible" should be omitted, however, since the Korean negotiators

believed that it would always be possible to report in advance. Furthermore, if the US armed forces found that they could not corform to the ROK labor laws, they should always refer the matter to the Joint Committee in advance.

19. Mr. Habib replied that if it is always possible to report in advance, then the Korean position was met by the US language and no problem existed. The US armed forces did not intend this provision to be a means of avoiding conformity to the Korean labor laws. They did believe, however, that in times of emergency it might not always be possible to notify the Joint Committee in advance of non-corformity. There had to be some qualifying phrase; otherwise the provision would be unreasonable.

20. Mr. Chang said he wished to close his preliminary remarks by stating that the Korean negotiators noted and appreciated the sincerity of the US negotiators in submitting their revised drafts.

21. Mr. Habib said that he wished to reply briefly to Mr. Chang's comments regarding Paragraph 4(e). The US negotiators wished to reiterate that

- 133 -

75

neither the US armed forces nor the ROK armed forces are ordinary employers. The phraseology of the revised US draft of this subparagraph had been carefully chosen from the standpoint of the Korean requirements as well as those of the US armed forces. The language is not unreasonable, given the unusual nature of the employers. Neither employer is an ordinary business enterprise. They are not in business to make money but to defend the Republic of Korea.

22. Regarding Paragraph 1, Mr. Habib pointed out that in revising the language, the US negotiators had done exactly what the Korean negotiators had desired - they had excluded members of the Korean Service Corps from the definition of employees and, therefore, from the coverage provided by this article. It appeared that both sides were substantially in agreement regarding this issue.

75TH MEETING (April 28, 1965)

1. Mr. Chang opened the meeting by stating that the Korean negotiators, as they had promised at the 73rd negotiating session, had carefully considered the revised draft of the Labor Article tabled by the US negotiators at that meeting. They would now table a revised draft of the entire article, in which the underlining indicates modifications of the draft which they had tabled at the 69th session. Mr. Chang said he would discuss the new revised draft on a paragraph by paragraph basis.

2. Paragraph 1 - Mr. Chang said the Korean negotiators accepted the US formula for defining an "employer," except as regards invited contractors. The Korean negotiators continued to maintain their position that invited contractors should be subject to Korean laws with regard to local employment relations and, therefore, they should be excluded from the provisions of this Article.

3. With regard to the definition of an "employee," Mr. Chang continued, the Korean

negotiators similarly had modified the language of their draft, taking into account the US suggestion of excluding members of the civilian component. They believed that it is unnecessary to mention domestics in this paragraph because domestics are not covered by Korean labor legislation (e.g. Article 10, Labor Standards Law). The Korean negotiators believed that members of the Korean Service Corps should be considered as employees coming under the provisions of this Article. KSC personnel have been recruited from the free labor market as manual laborers serving for the US Army since September, 1955, said Mr. Chang.

4. Referring to Agreed Minute #1, Mr. Chang said that the Korean negotiators consider that its provisions are already covered in Paragraph 2 of the Article. Under the terms of Paragraph 2, the ROK Government, as it has done in the past, will make available, on the request of the US armed forces, Korean personnel not only for the Korean Service Corps but also for any employment, insofar as possible, to meet the

requirements of the US armed forces.

5. Paragraph 3 and Agreed Minute #4 - Mr. Chang said that the Korean negotiators had made some self-explanatory modifications of the language in Paragraph 3 to satisfy the needs of the US negotiators. There had also been some changes in Agreed Minute #4. The Korean negotiators believe it is reasonable to provide that any deviation from Korean law shall be referred to the Joint Committee in advance for mutual agreement. In this regard, the Korean negotiators recalled that the US negotiators had in mind deviation from Korean law during times of emergency. In order to cover such situations, the Korean negotiators had drafted a new Paragraph #5, which they would explain shortly. They did not foresee any difficulty on the part of the US authorities in referring in advance any deviation from Korean law to the Joint Committee for mutual agreement.

6. Paragraph 4 - Mr. Chang said the Korean revised draft had deleted subparagraph (a) of the US draft, regarding the resolution of employee grievances, for such provisions are fully

described in Korean legislation. Also, the Korean negotiators could not accept the US versions of subparagraphs (b) and (c) because the employees' rights of union organization and consultation are provided for to a satisfactory extent in Korean labor legislation. Also, in a sense, any formula of recognizing the organization of labor unions is against the spirit of Korean labor legislation.

7. Regarding the issue of settlement of disputes, Mr. Chang said that the Korean negotiators had made a significant concession by providin in subparagraph (a)(4) of Paragraph 4 that the cooling-off period shall begin after the dispute is referred to the second stage, i.e. the specially-designated committee. This implies, he continued, prolongation by many more days of the prohibition against disruptive practices by the employees. The Korean negotiators believed this formula would satisfy the US desires.

8. Mr. Chang said the Korean negotiators had drawn up a new formula with regard to the right to strike. This was contained in subpara-

graph (b) of Paragraph 4, which would provide that the right to strike shall be accorded to employees except those whose exercise of this right is prohibited by the Joint Committee. There had been a great many deliberations on the right to strike and now the Korean negotiators were proposing to settle the matter by providing in their draft that the Joint Committee would resolve the question. The US negotiators had held the position that certain employees should not exercise the right to strike. The Korean negotiators agree that there would be some employees of the US armed forces who should not exercise that right. Therefore, Mr. Chang said, the Korean negotiators were proposing that the Joint Committee designate such persons.

9. Paragraph 5 - Mr. Chang said that the Korean negotiators, taking into account the worries of the US negotiators concerning deviation from Koran law during times of emergency, had introduced a new paragraph, which would provide that the application of the labor Article may be suspended, in whole or

in part, in accordance ~~with the extent~~ promulgated in the emergency measures taken by the Government of the Republic of Korea. The Korean negotiators believed that this formula would relieve the worries of the US negotiators and that they would accept Paragraph 5 and Agreed Minute #4 of the Korean draft without any objection.

10. Mr. Chang said the Korean negotiators had no problems with regard to subparagraph (a) of Paragraph 5 of the US draft. In subparagraph (b), the Korean negotiators had inserted the words "through mutual agreement" in order to clarify the points agreed upon at the previous meetings.

11. Mr. Chang said that the Korean negotiators' final comments were directed toward the second sentence of Agreed Minute #3 of the US draft. The US negotiators held the view that nowhere in the Article is there provision for the right of employers to terminate employment of employees. The Korean negotiators wished to call the attention of the US negotiators to the first sentence of Paragraph 2, which reads:

"Employers may recruit, employ and administer their personnel." The Korean negotiators understand that the word "administer" indicates the stages of personnel administration from hire to fire, as explained by the US negotiators at the 65th meeting. The US authorities would have the right to terminate employment under the provisions of Paragraph 2, when, under the provisions of Paragraph 3, there were justifiable reasons. If the US negotiators insist on the inclusion of the second sentence of Agreed Minute #3, then many more rights of employers in the field of personnel administration should be specifically spelled out in the Article. For that reason, the Korean negotiators maintain that this provision is unnecessary.

12. Mr. Habib stated that the US negotiators would reserve discussion of the revised Korean draft of the Labor Article until the next meeting.

78TH MEETING(May 7, 1965)

1. Mr. Habib opened the meeting by stating that at this session the U.S. negotiators wished to concentrate on the principal remaining point at issue in the Labor Article. There were a number of differences still unresolved but at this meeting the U.S. negotiators wished to present their reviews on the question of the status of the Korean employees of the U.S. armed forces. The U.S. negotiators have been seeking to establish in this Article a relationship between the U.S. armed forces and their employees which would support the mission of the armed forces and at the same time safeguard the rights and privileges of their employees. The U.S. draft of the Labor Article would protect and preserve all of the basic rights currently enjoyed by those employees. The principal difference between the two drafts centers on the question of the right to strike.

2. This question, Mr. Habib continued, should be viewed in connection with the disputes settlement procedures established in the U.S. draft. Through these procedures, the U.S. negotiators have sought

to provide for the amicable settlement of any disputes which may arise. They would establish a consultative and conciliation process which would operate at the governmental and Joint Committee level. Provision would be made for representation of the employees through recognition of the right to organize.

3. The Korean negotiators recognize the necessity for procedures for the settlement of disputes but the Korean draft goes beyond this, Mr. Habib continued. The Korean draft contradicts the settlement procedures provided for by quoting the Korean Labor Dispute Adjustment Law, which, in effect, says that a decision of the Joint Committee would not be binding. The Korean draft also provides that employees of the U.S. armed forces shall have the right to strike. Nowhere in their draft have the Korean negotiators recognized what the U.S. negotiators have been trying to stress - that Korean employees of the U.S. armed forces are not comparable to ordinary employees of commercial enterprises.

4. Mr. Habib reiterated the position of the U.S. negotiators that the Korean employees of the

U.S. armed forces have a status and importance comparable to that of employees of the Korean armed forces. The U.S. armed forces in Korea have exactly the same mission as the ROK armed forces - the defense of the Republic of Korea.

5. Mr. Habib pointed out that the paragraph in the U.S. draft dealing with strikes (Paragraph 4(e) simply states that "an employee shall be subject to the same legal provisions concerning strikes and other work stoppages as an employee in a comparable position in the employment of the armed forces of the Republic of Korea". This provision is not only sound with respect to the mission of the U.S. armed forces. It is also justifiable, not only in terms of military requirements but also in comparability with Korean procedures. Korean recognition that certain operations require special provisions extends beyond the armed forces, for employees of certain utilities in the Republic of Korea do not have the right to strike. The U.S. negotiators would also like to point out that staff functions of certain of the Korean employees of the U.S. armed

forces serve the Korean armed forces as well as the U.S. armed forces, particularly in the fields of supply and transport. The U.S. negotiators do not understand why the Korean negotiators attempt to apply different sets of rules to employees of the U.S. armed forces and employees of the Korean armed forces when the mission, functions, and command of the two armed forces are indentical.

6. Mr. Habib stated that the U.S. negotiators agree with the reasoning that leads the Korean negotiators to the conclusion that a requirement exists to restrict the rights of Korean employees of the ROK armed forces. The U.S. armed forces desire the same treatment, not discriminatory treatment, so that the achievement of the mission of the U.S. armed forces is not interfered with. The position of the U.S. negotiators is consistent with the past and present practice and rules of both the U.S. and ROK Governments.

7. Mr. Habib pointed out that the U.S. negotiators were not attempting to deny the rights of labor to organize and to be dealth with through

established procedures. They were trying to preserve rights equivalent to those held by employees of the Korean armed forces in order to permit the U.S. armed forces to fulfill their mission without unnecessary interference. The mission of the U.S. armed forces is all-important.

8. The U.S. negotiators believe that disputes should be conciliated, Mr. Habib continued. The formula contained in the U.S. draft permits the U.S. armed forces to meet their requirements and enables the Korean negotiators to justify these provisions to the Korean authorities and people. That jurisdiction is found in the phraseology which provides for resolution of the issue in the same fashion in both armed forces.

9. Mr. Habib remarked that the principal argument of the Korean negotiators has been that the right to strike exists elsewhere. This argument is not persuasive for a number of reasons. The primary mission of the U.S. armed forces in Korea is considerably different than that of such forces elsewhere. The U.S. negotiators believe

that the procedures set forth in the U.S. draft will fully meet the requirements of both sides for amicable relations. For all of the reasons which he had just cited, Mr. Habib concluded, the U.S. negotiators are unable to agree to the Korean proposal to delete Paragraph 4(e) from the U.S. draft.

10. Mr. Chang replied that the Korean negotiators would consider the position stated by the U.S. negotiators and would respond at a later meeting.

- 147 -

69

79TH MEETING(May 12, 1965)

1. Mr. Chang opened the 79th meeting by indicating that the Korean negotiators have carefully reviewed the position taken by the US negotiators at the 78th session in order to pave a way for resolving the stalemate, with a view to concluding the SOFA negotiations as early as possible. To this end, intensive consultation has taken place among the responsible authorities of the Korean Government with respect to the labor problem. As a result of this consultation, the new ROK proposal is ready to present. This proposal is honest evidence of Korean side's desire to make a significant concession with regard to the Labor Article.

2. Prior to explaing the new proposal, Mr. Chang stated that the Korean negotiators would like to make two principles clear to the US negotiators. First, the two sides are now negotiating to decide the status of Korean laborers working for the United States Armed Forces. Such laborers should not be considered either as Korean Government employees or military personnel of any state. Secondly, since they are simple laborers working for emoluments, their rights concerning labor relations should be protected along the lines of established

and world-wide standards. The Korean negotiators, however, are prepared to coopeyate with the US Armed Forces to enable them to carry out our common defense mission to the maximum extent possible on the basis of the foregoing two basic principles. Therefore, the ROK negotiators have already agreed to possible deviation of the US Armed Foreces from ROK labor legislation on account of the military requirements under normal situation as well as in time of emergency.

3. Mr. Chang stated, that, in this spirit of cooperation and with the foregoing two principles in mind, the Korean side now wishes to make further significant concessions relating to procedures to settle labor disputes and concerning the exersice of the right to strike.

4. With regard to procedures to settle any labor dispute, the ROK side proposes amendments to paragraph 4 (a), as follows:

Paragraph 4. (a)

"(2) In the event that the dispute is not settled by the procedures desribed in (1) above within twenty (20) days, the dispute shall be referred to the Joint Committee, which may refer the matter to the Labor Sub-Committee or to a specially-designated committee, for further conciliation efforts."

"(4) Neither employee organizations nor employees shall engage in any practice disruptive of normal work requirements unless a period of seventy(70) days has elapsed without settlement after the dispute is referred to the Office of Labor Affairs mentioned in (...) above."

5. Mr. Chang explained that this new language provides for a complete prohibition of disruptive practices for a maximum period of 70 days while any dispute is referred for settlement to the ROK Labor Office and to the Joint Committee. This new proposal is based on the ROK belief that there would be no dispute which could not be settled during 70 days. Under this formula, the ROK negotiators envisage no dispute would lead to a strike in a practical sense, although employees would retain the ultimate, but almost non-practical, right to strike. Concerning the right to strike, Mr. Chang said that the Korean side holds the view that there would be no need to set forth special provisions on this right, because the exercise of this right had heretofore been prohibited for 70 days under the provisions of Paragraph 4(a). As the ROK negotiators have already committed themselves at the 75th session, they are prepared to agree with the US side to prohibit the

exercise of the right to strike by certain categories of Korean employees working for the US Armed Forces, when such disruptive practices would be greatly detrimental to the military mission of the US Armed Forces.

6. In conclusion, Mr. Chang emphasized that the Korean negotiators believe that the foregoing proposal will meet the requirements of the US Armed Forces and they hope that the US side will accept these new proposals as a whole.

7. Mr. Habib asked to have the two principles enunciated in paragraph 2 above repeated and then he asked, if these principles were consistent with paragraph 4 (b) of the ROK draft. Mr. Chang stated that these principles are subject to modification, and in paragraph 4 (b) the ROK Government agrees that the right to strike shall be accorded to employees, except those whose exercise of this right is prohibited by the Joint Committee.

8. Mr. Habib asked if these two principles are consistent with US-ROK military requirements for the defense of the Republic of Korea. The Korea negotiators refer to these USFK employees as laborers, but as explained at the 72nd negotiating session, less than 5 percent of the present USFK employees are in the unskilled labor-pool category, while

- 151 -

93

most are skilled workers performing functions important to the joint defense position of the US and ROK armed forces.

9. Mr. Habib emphasized that it was in the mutual interest of our two governments to establish procedures for settling labour disputes amicably and without adversely affecting the defense of the Republic of Korea. That is what the US draft is designed to accomplish. We seek non-discrimination against USFK employees. We compare the USFK employees with ROK armed forces employees because they are similar employees performing similar functions for similar objectives. The US has agreed to conform to ROK labor legislation, taking into consideration special military requirements. We recognize the right of USFK employees to have a union and the USFK deals with it on matters of mutual concern. We have ... proposed comprehensive procedures for the amicable settlement of disputes. All the US is asking is that the ROK Government apply the same legal provisions in the one area of strikes and work stoppages to USFK employees working in the defense of their country as the ROK applies to Korean Government armed forces employees. We do not think this position is unreasonable.

10. Mr. Chang replied that the ROK negotiators

had agreed that special conditions and procedures would be applicable to USFK employees in the Article because of the role of such employees in the defense of the Republic. But the ROK Government cannot agree that such USFK employees are comparable to ROK Army employees, including the civilian component (mun-kwon), Government officials or employees, and it cannot agree that such employees will be denied their constitutional rights. Mr. Chang emphasized that, in providing for 70 days for the arbitration procedures to operate, the Korean negotiators firmly believe that chances of strikes would be almost non-existent in a practical sense. In the past the ROK Office of Labor Affairs has cooperated with USFK authorities to prevent strikes and this office will continue to do so. Furthermore, the ROK Government has provided that the Joint Committee can establish categories of essential employees who will be prohibited for exercising the right to strike. Thus, although the ROK draft avoids any particular provisions which specifically denies all USFK workers the right to strike, the ROK proposal in effect limits the possibility of strikes to the extent reasonable. Mr. Chang urged that the US side give careful consideration to the Korean proposals

- 153 -

95

11. Mr Habib answered that the Korean views would be carefully considered. He asked in turn for the ROK Government's understanding of the role of USFK's Korean employees. The US side firmly believes that the long term interests of both the US and ROK Governments, as well as the welfare of USFK employees, requires that both sides accept the realities of their important role in the defense of the Republic of Korea.

80TH MEETING (May 28, 1965)

1. Mr. Fleck stated that the US negotiators were tabling a revised Labor Article, which incorporates compromise language in keeping with the recent agreement by the leaders of the two governments in Washington. In this new draft, Paragraph 4 has been revised. The previous subparagraphs 4(a), 4(c), and 4(e), have been deleted, as suggested by the ROK authorities. A new subparagraph 4(a) (5) has been included, incorporating the concept of the Korean proposal made at the 79th negotiating session, and providing for a 70-day cooling-off after a labor dispute has been referred to the Joint Committee. The new subparagraph 4(b) incorporates the substance of the ROK draft of subparagraph 4(b). It gives the Joint Committee the responsibility for determining those categories of essential employees who shall not exercise the right of further collective action in the event a labor dispute is not resolved by the mediation procedures. A new subparagraph 4(c) incorporates the language previously tabled by the Korean negotiators in Paragraph 5. It provides that in a national emergency, application of this article will be limited

- 155 -

97

in accordance with emergency measures taken by the Government of the Republic of Korea. In connection with this new subparagraph, it is the understanding of the US negotiators that it was proposed by the Korean negotiators in order to assist in our joint defense effort in case of national emergency. During such an emergency every resource must be utilized to meet the crisis. Therefore, it is the understanding of the US negotiators that the limitation of the Labor Article would be selective. In other words, those provisions which might hamper US operations during such a national emergency would be suspended. At the same time those provisions which would further our joint defense efforts and would be of assistance would remain in effect. The substance of the previous subparagraph 4(b) of the US draft, which is an essential provision, had been incorporated as a new Agreed Minute No. 5 in this draft.

2. Mr. Fleck stated that this revised draft incorporates the Korean proposal to exclude the Korean Service Corps from coverage of the Labor Article. The KSC personnel are to be covered by a separate agreement. Therefore, the revised US draft on this

subject merely affirms that they are not covered by the Article. The US negotiators agree to delete Agreed Minute No. 1, on the basis that a separate agreement for the KSC will be negotiated. This deletion of Agreed Minute No. 1 is made with the understanding that, pending conclusion of a separate agreement, KSC personnel will continue to be made available by the ROK Government as at present. In other words, the 1960 US-Korean agreement will remain in effect until it is superseded by a new agreement, separate from the SOFA.

3. In tabling this revised US draft, Mr. Fleck continued, the US negotiators believe they have met the Korean requirements on the key point of difference in the two drafts. In making this concession, they would like to reiterate that the US armed forces are here solely for the defense of Korea. Their Korean employees are vital to the joint US-ROK defense mission. As the US negotiators had explained, the US armed forces are relying more and more on their Korean employees in semi-skilled and skilled occupations. Many of these employees are engaged in work which is essential to the combat readiness of both the US and

- 157 -

99

Korean armed forces. Therefore, the US negotiators were making these important concessions with the understanding the Korean negotiators would accept the remainder of the US draft of the Labor Article, and that in future the Joint Committee, when considering the role of the Korean employees of the US armed forces under subparagraph 4(b), will take into full consideration the importance of the US armed forces' Korean employees in the defense of their homeland and the special status of these employees.

4. Mr. Chang thanked Mr. Fleck for his presentation and indicated that the Korean negotiators would respond at the next negotiating session. The Korean negotiators asked questions about the meaning of Paragraph 4(a) (5) of the Labor Article, especially whether the reference therein should not be to subparagraph (2) rather than to subparagraph (3). Mr. Fleck explained that reference of a dispute to the special committee, provided for in subparagraph (2), was not intended to be compulsory or automatic. Under the provisions of the US draft, if the Joint Committee decides to refer the dispute to the special committee and the special committee, having failed to resolve the dispute,

then returns the dispute to the Joint Committee, the 70-day period would begin when the special committee returns the dispute to the Joint Committee. However, if the Joint Committee should decide not to refer the dispute to a special committee, the 70-day period would begin from the date the dispute was referred to the Joint Committee by the Office of Labor Affairs. The Korean negotiators expressed the opinion that the subparagraph (5) appeared to be faultily drafted, since it does not clearly provide for procedure explained by the US negotiators.

101

81ST MEETING (June 7, 1965)

1. Turning to the Labor Article, Mr. Chang said that the Korean negotiators, with a view to reaching prompt agreement, were prepared to accept the US draft as a whole, with modifications of the following provisions: Paragraphs 1(b), 3, 4(a), 5(b), and Agreed Minute #4 and #5. Most of the proposed modifications, he pointed out, were technical in nature rather than substantive and the Korean negotiators believed they would present no difficulty to the US negotiators since they are all valid and reasonable.

2. Paragraph 1 (a) and (b)

Mr. Chang stated that the Korean negotiators were now prepared to agree to inclusion of the invited contractors in the provisions of this article. The Korean negotiators were prepared to accept subparagraph (b) of the US draft if the US negotiators would agree to the addition of the following sentence:

"Such civilian personnel shall be nationals of the Republic of Korea."

By accepting the US draft of subparagraph (b), Mr.

Chang stated, the Korean negotiators were acceding to the specific exclusion of KSC personnel and domestics from the definition of employees. In making this most significant concession, the Korean negotiatots wished the Agreed Joint Summary to clearly indicate that exclusion of KSC personnel from the definition of employee shall not be considered as a change in the position taken by the Korean negotiators with reg rd to the status of KSC personnel. Moreover, the addition of the second sentence, proposed by the Korean negotiators, with regard to the nationality of the employees is considered necessary by the Korean negotiators to minimize the employement of third-country nationals in Korea.

3. Paragraph 2 and Agreed Minute #2

Mr. Chang said the Korean negotiators were now prepared to accept the US draft of this paragraph and Agreed Minute, with following understanding:

"The termination of employment on account of the US military requirements referred to in the second sentence of Agreed Minute #2 shall be referred to the Joint Committee, in advance whenever poss-

- 161 -

103

ible, for mutual agreement, as provided for in Agreed Minute #4. But such termination of employment as may be made in accordance with the relevant provisions of labor legislation of the Republic of Korea will not be subject to mutual agreement at the Joint Committee."

4. Paragraph 4(a)

Mr. Chang stated that the Korean negotiators were prepared to accept the US draft of Paragraph 4(a) except for subparagraph (5). They proposed that subparagraph (5) be altered to read "as stipulated in subparagraph (2), above" instead of "subparagraph (3), above". Although they maintain that the cooling-off period should comprise 70 days after the dispute is referred for conciliation, the Korean negotiators now proposed, as a compromise, to fix the starting date of the cooling-off period at the second stage of the conciliation process, regardless of whether the Joint Committee deals with the dispute itself or refers it to a specially designated committee. The US draft of this paragraph does not clearly accommodate the case when the Joint Committee takes up the dispute itself without having referred the matter to the special committee. Therefore, the

Korean negotiators urge that their compromise proposal be accepted.

5. Paragraph 4(b) and (c)

Mr. Chang said the Korean negotiators accepted the US draft of Paragraph 4(b) and (c), relating to collective action and emergency measures, without any change of wording.

6. Paragraph 5(b)

Turning to Paragraph 5(b), Mr. Chang said the Korean negotiators were now prepared to accommodate the contention expressed by the US negotiators by accepting the word "shall" instead of "will" and by substituting the phrase "through mutual consultation" for the phrase "through mutual agreement". The language in question would then read as follows:

> "...employees who have acquired skills essential to the mission of the United States Armed Forces shall, upon request of the United States Armed Forces, be deferred through mutual consultation from Republic of Korea military service or other compulsory service."

The Korean negotiators hoped, Mr. Chang continued, that through amicable consultation no disagreement would arise between the appropriate authorities of both sides in deferring skilled employees essential to the mission of the US armed forces.

7. Agreed Minute #5

Mr. Chang said the Korean negotiators believe that the words "interests of the United States" referred to in the phrase "inimical to the interests of the United States" in the US draft of Agreed Minute #5 do not imply interests in terms of wages, compensation, or other forms of "payments protection". Rather, they imply those interests of a political nature, such as when the leadership of a union is dominated or influenced by leftist or communist elements. The Korean negotiators believe that if such an unlikely situation should develop, it would undoubtedly be inimical to the interests of the Republic of Korea. Therefore, they would like to change the languge to read as follows:

"....inimical to the common interests of the United States and the Republic of Korea..."

8. Paragraph 3 and Agreed Minute #4

The Korean negotiators tabled the following proposed revision of Paragraph 3:

"3. To the extent not inconsistent with the provisions of this Article or the military requirements of the US armed forces, the conditions of employment, compensation, and labor-management relations established by the United States armed forces for their employees shall conform with provisions of labor legislation of the Republic of Korea."

They also tabled the following proposed revision of Agreed Minute #4:

"4. When employers cannot conform with provisions of labor legislation of the Republic of Korea applicable under Paragraph 3 on account of the military requirements of the United States armed forces, the matter shall be referred, in advance whenver possible, to the Joint Committee for mutual agreement."

Mr. Chang noted that in order to meet the US requirements, the proposed revision of the Agreed Minute retains the phrase "whenever possible". However, the Korean negotiators believe that "under Paragraph 3" is preferable to "under this Article" because the latter phrase might lead to dual application of an

- 165 -

107

already agreed-upon deviation which the Korean negotiators believe to be irrelevant and unnecessary. With regard to the phrase "whenever possible", Mr. Chang said the Korean negotiators wished to include in the Agreed Joint Summary the following understanding:

"The deviation from Korean labor legislation shall be referred to the Joint Committee for mutual agreement in advance, except in the case when reaching advance agreement by the Joint Committee would seriously hamper military operations in an emergency."

Mr. Chang said the Korean negotiators believed this understanding would present no difficulty to the US negotiators in view of the statement made by the latter at the 71st meeting.

82ND MEETING (July 8, 1966)

1. **Mr. Ericson** tabled a revised Labor Article, which he stated was responsive to the proposals made by the ROK negotiators at the 81st session, and at subsequent informal meetings. He expressed the belief that this revised Labor Article fully meets the ROK requirements, and he anticipates full agreement can now be reached on the revised text of the Labor Article.

2. Mr. Ericson stated that the following comments refer to specific changes in the previously tabled United States draft, made in response to the Korean proposals at the 81st session:

a. Paragraph 1(b). The US negotiators accept the ROK proposal for the inclusion of a new sentence in Paragraph 1(b), as follows: "Such employees shall be nationals of the Republic of Korea." This sentence is accepted on the condition of ROK acceptance of two understandings for the Agreed Summary Record, as follows:

(1) "Local residents, who are third-country nationals and are also local-hire USFK employees and local-hire contractor employees paid in won, on the effective date of the agreement, shall be excluded from the application of this provision.

109

There are only a few USFK employees in this category, who have been working with USFK in good faith for some years, and the US negotiators feel their exclusion from this provisi would not present problems and would only be fair to all concerned.

(2) The second understanding is as follows: "The provisions of Paragraph 1(b) do not preclude the United States armed forces bringin into Korea, without privileges, third-country contractors employees possessing special skills not available from the Korean labor force."

The US negotiators believe general US-ROK agreement on this point is reflected in previous informal discussions. In adding the new sentence to Paragraph 1(b), it is also necessary to add, in the parenthetical phrase "(other than a member of the civilian component)" the phrase "or a contrac employee under Article XV," to enable invited contractors to hire American personnel. Mr. Ericson pointed out that invited contractors employees are not included as part of the civilian component in the Definitions Article (1). Therefore, this added phrase is made necessary by the ROK-proposed added sentence, and it makes it clear that the word "employee" as u in this Article does not refer to non-Korean employees of inv ntractors.

b. Paragraph 2 and Agreed Minutes No. 1,2,3. The egotiators believe the two sides are now in full agreement rding Paragraph 2 and Agreed Minutes 1,2 and 3 as previously ed by the US. Mr. Ericson noted that, during the rmal discussions which took place since the 81st meeting, as mutually agreed that the ROK-proposed understanding ting to Agreed Minute No. 2, reported in Paragraph 27 he Agreed Summary Record of the 81st meeting, would be drawn.

c. Paragraph 3 and Agreed Minute No. 4. Mr. Ericson ed that the US negotiators accept the revisions in Paragraph s tabled by the ROK negotiators at the 81st meeting. regard to the related Agreed Minute No. 4, subsequent to 81st meeting the ROK negotiators proposed revision of the of this Agreed Minute which they had previously tabled. r new proposal is as follows:

"4. When employers cannot conform with provisions of labor legislation of the Republic of Korea applicab under this Article on account of the military requirements of the United States armed forces, the matter shall be referred, in advance, to the Joint Committee for consideration and appropriate action. In the event mutual agreement cannot be reached in the Joint Committee regarding appropriate action, the

- 39 -

issue may be made the subject of review through discussions between appropriate officials of the Government of the Republic of Korea and the diplom mission of the United States of America."

Mr. Chang noted that the ROK negotiators had revised their previously tabled Agreed Minute No. 4, deleting the words "Whenever possible". In proposing this revised language, Mr. Chang stated that the ROK Government is appreciative o the need for the United States armed forces to have the flexibility in an emergency to deviate from ROK labor legi without referral to the Joint Committee, as presented by t US negotiators at the 71st meeting (Paragraph 15 of the Ag Joint Summary) and at the 73rd meeting (Paragraph 5 of the Agreed Joint Summary). Therefore, the ROK negotiators pro the following agreed understanding which will be included i the Agreed Joint Summary, as follows:

"It is understood that the deviation from Korean labor legislation need not be referred to the Joi Committee in cases when such referral would serio hamper military operations in an emergency."

Mr. Ericson stated that the US negotiators were authorized accept the ROK proposal to delete the phrase "Whenever pos in Agreed Minute 4 on the basis that the ROK-proposed agre understanding, which the US accepts, clearly indicates the nited States military authorities can deviate from Korean abor legislation without referral to the Joint Committee when uch would seriously hamper military operations in an nergency. Mr. Chang stated that whenever the matter is eferred to the Joint Committee after the deviation had lready been made on account of military requirements in an mergency, it is presumed that the Korean side could raise bjection in the Joint Committee to the action taken by the mployer and request that appropriate action, i.e., corrective ction or measures for remedy be taken. It is understood hat such corrective action will be taken as and when the oint Committee so directs. In the event that mutual agreement annot be reached in the Joint Committee regarding appropriate tion, the matter may be discussed between officials of the overnment of the Republic of Korea and the US diplomatic ssion. Mr. Chang indicated that these remarks are not ntended to introduce any new understanding, but rather are ntended to provide guidance to the members of the Joint ommittee in their interpretation and implementation of the ew agreed Labor Article.

d. Paragraph 4: The US side concurs in the proposed OK changes at the end of Paragraph 4(a) (5), changing the umber in parentheses from "3" to "2" in the following phrase: as stipulated in subparagraph (2), above."

(17)

The US side also accepts the revised Paragraph 4(b), as proposed by the ROK side, as follows:

"Employees or any employee organization shall have the right of further collective action in the event a labor dispute is not resolved by the foregoing procedures except in cases where the Joint Committee determines such action seriously hampers military operations of the United States armed forces for the Joint defense of the Republic of Korea. In the even an agreement cannot be reached on this question in the Joint Committee, it may be made the subject of review through discussions between appropriate offic of the Government of the Republic of Korea and the diplomatic mission of the United States of America."

In accepting this ROK proposal on this important point, the U side should like it understood and agreed that the Joint Comm will take up as one of its earliest items of business the delineation of those activities the interruption of which wou seriously hamper military operations of the United States arme forces for the joint defense of the ROK. In the Joint Commit consideration of this matter, the Korean Labor Disputes Act of 1953 should be used as a general guide.

e. Paragraph 5: The US side accepts the ROK-propos ied phrase, "through mutual consultation," after the word

114

deferred."

f. Agreed Minute No. 5: The US negotiators also accept the modifications of Agreed Minute No. 5, asproposed by the ROK negotiators at the 81st meeting, with the addition of the phrase "by the employers" as agreed upon in informal discussion. The full text of Agreed Minute No. 5 is as follows:

"5. A union or other employee group shall be recognized by the employers unless its objectives are inimical to the common interests of the United States and the Republic of Korea. Membership or non-membership in such groups shall not be a factor in employment or other actions affecting employees."

3. Mr. Ericson states that he felt that the revisions of text of the Labor Article, as tabled by the US side at this meeting, will be fully acceptable to the ROK negotiators. These proposals are presented as a package and the US revisions of its draft in response to ROK proposals are contingent upon ROK acceptance of the rest of the text and understandings.

4. Mr. Chang stated that the Korean negotiators appreciate the general acceptance of the revised draft of the Labor Article, as tabled at 81st session and as revised as a result of informal discussions. The Korean side accepts the modifications effected in Paragraph 1(b) and Agreed Minutes No. 4 and No. 5, as well as in the agreed understandings, and therefore full agreement has been reached on the Labor Article.

- 173 -

115

These minutes are considered as official documents pertaining to both Governments and will not be released without mutual agreement.

REPUBLIC OF KOREA - UNITED STATES
LABOR SUBCOMMITTEE

MEMORANDUM FOR: THE JOINT COMMITTEE

JUL 0 2 1970

1. Subcommittee Members:
분과 위원:

United States	Republic of Korea
COL E. N. Hathaway, Chairman	Mr. Han Jin Hui, Chairman
COL R. C. Dufault, G1 Eighth Army	Mr. Pak Pil Su, Office of Labor Affairs
COL D. W. Langham, KPA	Mr. Um Ki Sup, Office of Labor Affairs
CPT F. M. Romanick, J5, USFK	Mr. Min Seok Ky, Ministry of Justice
COL N. Jabbour, USAF	Mr. Kim, Kyu-hwan, Ministry of Justice
MAJ A. D. Adams, SJA Eighth Army	COL Oh Chul, Ministry of National Defense
MR. G. A. Seamster, Eighth Army	Mr. Kang Tu Hyon, Ministry of Home Affairs
	Mr. Paik Sun Wol, Ministry of Foreign Affairs
	Mr. Sim Tae Sup, Office of Labor Affairs

2. Subject of Recommendation: Procedures for Implementation of Paragraph 4(b) of SOFA Article XVII.
건의 안건: 행협 제 XVII 조 4(ㄴ)항 시행 절차

3. Recommendation: Recommend that the SOFA Joint Committee approve conclusions and recommendations arrived at by the Joint Labor Subcommittee as outlined in the attached appendix.
건의: 첨부물에 제시된대로 노동 분과 위원회가 의결한 결론과 건의를 한미 합동 위원회에서 승인할것을 건의함.

4. Security Classification: Not applicable.
보안 구분: 해당 무.

Han Jin Hui	Edward N. Hathaway
Mr. Han Jin Hui Chairman Republic of Korea Component Labor Subcommittee	COL Edward N. Hathaway Chairman United States Component Labor Subcommittee

116

These minutes are considered as official documents pertaining to both Governments and will not be released without mutual agreement.

APPROVED BY THE JOINT COMMITTEE ON
10 JULY 1970

HAHM YOUNG HUN Republic of Korea Representative	ROBERT N. SMITH Lieutenant General United States Air Force United States Representative

These minutes are considered as official documents pertaining to both Governments and will not be released without mutual agreement.

APPENDIX

첨부문

1. The Joint Labor Subcommittee concludes that concerned officials of the
한미 노동 분과 위원회는 대한 민국과 주한 미군관계 당국자가

Republic of Korea and the United States armed forces (USFK) will jointly
한미 행협 제 XVII 조 4(ㄱ) 항 범위내에서 종업원이나 종업원

endeavor to complete settlement of any disputes being filed by employees
조직체가 제기한 쟁의를 종결하도록 노력할것을 의결한다.

or recognized employee organizations within the procedures as stipulated in

paragraph 4(a), Article XVII, ROK-US SOFA.

2. This Subcommittee has jointly developed and agreed upon the following
당 분과 위원회는 다음과같이 협의하여 합의를 보았다.

statement:

"That USFK Korean employees are essential at all times in conducting
주한 미군 한국인 종업원은 대한 민국 공동 방위를위한 군사 업무

military operations of the United States armed forces for joint defense of
수행에 항시 긴요하다. 따라서 한미 합동 위원회는 한국인 종업원의

the Republic of Korea. Therefore, it is the determination of the Joint
계속 근무가 상기 공동 방위를위한 주한 미군의 군사 업무에 긴요한

Committee that the continued availability of these employees is essential
것으로 의결한다.

to the military missions of USFK for such joint defense."

3. This Subcommittee recommends that the ROK-US Joint Committee approve
당 분과 위원회는 한미 합동 위원회가 상기 합의 사항을 승인하고

the above statement which will be used for reference if and when needed for
한미 행협 제 XVII 조 4(ㄴ)항에있는 노동 조합이나 종업원의 단체

restraint of employee organizations or employees from exercising the right
행동권 행사를 삼가하게함이 혹시 필요할 때 참조하도록 건의를 한다.

of further collective action discussed in paragraph 4(b), Article XVII, ROK-

US SOFA.

118

(72) 8852.

REPUBLIC OF KOREA - UNITED STATES
LABOR SUBCOMMITTEE

MEMORANDUM FOR: THE JOINT COMMITTEE

JUL 0 2 1970

1. Subcommittee Members:
분과 위원:

United States	Republic of Korea
COL E. N. Hathaway, Chairman	Mr. Han Jin Hui, Chairman
COL R. C. Dufault, G1 Eighth Army	Mr. Pak Pil Su, Office of Labor Affairs
COL D. W. Langham, KPA	Mr. Um Ki Sup, Office of Labor Affairs
CPT F. M. Romanick, J5, USFK	Mr. Min Seok Ky, Ministry of Justice
COL N. Jabbour, USAF	Mr. Kim, Kyu-hwan, Ministry of Justice
MAJ A. D. Adams, SJA Eighth Army	COL Oh Chul, Ministry of National Defense
MR. G. A. Seamster, Eighth Army	Mr. Kang Tu Hyon, Ministry of Home Affairs
	Mr. Paik Sun Wol, Ministry of Foreign Affairs
	Mr. Sim Tae Sup, Office of Labor Affairs

2. Subject of Recommendation: Procedures for Implementation of Paragraph
건의 안건: 행협 제 XVII 조 4(ㄴ)항 시행 절차

4(b) of SOFA Article XVII.

3. Recommendation: Recommend that the SOFA Joint Committee approve
건의: 첨부물에 제시된대로 노동 분과 위원회가 의결한

conclusions and recommendations arrived at by the Joint Labor Subcommittee
결론과 건의를 한미 합동 위원회에서 승인할것을 건의함.

as outlined in the attached appendix.

4. Security Classification: Not applicable.
보안 구분: 해당 무.

Han Jin Hui

Mr. Han Jin Hui
Chairman
Republic of Korea Component
Labor Subcommittee

Edward N. Hathaway

COL Edward N. Hathaway
Chairman
United States Component
Labor Subcommittee

118-1

APPROVED BY THE JOINT COMMITTEE ON
10 JULY 1970

HAHM YOUNG HUN	ROBERT N. SMITH
Republic of Korea	Lieutenant General
Representative	United States Air Force
	United States Representative

118-2

APPENDIX

첨부문

1. The Joint Labor Subcommittee concludes that concerned officials of the
한미 노동 분과 위원회는 대한 민국과 주한 미군관계 당국자가

Republic of Korea and the United States armed forces (USFK) will jointly
한미 행협 제 XVII 조 4(ㄱ) 항 범위내에서 종업원이나 종업원

endeavor to complete settlement of any disputes being filed by employees
조직체가 제기한 쟁의를 종결하도록 노력할것을 의결한다.

or recognized employee organizations within the procedures as stipulated in paragraph 4(a), Article XVII, ROK-US SOFA.

2. This Subcommittee has jointly developed and agreed upon the following
당 분과 위원회는 다음과같이 협의하여 합의를 보았다.

statement:

"That USFK Korean employees are essential at all times in conducting
주한 미군 한국인 종업원은 대한 민국 공동 방위를위한 군사 업무

military operations of the United States armed forces for joint defense of
수행에 항시 긴요하다. 따라서 한미 합동 위원회는 한국인 종업원의

the Republic of Korea. Therefore, it is the determination of the Joint
계속 근무가 상기 공동 방위를위한 주한 미군의 군사 업무에 긴요한

Committee that the continued availability of these employees is essential
것으로 의결한다.

to the military missions of USFK for such joint defense."

3. This Subcommittee recommends that the ROK-US Joint Committee approve
당 분과 위원회는 한미 합동 위원회가 상기 합의 사항을 승인하고

the above statement which will be used for reference if and when needed for
한미 행협 제 XVII 조 4(ㄴ)항에있는 노동 조합이나 종업원의 단체

restraint of employee organizations or employees from exercising the right
행동권 행사를 삼가하게함이 혹시 필요할 때 참조하도록 건의를 한다.

of further collective action discussed in paragraph 4(b), Article XVII, ROK-US SOFA.

118-3

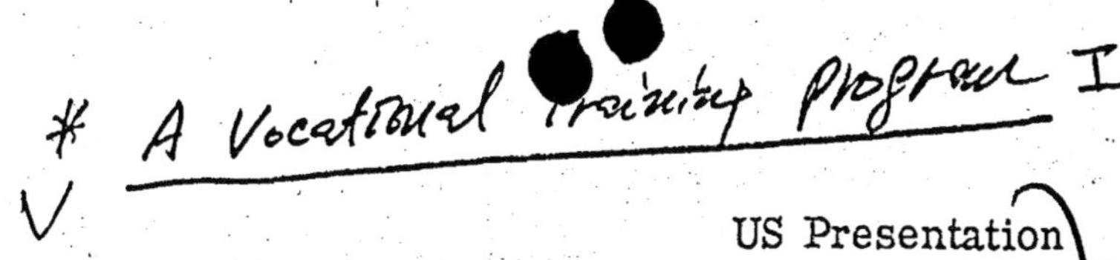

AGENDA ITEM VI V US Presentation

(1. FOR YOUR INFORMATION: This presentation is designed to put into the Joint Committee record a brief statement concerning the coordinated USFK-ROK Government Korean Nationals Outplacement Program (KNOP) and to seek maximum ROK Government cooperation and assistance in the implementation of this program. In discussions with MOFA personnel, they indicated ROKG dislike of the name of the program (KNOP) and strongly suggested it merely be termed a vocational training program. This item has been amended to conform to this ROK suggestion).

2. The United States Forces, Korea, in coordination with the appropriate authorities and organizations of the Republic of Korea, has developed a vocational training program. This program is designed to assist Korean national employees of the United States Forces, Korea, who face possible loss of their jobs as the result of the United States troop reductions in Korea, to obtain continued employment in jobs which contribute to the economic growth and mutual defense of the Republic of Korea. These Korean employees are an effective and industrious work force, engaged in about 200 different occupations involving a wide range of skills. Special training is being provided, as required, to assist in the placement of such Korean workers in new jobs in the Republic of Korea. The Commander of the United States Forces, Korea, General J. H. Michaelis, has written letters to the Minister of National

119

Defense and the Minister of Health and Social Affairs outlining this program and soliciting their assistance and support to insure its successful implementation. I would like to propose that these letters be included in the minutes of this meeting.

3. This program is now getting underway in various parts of the Republic. For example, the Commanding General, I Corps (Group), Eighth US Army, in cooperation with the Governor of Kyonggi Province, now has in operation vocational training programs which include classes in drivers' training, cooking, barbering, radio and TV repair and maintenance, operation of heavy equipment, and English typing.

4. The program should materially assist the employees of the United States Forces, Korea, who may be required to change their employment, to continue to utilize their natural talents and special skills for the continued benefit of the Republic of Korea and of themselves and their families. The cooperation of the various agencies of the Government of the Republic of Korea in the successful implementation of this program is greatly appreciated.

(5. FOR YOUR INFORMATION: The ROK Representative will respond as follows:

120

HEADQUARTERS, UNITED STATES FORCES, KOREA
APO SAN FRANCISCO 96301

CC

9 NOV 1970

Dear Minister KIM:

Troop reductions in Korea will result in a drastic curtailment of support activities and a concurrent reduction in the number of Korean civilian employees working for United States Forces, Korea.

Our Korean nationals have demonstrated through the years that they are a highly effective, loyal, and industrious work force. These employees are engaged in almost 200 different occupations involving a wide range of skills, and I feel that it is extremely important that their skills and proven abilities continue to be utilized after their service with United States Forces, Korea is completed. This is important for the impetus they can offer to the continued economic growth of the Republic of Korea and for the welfare of the employees themselves.

To meet this objective, the U. S. Forces have established a Korean Nationals Outplacement Program (KNOP) which includes plans for providing continued job opportunities for surplus personnel through specialized skills training, and it places maximum effort on placement efforts in collaboration with appropriate agencies of your government.

I solicit your personal support of this program to assure its successful implementation. For example, you may wish to consider prompt testing and certification of our skilled Korean employees, thereby enabling the Office of Labor Affairs to provide priority outplacement efforts in the public and private sectors.

121

I believe that it is to our mutual benefit that we provide continued employment for the highly effective Korean nationals of the U. S. Forces in meeting the civilian staffing requirements of the Republic of Korea.

I hope that the above information will be of assistance to you in your plans to help the U. S. Forces minimize the economic impact of the military drawdown on Korean employees.

Please rest assured, Mr. Minister, of my warmest personal regards.

Sincerely,

J. H. MICHAELIS
General, United States Army
Commander

The Honorable KIM, Tae Dong
Minister of Health and Social Affairs
Republic of Korea
Seoul, Korea

2

122

HEADQUARTERS, UNITED STATES FORCES, KOREA
APO SAN FRANCISCO 96301

CC

9 NOV 1970

Dear Minister JUNG:

Troop reductions in Korea will result in a drastic curtailment of support activities and a concurrent reduction in the number of Korean civilian employees working for United States Forces, Korea.

Our Korean nationals have demonstrated through the years that they are a highly effective, loyal, and industrious work force. These employees are engaged in almost 200 different occupations involving a wide range of skills, and I feel that it is extremely important that their skills and proven abilities continue to be utilized after their service with United States Forces, Korea is completed. This is important for the impetus they can offer to the continued economic growth of the Republic of Korea and for the welfare of the employees themselves.

To meet this objective, the U.S. Forces have established a Korean Nationals Outplacement Program (KNOP) which includes plans for providing continued job opportunities for surplus personnel through specialized skills training, and it places maximum effort on placement efforts in collaboration with appropriate agencies of your government.

I solicit your personal support of this program to assure its successful implementation. For example, you may wish to consider employing our skilled Korean workers at the U.S. camps and installations which will be occupied by Republic of Korea Forces, or perhaps hiring our excess personnel for your Pusan support activity which, I understand, is experiencing a 20 percent turnover rate.

123

I believe that it is to our mutual benefit that we provide continued employment for the highly effective Korean nationals of the U.S. Forces.

I hope that the above information will be of assistance to you in your plans to help the U.S. Forces minimize the economic-impact of the military drawdown on Korean employees.

Please rest assured, Mr. Minister, of my warmest personal regards.

Sincerely,

J. H. MICHAELIS
General, United States Army
Commander

The Honorable JUNG, Nae Hiuk
Minister of National Defense
Republic of Korea
Seoul, Korea

124

4 The Japan Times 18 NOV 1970

Training Offered Employes Facing Dismissal at U.S. Bases

YOKOHAMA—Kanagawa Prefecture, which has a large number of U.S. installations, last week opened four training schools for Japanese employes who face dismissal by U.S. authorities.

The vocational schools were opened under the auspices of the Kanagawa Prefectural Government at the U.S. Naval Base in Yokosuka, the U.S. North Pier in Yokohama Port, the U.S. supply depot at Sagami and the U.S. camp at Zama.

The schools were opened for the period from Nov. 9 to Feb. 19, offering training for such work as welding, painting and accounting.

It is reported that Kanagawa Prefecture alone has some 21,000 people working at U.S. installations and some 3,000 of them have received dismissal notices so far.

Out of the 3,000 persons, some 1,600 have already found other jobs.

Prefectural Government officials expect the schools to be of benefit not only to those having difficulty in obtaining other jobs, but to those seeking to become more adept in their work.

The schools will award certificates, to persons finishing the courses offered, equivalent to those given graduates of Japanese vocational schools.

21000명 중
3000 해고

125

Base Retraining Classes Opened

S&S Korea Bureau　S&S. 70. 11. 23

UIJONGBU, Korea—A helping hand has been extended to Korean civilian employes losing their jobs with U.S. Forces installations in the Uijongbu area because of cutbacks in American military strength here.

With Lt. Gen. Edward L. Rowney, I Corps commander, and Kyonggi Provincial Gov. Nam Bong Jin participating, the first phase of a cooperative vocational retraining school was opened at Camp Red Cloud on Thursday.

The first two classes began with 45 students, who will learn to drive or to acquire American-style cooking skills. The evening classes meet for four hours, five days a week, in classrooms on the Camp Red Cloud Corps headquarters post.

Other courses slated to start soon will include ones on heavy equipment operation and care, radio and television repair, typing, electrical installation and barbering.

The training is designed to teach new skills to recently-released employes and to help the general economic development of the province.

Rowney told students at the opening classes that he and the governor are also looking into the possibility of establishing training centers in other cities. He said Tongduchon and Paju County have ample U.S. military men to teach classes.

Rowney pledged "all the resources" of the Corps to provide training needed by the jobless of Kyonggi Province.

The training course will use U.S. equipment and the instructors, all members of U.S. units in the area, will be teaching curricula designed or approved by the province.

The specially-qualified instructors were presented letters of appointment at the opening ceremony for the training center this week.

Province officials hope to later expand the program to include better English-language instruction in all high schools and to provide special vocational training in some of the scholls.

There are also plans to provide instruction for other persons who, although they do not work directly for the U.S. Forces, will be affected by current and proposed reductions.

1970. 11. 23
SOFA
노무분과 위원회

126

EADCS DEC 0 1 1970

Mr. Han Chin Hui
Chairman
ROK Component
Labor Subcommittee, SOFA

Dear Mr. Han:

Reference your letter of 5 November 1970 requesting a full scale US-ROK Labor Subcommittee meeting.

Business on the task - procedures for implementation of paragraph 4(b) of SOFA Article XVII - was closed on 2 July 1970, when representatives of US and ROK components officially approved the recommendation for action by the Joint Committee.

If the ROK component of the Labor Subcommittee has a counter proposal for the solution of this task for consideration, it is suggested that the new proposal be submitted to the US component of the Subcommittee for study prior to the next Labor Subcommittee meeting.

Sincerely yours,

EDWARD N. HATHAWAY
Colonel, GS
Chairman
US Component Labor Subcommittee

127

HEADQUARTERS EIGHTH UNITED STATES ARMY
APO SAN FRANCISCO 96301

EACP 15 December 1970

Mr. Lee Kwang Cho
President
Foreign Organizations Employees Union

Dear Mr. Lee:

With regard to the announced strike vote of the Foreign Organizations Employees Union on 14-15 December 1970, I wish to call your attention to the provisions of the Republic of Korea - United States Status of Forces Agreement (SOFA), Article XVII, Para 4(a)(iv): "Failure of any recognized employee organization or employee to abide by the decision of the Joint Committee on any dispute, or engaging in practices disruptive of normal work requirements during settlement procedures, shall be considered just cause for the withdrawal of recognition of that organization and the discharge of that employee."

As you know, the SOFA provides for systematic and orderly procedures for the resolution of labor disputes, and any disruptive practices during settlement procedures will not be condoned by the US Forces, Korea.

I trust that you and the responsible members of your Executive Council fully understand the foregoing facts and will act accordingly. A copy of this letter is being sent to the ROK Ministry of Foreign Affairs and the Ministry of Health and Social Affairs.

Yours truly,

FREDRIC NEWMAN
Civilian Personnel Director

Info copy:
Min of Foreign Affairs
Min of Health & Social Affairs

128

AGENDA ITEM III 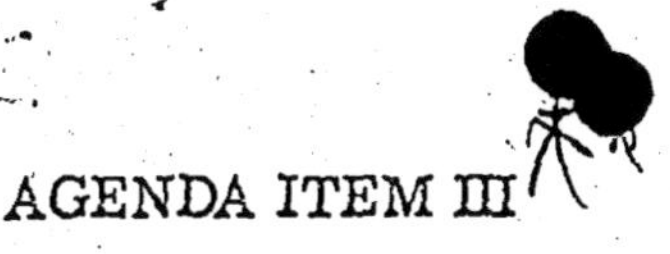 US Presentation

(1. FOR YOUR INFORMATION: The Foreign Organizations Employees Union (FOEU) on 28 November 1970 initiated a labor dispute against the United States Forces, Korea with the Republic of Korea Office of Labor Affairs (OLA), in accordance with the provisions of Article XVII of the Status of Forces Agreement. This labor dispute was terminated on 30 December 1970 with the signing of a Memorandum of Understanding (copy attached) by CPO officials of USFK and the FOEU. This Memorandum was countersigned by the Chief, OLA, who serves concurrently as the Republic of Korea Chairman of the Joint Committee's Labor Subcommittee).

2. The United States Representative would like to propose that the Memorandum of Understanding of 30 December 1970, which terminated the recent labor dispute between the United States Forces, Korea and the Foreign Organizations Employees Union, be recorded in the minutes of this Joint Committee meeting. This dispute had been referred for conciliation to the Office of Labor Affairs of the Government of the Republic of Korea, in accordance with paragraph 4 of Article XVII of the Status of Forces Agreement. The Memorandum of Understanding was signed by officials of the Foreign Organizations Employees Union and of the United States Forces, Korea, and was countersigned by Mr. HAN Chin Hui, Chief, Labor Affairs Bureau of the Office of Labor Affairs.

3. The United States Representative would like to express his deep appreciation for the assistance of officials of the Government of the Republic of Korea in the amicable settlement of this labor dispute, in accordance

129

with the provisions of the Labor Article of the Status of Forces Agreement. The resolution of this labor dispute is another in a series of demonstrations, since the entry into force of the Status of Forces Agreement on 9 February 1967, of the fairness and effectiveness of the provisions of the Labor Article in helping to maintain friendly and stable labor relations between the United States Forces, Korea and its Korean employees in the Republic of Korea. The continued maintenance of such cooperative labor relations and the efficient utilization of the provisions of the Labor Article are believed to be strongly in the mutual security interest of our two Governments.

(4. FOR YOUR INFORMATION: ~~The ROK SOFA Secretary has indicated that~~ the ROK Representative ~~will~~ is happy to concur in the inclusion of the Memorandum of Understanding of 30 December 1970 in the minutes of this Joint Committee meeting).

130

MEMORANDUM OF UNDERSTANDING

1970.12.30

1. With regard to issues in the current dispute, the following actions are being taken.

a. Recently-approved wage schedules (Incl 1), covering all USFK Korean employees, will be implemented effective 1 January 1971.

b. One additional paid holiday is approved to be 2nd January for New Year.

2. USFK advises that a study on the current minimum 30 day advance notice period in RIF will be undertaken for possible extension of the period.

3. USFK advises that the matter of Korean legal holidays will be reexamined to determine whether benefits can be further expanded, particularly when certain legal holidays fall on Saturday or Sunday.

4. USFK advises that efforts will be made to provide more advance RIF information to National FOEU officials, thereby improving long range planning for specialized training and outplacement actions under KNOP.

5. FOEU and USFK agree that a major future objective is to maintain and further develop cooperative and responsible labor relations, thus helping to promote effective manpower support to USFK missions and an effective sharing of responsibilities in support of joint ROK-US security objectives. Included in this objective are appropriate improvements in employee welfare and working conditions and positive employee relations and Korean-American relations at work sites.

6. The labor dispute initiated by FOEU on 28 November 1970 is terminated.

FOR UNITED STATES FORCES, KOREA:

FREDRIC NEWMAN
Chairman
Joint Labor Affairs Committee

ROLAND E. BELDON
Executive Secretary
Joint Labor Affairs Committee

FOR FOREIGN ORGANIZATIONS EMPLOYEES UNION:

KANG CHU WON
President

CHANG SU TOK
Secretary General

HAN CHIN HUI
Chief, Labor Affairs Bureau
Office of Labor Affairs, ROKG

131

US FORCES WAGE SCHEDULE

KOREA
MANUAL (KWB) WAGE SCHEDULE
LOCALLY HIRED, NON-US CITIZEN EMPLOYEES

HOURLY STEP RATES (KOREAN WON)

KWB GRADE	STEP A	STEP B	STEP C	STEP D	STEP E	STEP F	STEP G	STEP H	STEP I	STEP J
1	77	80	84	87	91	95	98	102	105	109
2	97	102	107	111	116	121	125	130	135	139
3	119	125	131	136	142	148	153	159	165	170
4	136	143	149	156	162	168	175	181	188	194
5	153	160	167	175	182	189	197	204	211	218
6	171	179	187	195	203	211	219	227	235	244
7	188	197	206	215	224	233	242	251	260	269
8	206	216	225	235	245	255	265	274	284	294
9	223	234	245	255	266	277	287	298	309	319
10	240	252	263	275	286	297	309	320	332	343
11	294	308	322	336	350	364	378	392	406	420
12	345	362	378	395	411	427	444	460	477	493
13	396	415	434	453	472	491	510	529	548	566

Effective Date: 1 January 1971

BEN B BEESON
Asst DCSPER (Civ Per)
US Army, Pacific

JOHN E. TAYLOR
Director Civilian Personnel
US Pacific Air Forces

WILLIAM M. MEAUT
Fleet Civilian Personnel Director
US Pacific Fleet

132

US FORCES WAGE SCHEDULE

KOREA
NON-MANUAL (KGS) WAGE SCHEDULE
LOCALLY HIRED, NON-US CITIZEN EMPLOYEES

HOURLY STEP RATES (KOREAN WON)

KGS GRADE	STEP A	STEP B	STEP C	STEP D	STEP E	STEP F	STEP G	STEP H	STEP I	STEP J
1	82	86	90	94	98	102	106	110	114	118
2	109	114	120	125	130	135	140	146	151	156
3	135	142	148	155	161	167	174	180	187	193
4	162	170	178	185	193	201	208	216	224	232
5	189	198	207	216	225	234	243	252	261	270
6	215	225	236	246	256	266	276	287	297	307
7	242	253	265	276	288	300	311	323	334	346
8	268	281	293	306	319	332	345	357	370	383
9	305	319	334	348	363	378	392	407	421	436
10	342	358	374	391	407	423	440	456	472	488
11	379	397	415	433	451	469	487	505	523	541
12	452	473	495	516	538	560	581	603	624	646
13	526	551	576	601	626	651	676	701	726	751

Effective Date: 1 January 1971

BEN B BEESON
Asst DCSPER (Civ Per)
US Army, Pacific

JOHN E. TAYLOR
Director Civilian Personnel
US Pacific Air Forces

WILLIAM M. MEAUT
Fleet Civilian Personnel Director
US Pacific Fleet

133

US FORCES WAGE SCHEDULE

KOREA
MARINE (KM) WAGE SCHEDULE
LOCALLY HIRED, NON-US CITIZEN EMPLOYEES

HOURLY STEP RATES (KOREAN WON)

KM GRADE	STEP A	STEP B	STEP C	STEP D	STEP E	STEP F	STEP G	STEP H	STEP I	STEP J
1	113	118	123	129	134	139	145	150	155	161
2	125	131	137	143	149	155	161	167	173	179
3	140	147	154	160	167	174	180	187	194	200
4	153	160	167	175	182	189	197	204	211	218
5	179	187	196	204	213	222	230	239	247	256
6	202	211	221	230	240	250	259	269	278	288
7	239	251	262	274	285	296	308	319	331	342
8	277	290	304	317	330	343	356	370	383	396
9	363	380	397	415	432	449	467	484	501	518
10	415	435	454	474	494	514	534	553	573	593

Effective Date: 1 January 1971

BEN B BEESON
Asst DCSPER (Civ Per)
US Army, Pacific

JOHN E. TAYLOR
Director Civilian Personnel
US Pacific Air Forces

WILLIAM M. MEAUT
Fleet Civilian Personnel Director
US Pacific Fleet

134

3. 1971

135

二四〇명 減員통고

美제20일반지원단

【부평】속보=七일 미제二〇일반 지원단은 산하 三千五百여 한인종업원중 약一〇%에 해당하는 二百四十명에 대해 오는二월九일자로 해고하겠다는 감원통고를 해당종업원들에게 개별발송했다。대부분 十년이상 공병대와 항공대 사무직등에서근무해온 이들 종업원들은 부대기구가 축소된것도아니고 기지가 폐쇄된것도 아닌데 엄동설한에 내쫓는다는것은 있을수없는 일이라고 반발하고있다。

美軍二師六百여從業員 外機에減員反對를호소

【문산】七일 미二사단 예하부대소속六百여 막사종업원들은 집단감원계획에반대、이를철회해달라고 외기노조 파주지부와 사단노무처등 요로에 진정하는 한편、중재를 호소했다。

미二사단 九보병一대대소속李梁煥씨 (四二) 를비롯 각부대별 막사에 근무하는 六百여 미충당종업원들은 동두천등 부대이동지까지 따라가 계속취업하기를 희망하고있으나 미二사단당국은 소속부대장의 개인고용방침을 억제하고 오는 二월말까지 지역별로 전원감원할 방침을 밝힌바있다。

美軍산하韓国人종업원失業대비

短期직업訓鍊실시

労動庁

노동청은 17일 주한미군 감축에따른 미군산하 한국인 종업원의 실업사태에 대비, 미8군및 외기노조와 합의아래 4만여 종업원에게 전직할수있도록 단기직업훈련을 실시키로했다.

사무직은 외국인투자기업체와 무역상사로, 특수기술직은 수요가 절대부족한 국내기능직으로, 서비스직은 관광업체로, 단순노무직은 공공토목사업및 단기취업으로 알선한다는 것이다.

노동청의 단기훈련계획은 ①미군의직업훈련소에서 양성하는 운전사, 조리사, 중기조정공등 42개 직종에 걸친 훈련을 활용, 전문기능공을 키우고 ②금해 6월말까지의 감원대상자 1만6천명을 전국 25개직업안정소를 통해 취업알선하며 ③해외개발공사를 통해 보르네오, 인도네시아, 괌도, 사이판등지에 약9백명을 내보내고④상공부, 건설부, 국방부등과 협조, 국영기업체, 각종공공토목사업, 한국군군속으로 흡수시키는 것등을 내용으로하고 있다.

137

Call on Lions To Aid KNOP

71.2.3. 5&S.

BUPYONG, Korea (Special) — In a recent address presented to the members of the Inchon Lions Club, Charles G. Farmer, ASCOM civilian personnel officer, praised the long, faithful and qualitative services of 8th Army employes and requested the Lions' membership to assist in the 8th U.S. Army's Korean National Outplacement Program (KNOP) efforts during the current personnel reductions.

Vice Mayor of Bupyong, Han Yong Su affirmed Farmer's request saying, "Qualified ASCOM area employes should be given all support possible as members of the Inchon community."

Currently, 92 employes of the 20th General Support Group and 69th Transportation Bn. are availing themselves of KNOP training courses being conducted at Ascom.

Korean employes and instructors are devoting their off-duty time to prepare themselves for Republic of Korea government licenses as auto mechanics and plumbers. Farmer stated that many other types of skills training and testing for ROK government certificates and licenses will be available shortly.

138

현 황

1971. 3. 31. 현재

주한미군 한국인 종업원

총 수	39,467 명
(직종수)	(1,300)
중요직책요원	9,956 명
(직종수)	(265)
미8군에 근무	6,903 명
해 군	93 "
공 군	584 "
초청계약자	1,845 "
	807 "
	534 "
계	9,956 "

36개 직종이 파업할 경우 군사작전상 심히 방해

139

사무 직종 명세

직 종 명

1. 전자계산관계 도서관원 5
2. 항공 관제사 7,8
3. 방역 검역관및 감독 5,10
4. 통병 보좌관 7,9
5. 지구고용 관리관 9
6. 부 소방서장 9,10
7. 경비 보좌관 9
8. 개인 화물 주임서기 4–6
9. 숙사 행정관 4–6
10. 마약검수원 및 감독 4–7
11. 마약 검사관 7–9
12. 현금 출납원 감독 5–7
13. 민사 전문관 9,10
14. 숙사 주임서기 4–6
15. 전화 번호부 주임서기
16. 방송국 주임서기 4–6
17. 번역주임서기(병원) 4–6
18. 식당 매니저 5–11
19. 가미세리 감독 5–8
20. 통신 전문관 7–12
21. 대민관계 전문관 7–9
22. 건축 설계기사 및 감독 [illegible]
23. 건축 검사관 [illegible]
24. 범죄 수사관및 감독 9,11
25. 통관 전문관 7–11
26. 전자계산기 자료 처리 서기 및 감독 5–11
27. 치과 조수 5
28. 치과 위생관 5
29. 치과 의사 11
30. 의치술사 7
31. 드라이크리닝종 감독 9
32. 교육 행정관 7–12
33. 교육 보좌관 5–7
34. 전기 공학기사 5–12
35. 전자공학 기사 5–11
36. 전자 기술원 및 감독 5–11
37. 노동 고문관 5–12
38. 공학 기사 9–12
39. 근흥 전문기사 9–11
40. 장비 지술관 5–11

140

1. 화재 [illegible]	5-7	64. [illegible]	[illegible]
2. 화재예방 검열관	5-7	65. [illegible]	5-7
. 화재 예방 전문관	7-11	66. 법원서류 [illegible]	4-8
4. 외국정보 전문관	7-11	67. 의료 기술원 및 감독	7-10
5. 무장 경비원	3,4	68. 도서관원(음악)	5-7
6. 무장경비원 감독	5-10	69. 콘솔 조작원(음악)	4-6
. 군견 경비원 및 감독	4-8	70. 방송원고 편집자	7-11
8. 고 관	5-9	71. 기 자	9-11
9. 정보 보좌관	5-11	72. 보조 간호원	5,6
0. 정보조사 전문관 및 감독	7-12	73. 간호원	7
1. [illegible]	11-12	74. 급여 주임서기및 감독	5-10
2. 통 번역관	5-13	75. 유류품질 통제관리관감독	9-11
3. 보급관리관 및 감독	7-12	76. 유류탱크 조사원및 감독	4-6
4. 조사관 및 감독	5-11	77. 약제사	4-7
5. 실험실 기사	5-7	78. 물리요법사	7
56. 세탁 전문관	8	79. 부두장	7-11
57. 세탁소 지배인	9	80. 유류 저장감독	5-7
58. 법률 보좌관	9-11	81. 우편주임서기 및 감독	4-6
59. 도서관원	7-9	82. 공중위생 전문관	7-11
60. 도서관 보좌관 및 감독	4-7	83. 공보관	9-12
61. 해상무역 선적 전문관및감독	7-11	84. 품질관리 통제관	7-11
62. 기계 공장장(해상)	11	85. 품질 검사관	7-1
63. 의료 보좌관		86. 아나운서	7-9

141

87. 라디오 프로듀서 9–11
88. 방송원고 집필및 편집원 9–11
89. 철도수송 주임서기 및 감독 4–7
90. 철도 수송전문관 7–9
91. 졸병 보좌관 4–8
92. 졸병 조장 4–9
93. 졸병 전문관 7–9
94. 안전관 5–12
95. 위생 검열관 7–9
96. 판매서기 및 감독 5–7
97. 수석비서(타자) 5
98. 수송 보좌관 5,7
99. 수송 주임서기 및 감독 4–7
100. 수송 전문관 및 감독 7–9
101. 소형 선박 배차계 5
102. 저장 주임서기 및감독 4–7
103. 보급 주임서기 및 감독 4–7
104. 보급청구 주임서기 및감독 4–6
105. 고 사 7–8
106. 텔렉스 조작원 4,5
107. 주임교환수 및 감독
108. 현금 출납원 4–6
109. 부두 운영관리관
110. 교통관리관 및 보좌관 9–12
111. 교통관리 전문관 7–11
112. 번 역 관 7–9
113. 수송 보좌관 6–7
114. 수송 주임서기 및 감독 4–7
115. 수송관리 전문관 7–11
116. 수송 전문관 7–9
117. 출장 전문관 5–7
118. 출장 주임서기 4–6
119. 수의사 11
120. 별관 매점지배인 및 부지배인 5–10
121. 제과공장 지배인 및 부지배인 9,10
122. 간이식당 지배인 및 부지배인 5,10
123. 위탁판매 전문관 7–11
124. 고객업무 전문관 5–7
125. 백화점 지배인 6–8
126. 상품진열 전문가 및 감독 5–10
127. 매점 출납계원 5,6
128. 식당운영관리 지배인 및 부지배인 11,12
129. 보험 및 청구 주임서기 4–7
120. 상품 조정관 10–12

142

131. 상품 검사원 및 감독	5—8
132. 소매상 지배인 및 부지배인	7—11
133. 위탁영업관리 지배인 및 부지배인	9—12
134. 스낵바 지배인 및 부지배인	5—8
135. 보급소 감독	7—9
136. 가격표시 감독	6
137. 전자계산기 조작관리관	12
138. 식품기술 고문	11—12
139. 판매기술 고문	11,12
140. 위탁영업 기술고문	11,12
141. 보급창고 감독	5—11
142. 운동교관	7 [illegible]
143. 보우링지배인 및 부지배인	6—9
144. 예약주임서기 및 감독	4—7
145. 크럽지배인 및 부지배인	4—10
146. 크럽 운영자	4,5
147. 크럽주방장 및 부주방장	4—9
148. 구매원	8
149. 기상 관측사	9—11
150. 기상 예보관	5—7

143

기능패출

41. 중장비 운전사 및 감독 5—10
42. 탄약 취급공 및 감독 6—10
43. 고압 보이라공 및 감독 6,9
44. 소방원 5
45. 소방원(조장) 6
46. 소방차 운전사 6
47. 소방원 감독 10
48. 소방물차 운전사 5
49. 시설장비 정비공 및 감독 6—11
50. 감독(전기술 계통) 9—13
51. 중기계차 운전사 6
52. 살균기계 조작원 6
53. 개솔린 모타 수리공 및 감독 6,7
54. 발전기 수리공 6
55. 난방장비 정비공 및 감독 6—10
56. 난방장비 검사원 7
57. 배리큐 터 정비공 및 감독 6—8
58. 전기 수리공 및 감독 6—8
59. 취사도구 장비수리공 6
60. 세탁공 감독 8—10
61. 세탁기계공 및 감독 5—10
62. 드라이크리닝 장비 정비공 및 감독 6,7
63. 세탁부 감독 6
64. 전기술 계통 반장 6,9
65. 측량수문 조작원 및 감독 6—11
66. 부분품 제조 검사원 8
67. 선반공 및 감독 7—11
68. 선박엔진 및 장비경비공 및 감독 7—12
69. 의료장비 수리공 6
70. 금속차체 수리공 및 감독 6—7
71. 자체운행장비 정비공 및 감독 6—11
72. 사무용품기계 수리공 및 감독 6—9
73. 포장공 및 감독 5—8
74. 포장 처리공 및 감독 5—9
75. 포장 검사원 5
76. 화약 및 곤충약 살포원 및 감독 6—10
77. 유류 검사원 5
78. 철근공 및 감독 6—10
79. 연관공 및 감독 6—11
80. 지상동력 장비 수리공 및 감독 6—10
81. 예방 정비공 및 감독 6—10
82. 인쇄기정비공 및 감독 6

144

83. 인쇄기 조작원 및 감독 6—9
84. 영사기 수리공 6
85. 병참 장비 검사원 7
86. 레이다 수리공(고압) 8
87. 냉동기 정비공 및 감독 6—10
88. 리거 및 감독 5,9
89. 분비물 처리 기계공 및감독 6—9
90. 철판공 및 감독 6—11
91. 선박 연관공 및 감독 6—11
92. 군화수선 기계 수리공 6
93. 군화 수선공 및 감독 5—8
94. 소총 검사원 7
95. 소총 수리공 및 감독 6—9
96. 안경 렌스공 7
97. 고압 연관공 및 감독 6—9
98. 수신타자 설치 및 수리공 6
100. 급수 공급공 및 감독 6—12
101. 지게차 운전사 5,6
102. 창고계 및 감독 5—9
103. 식수공 및 감독 6—11
104. 용접공 및 감독 6—10
105. 용접 검사원 7
106. 윈치 조작원 5
107. 제과제품 생산지배인 7—11
108. 보수공 감독 6—9
109. 텔레비 수리공 및 감독 7—11
110. 항공화물 적재원 감독 6—9
111. 항공기 지상정비 수리공 및 감독 6—9
112. 송유 배관공 및 감독 7—[illegible]
113. 열쇠 수리공 및 감독 6—9
114. 식당 감독 및 부감독 8—10
115. 이동 판매차량 운전사 7
116. 자동 판매기 기술원 7
117. 자동판매기 조작공 5
118. 자동판매 반장 8

1145

제 삼 사 용 직 서

직 책 명	등 급
1. 밧지 품투공(급수—유류)	6
2. 밧지 품투공(급수—유류)	7
3. 갑판장	5
4. 기관장	9
5. 기중기 기사	8
6. 기중기 선장	9
7. 기중기 운전사	8
8. 기관사 (소형 선박)	6
9. 기관사(급수—유류 밧지)	8
10. 소방원 (해상)	4
11. 일등 기관사	8
12. 일등 항해사	8
13. 선 장	10
14. 조기원	4
15. 무선 통신사	6
16. 이등 기관사	7
17. 이등 항해사	7
18. 소형 선박 항해사	7
19. 삼등 기관사	6
20. 삼등 항해사	6

146

Agenda Item II

노동청기준(한국)

외 무 부

27-2556

년 월 일

김세국 사무관
(노동청)

1. VTP 目的.

i) 부가 技術연마

ii) 시험 및 면허취득.

iii) 해고 노무의 취직알선.

2. the commander of USFK 사업요청(외무부)

3. 현황.

① 11개 직업훈련소 실시할수. — 1군산하 (I corp)

② 1,450名 양성중임. — 86개 새교실 신설계획. —2,000명 수용計劃.

③ Key punch, driving, welding, electricity.

④ 교관 : 미군 강사(?), 미간인강.

4. outplacement 向 2과 General orientation for new job for those Korean employees

147

AGENDA ITEM US Presentation

(1. FOR YOUR INFORMATION: This presentation is designed to put into the Joint Committee record a brief statement concerning the coordinated USFK-ROK Government Korean Nationals Outplacement Program (KNOP) and to seek maximum ROK Government cooperation and assistance in the implementation of this program. Since the joint US-ROK announcement of the troop reduction plans, the ROKG has been giving vigorous attention to the problem of placement of USFK's Korean employees.)

2. The United States Forces, Korea, in coordination with the appropriate authorities and organizations of the Republic of Korea, has developed a vocational training program for its Korean employees. This program is designed to assist Korean national employees of the United States Forces, Korea, who face possible loss of their jobs as the result of the United States troop reductions in Korea, to obtain continued employment in jobs which contribute to the economic growth and mutual defense of the Republic of Korea. These Korean employees are an effective and industrious work force, engaged in about 200 different occupations involving a wide range of skills. This program has three primary objectives, as follows:

a. Vocational training to develop additional skills of employees to prepare them for eventual outplacement opportunities in the Korean economy when their employment is terminated;

148

b. Testing and licensing of employees, as required by Korean ~~labor laws,~~ for specific crafts, trades, and other vocations; and

c. ~~Outplacement~~ of Korean employees declared surplus by reduction in force.

3. It is hoped that this program will help insure that the skills and proven abilities of these workers will continue to be utilized by the Republic of Korea after their service with the United States armed forces is completed. This is important both for the valuable impetus they can offer to the continued economic growth of the Republic, and for the welfare of the employees themselves. The Commander of the United States Forces, Korea, General J. H. Michaelis, has written letters to the Minister of National Defense and the Minister of Health and Social Affairs outlining this program and soliciting their assistance and support to insure its successful implementation. I would like to propose that these letters be included in the minutes of this meeting.

4. This program has gotten off to a good start in various parts of the Republic. Eleven vocational training centers have been established throughout Korea, and surveys have been conducted to determine vocational training needs and certification requirements. Classes have been organized and thus far approximately 1,450 employees are either undergoing training, or have already completed training, with 86 new classes scheduled to start at an early date for an additional 2,000

2

149

employees. Courses include such subjects as welding, plumbing, electricity, air conditioning and refrigeration, heavy duty engineering equipment operation, training for auto mechanics, driver's training, key punch operation, etc. Instructors include United States and Korean military and civilian personnel, many of whom are contributing their own time voluntarily as part of the joint civil affairs program. About 235 employees have already been tested for certification and 701 employees are currently scheduled to be tested. More vocational training centers will be established at additional locations, contingent upon employees' needs, and the availability of qualified instructor personnel.

5. This program should materially assist the Korean employees of the United States Forces, Korea, who may be required to change their employment, to continue to utilize their natural talents and special skills for the continued benefit of the Republic of Korea and of themselves and their families. The cooperation of the various agencies of the Government of the Republic of Korea in the successful implementation of this program is greatly appreciated.

(6. FOR YOUR INFORMATION: The ROK Government is cooperating with this USFK program and has launched various related projects. The ROK Representative will concur in the inclusion of General Michaelis' letters in the minutes of this meeting and appropriately respond to the US statement.)

3

150

「韓國人六千명減員」통보

駐韓美軍 내달90% 六月에10%

駐韓美軍부대 종업원 六千여명이 오는六月말까지 감원될것으로 밝혀졌다。

十八日 全國外機勞組에 의하면 최근 미군당국은 勞組측에 ▲陸軍세출자금종업원 三千七百명 ▲한국인노무단(KSC) 一千五百명 ▲영선업무를 맡고있는 초청청부업체 종업원八百명등 모두 六千명을 오는 六月말까지 감원하겠다고 통보해온것으로 밝혀졌다。

이六千명의 감원외에도 아직 수자가 결정되지않은 클럽 야전식당종업원등 非세출종업원가운데 예상되는 약一千명의 감원(蔡桂元위원장말)을 합치면 총감원수자는 七千명정도 되지만 노조가 지난 十五日까지 모집한 자원퇴직자 一千二百명을 빼면 駐韓美軍의 감축계획에따른 外機종업원들의 감원수자는 대체로 六千명선이될것같다。

그런데 이들 감원대상자六千여명중 거의九○%에 해당하는 종업원을 미군당국은 오는四月十五日에 감원할예정이며 나머지一○%는 六月말에 감원할것으로 계획하고있다는데 노조측은 空軍과 PX계통엔 감원이 없을것으로 보고있다。 노동청과 勞組 미군당국은 이들감원대상자들에게 현재 미군부대내에서 중장비운전등 轉職훈련을 실시하고있으며 노조측은 또 미군당국에대해 ㈠감축되지않은 부

151

오늘 KSC 總罷業

美軍당국감원에 항의 無期限으로

【坡州】전국 미군부대에 종사하고있는 한국인 노무자(KSC) 전원 (약3천명)이 7일 상오7시를 기해 총파업에들어갈 예정이다.

이들은 미군당국이 지난 4월초 노사협의회에서 전체한국인 노무자 5천여명중 1천명만감원, 4천명을 그대로 취업토록 하겠다고 약속해놓고 계속해서 일부 간부를포함하여 약1천명을 감원시킴으로써 노조기능을 와해시키고있다고주장, 요구조건이 관철될때까지 무기한파업에 들어가기로했다.

이들이 제시한 세가지요구사항은 ①노사협정을 이행할것 ②4천명선의 취업을 이행할것 ③부당한 인사방침을 철회하고 일반군속과 동일한 대우를해줄것 등이다.

기 안 용 지

분류기호 문서번호	미이 723 -	(전화번호)	전결규정 조 항 국 장 전결사항
처리기간			
시행일자	71. 5. 10.		
보존년한			장 관
보조기관	외무부	구미국장	
		북미 2과장	
기안책임자	외무사무관 권 찬		
경유 수신 참조	전국 외기노조 위원장	발신	발송 No. 8433 1971.5.11 외무부 / 검열 1971.5.11 통제관
제목	탄원서 송신		

대 : 전외노 제10-378

대호 건 주한미군 당국에 알아본 바에 의하면 미군 부산항만 수송사령부가 본건에 관해 한국군 당국과 실무진에서 일차 논의한바는 있었으나 아무런 결정도 내린바 없으며, 따라서 당분간은 현상에 변동이 없을 것이라고 합니다. 끝

정서

관인

발송

공통서식 1-2 (갑) 1967. 4. 4 승인

190mm×268mm 중질지 70g/m² 조달청 1000,000매 인쇄)

153

외 무 부

미이 723 - 71. 5. 11.

수신 : 전국 외기노조 위원장

제목 : 탄원서 응신

대 : 전외노 제 10 - 378

대호 건 주한미군 당국에 알아본 바에 의하면 미군 부산 항만 수송 사령부가 본건에 관해 한국군 당국과 실무진에서 일차 논의한 바는 있었으나 아무런 결정도 내린바 없으며, 따라서 당분간은 현상에 변동이 없을 것이라고 합니다. 끝

외 무 부 장 관

154

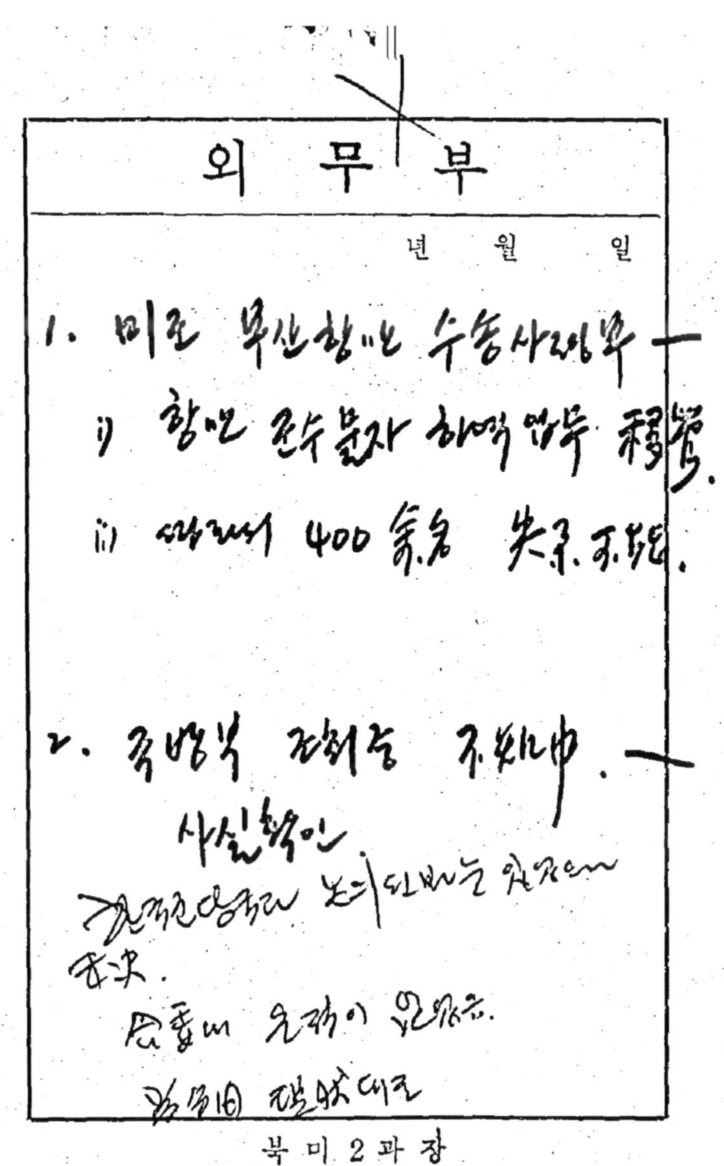

외 무 부

년 월 일

1. 미군 부산항에 수송사령부 —

i) 항만 관수물자 하역 업무 移管.

ii) 따라서 400余名 失業 予想.

2. [illegible] 조회중 [illegible]. —

사실확인

[illegible]

[illegible]

[illegible]

[illegible]

북 미 2 과 장

0155

전 국 외 국 기 관 노 동 조 합

전외노 제 10-378 호 (23-1564) 1971. 5. 6

수 신 외무부 장관

제 목 탄원서 제출

1. 주한 미군 부산 항만 수송 사령부가 관장해 오던 미 항만 군수 물자 하역 업무가 현재까지 그 작업량이나 물동량이 조금도 감소되지 않고 있음에도 불구하고 갑자기 한국군으로 이관될 계획이 진행중인바

2. 이의 즉시 중지로서 한국인 종업원 약 400 여명의 실직과 막대한 외화의 손실을 방지하여 주시옵기 별첨과 같이 탄원서를 제출하오니 적극적인 협조 있으시기 바랍니다.

유 첨 : 탄원서 1 부 끝

전 국 외 국 기 관 노 동 조 합

위 원 장 강 주

156

외 무	7	11:46
접수일시	197 . . . 시 분	지시사항
접수번호	제 18069 호	
주무과		
담당자		
위임근거		

탄 원 서

외무부 장관 귀하

요지 : 미 부산 항만 수송 사령부 하역업무의 한국군 이관 계획을 중지함으로서 400여 한국인 종업원의 실직과 막대한 외화(손실을 방지하여 주시기 바랍니다.

현재 주한 미군 제 2 수송단 부산 항만 수송 사령부가 관장해 오던 미 항만 군수물자 하역업무 및 하역장비가 한국군 제 3 수송 사령부로 이관되는 제반 계획이 점차 실시 과정에 있어 현지 종업원 약 400 여명이 20 년간 근무해 오던 직장을 잃게될 시급한 위기에 처하여 불안한 나날을 보내고 있어 본 조합 3 만여 조합원을 대표하여 귀하의 성의있는 관심과 협조로서 그들의 살길이 마련될 수 있도록 조치하여 주시기를 탄원하는 바입니다.

주한 미군 부산 항만 사령부가 지난 20 년간 관장해 오던 미 군수 하역업무가 현재까지 정책의 변동없이 수행되고 있는 현 실태임에도 불구하고 갑작스럽게 한국군으로 이관되어 아무런 대책없이 수백명의 종업원이 일시에 실직되는 사태는 조합의 문제이기 보다는 오히려 사회적 중대사라 하겠읍니다.

그간 주한 미군의 철수로 인한 한국인 종업원의 대량감원이란 대 시련을

-157

겪고 있는 외기노조 사상 최악의 시점에서 크나큰 혼란과 파동이 우려되었으나 본 조합은 국가의 대내외적 정책과 국제적 정세 변동을 감안하여 벌써 수천명 종업원의 감원을 별다른 파동없이 감수하였던 것입니다.

그러나 부산 미 항만 수송 사령부가 작업량 또는 물동량의 감소 또는 작업의 기계화 제도로 인한 감원실시 혹은 미군철수나 기구 통합등으로 인한 미 항만 작업 전반의 폐쇄인 경우에는 조합으로서도 부득이한 사태 이겠읍니다만 한국군으로 이관되거나 하청시킨다 함은 국가적으로 보아 외화의 막대한 손실 (400 여명 종업원의 년간 총 임금 ¥364,816,035) 이며 이로 말미암아 수백명의 종업원과 그들 가족의 생계에 큰 위협을 주게 될것이므로 조합은 도저히 좌시할 수 없어 자에 탄원하오니 미군의 부산 항만 하역 작업의 한국군 이관 계획이 즉시 중지됨으로서 400여 종업원과 그 가족의 생계가 보장되고 아울러 막대한 외화 손실이 방지될 수 있도록 적극적인 협조를 바랍니다.

1971. 5. 6

전 국 외 국 기 관 노 동 조 합

위 원 장 강 주

158

LABOR-MANAGEMENT AGREEMENT MAY 20 1971

CHAPTER I - GENERAL OBJECTIVES AND POLICIES

Art. 1-Introduction. a. This Agreement is made by and between the United States Forces, Korea, hereinafter referred to as the "Employer" and the Foreign Organizations Employees Union, hereinafter referred to as the "Union."

b. It is the intent of the parties hereto to establish a basic agreement governing labor-management relations which will provide a means of consultation and negotiations on certain designated matters of mutual interest to the Employer and the Union, thus helping to provide effective personnel support to USFK missions, better employee-management communications and improved working conditions.

c. Both the Employer and the Union will undertake necessary actions to assure compliance with this Agreement. In instances of noncompliance the involved party will take immediate steps to assure compliance with procedures for labor-management relations of this Agreement.

Art. 2-Definitions. For the purpose of this Agreement, the following definitions apply unless otherwise specified:

a. The Employer. Refers to USFK and to its Army, Air Force and Navy components (including KRE and other nonappropriated fund organizations) and to other activities associated with or under the jurisdiction of the USFK or one of its military components. Included are those organizations and persons (including invited contractors) designated as falling under paragraph 1a of Article XVII of the US-ROK Status of Forces Agreement.

b. The Employee. Korean national employees of the Employer.

c. The Union. An organized Korean employee group (Foreign Organizations Employees Union) which represents personnel employed by various organizations of the Employer cited above.

Art. 3-Relationship to the Labor Article, US-ROK, SOFA. Where there is any conflict between the provisions of this Agreement and the provisions of the SOFA, the provisions of the Labor Article in the US-ROK Status of Forces Agreement, Agreed Understandings and Agreed Minutes prevail.

Art. 4-Recognition of the Foreign Organizations Employees Union. The Foreign Organizations Employees Union is recognized by the Employer as the exclusive representative of Korean personnel employed by the Employer provided the following requirements are met.

159

Labor-Management Agreement (cont'd)

a. A copy of the organization's constitution and bylaws and a statement of objectives is presented to the Employer.

b. A current roster of the organization's officers and representatives is furnished the Employer.

c. The Union has a membership of not less than 50 per cent of the employees of the Employer.

d. Requirements of Republic of Korea labor laws concerning union certification and union activities are met.

Art. 5-Relationships to Established Personnel Policies and Working Conditions.

a. Current personnel policies governing wages, working conditions and personnel practices established by USFK and its components and activities continue in effect, except where SOFA Labor Article provisions apply.

b. Substantial changes to policies in areas for which consultation or negotiation is provided will be preceded by exchange of opinion with the Union. (See Article 13 of the Agreement.)

c. The Union may at any time request changes in policies where applicable under Article 13 of this Agreement. The limitation of Article 18 of this Agreement is not applicable to requests for changes in policies under this Article.

Art. 6-Status of Employees. a. Membership or non-membership in a labor union or other employee organizations will not be a factor in employment or other actions affecting employees.

b. Employees have the right freely and without interference, restraint, coercion or fear of penalty or reprisal to organize, join or assist any employee organization, or equally, to refrain from such activity.

c. Employees have the right to designate Union representatives for the purpose of consulting with management officials on individual grievances and appeals or to handle their own grievances and appeals and to choose their own representative in accordance with applicable regulations.

d. Because of special features involving nonappropriated fund employees (except employees of KRE) and certain invited contractors, a number of policy revisions and different union-management arrangements may be required between the two parties.

Art. 7-Status of Managerial Employees. a. Exclusions. Korean employees in the following positions who take action on behalf of the Employer and high level supervisory employees shall be considered managerial employees and shall not be members of the Union:

(1) Personnel Specialist (includes only positions of KGS-7 and above).

(2) Attorney and similar legal positions.

(3) Procurement Specialist and technical positions concerned with procurement (includes only positions of KGS-7 and above).

(4) Medical Officer.

(5) Confidential and investigative-type positions in security organizations.

(6) Investigative and inspection-type positions involving relations with the community or the workforce.

(7) Master.

(8) Officer of the Guard and Assistant Officer of the Guard.

(9) General Foreman and Assistant General Foreman.

(10) Other high-level supervisory positions whose titles include the word "Manager" or "Superintendent" (as for example "Club Manager", "PX Manager", "Pier Superintendent" and "Assistant PX Managers", and "Snack Bar Manager"), when supervision includes at least 10 subordinate personnel.

b. Union membership. Occupants of the following middle level supervisory and managerial positions are designated managerial employees, who may be union members but may not serve in an official position with the Union:

(1) Level III supervisors with functional responsibility for overall administrative operations, as defined in EA CPP 690-2, including Payroll Clerk Supervisor (Level III), Accounting Clerk Supervisor, Card Punch Operator Supervisor, Storekeeping Clerk Supervisor, Clerk Supervisor, Digital Computer and Systems Operator Supervisor, Telephone Operator Supervisor, Stock Control Clerk Supervisor, etc.

(2) Sergeant of the Guard.

c. Foreman and other supervisory personnel (Foreman, Lead Foreman and supervisor Level II, and managers and superintendent (see 7a(10) having 4-9 subordinates) not covered above are not excluded from union membership or office holding. However, they will not engage in union activities, including grievance representation, which affect employees under their supervision.

3

160-1

d. Both the Employer and the Union hold the right to further define supervisory and managerial personnel who are not eligible for union membership.

e. Employees under "b" above who are elected to a union office may serve as "full-time" union officials in accordance with Article 11g of this Agreement.

f. Incumbent union officials not eligible for union membership or to hold office under the preceding criteria will not be eligible to run for another term of office after this Agreement, unless they are to serve as "full-time" union officials in accordance with Article 11g of this Agreement.

Art. 8-Union Officials. a. No union official acting in an official capacity will be discriminated against for his acts as an officer so long as such acts are in accordance with this Agreement and the Labor Article of the Status of Forces Agreement, nor will there be any discrimination against any employee because of his authorized union activities.

b. The Union will not undertake any disciplinary measures or other actions intended to hinder any employee in the discharge of his official duties.

c. The Employer will inform the Union about adverse personnel actions affecting union officials who are elected by a general vote, so long as policy set forth under Article 6a is followed.

Art. 9-Policy Governing Union Activities. a. Activities concerned with internal management of employee organizations, union meetings, and conduct of union officer elections will be held off-post.

b. Distribution of union literature and collection of union dues will not be conducted during regular working hours. However, such activities may be conducted outside of regular working hours (such as lunch periods) on-post so long as such activities do not involve union or group meetings.

c. Material submitted by the Union for posting on bulletin boards may be posted at designated locations after obtaining consent of the appropriate commander or his representative.

Art. 10-Supporting Activities. a. The Employer will furnish copies of this Agreement to interested employees. Information on the Union's status as exclusive representative of employees will be provided by the Employer during orientation and similar activities.

b. Dues check-off applications and related union literature will be available at the employment offices of the Employer.

Art. 11-Time-Off for Union Officials. a. Union-management meetings will normally be conducted during regular working hours.

b. Time spent by union officials in attendance at official union-management meetings and other official union-management relations activities will be considered regular duty time. Union officials will be granted time-off (excused absence) during working hours without charge to leave or loss of pay for such meetings and activities, time spent in preparation for such meetings and activities, and for participation in those types of union activities which relate to union-management issues and not the Union's internal affairs. Time-off may be granted for participation in appeals board meetings. Generally speaking, the following criteria on use of time-off will apply:

(1) Subchapter Vice-Presidents - up to 10% of the regularly scheduled tour of duty during a pay period.

(2) Subchapter Presidents, Vice-Presidents of Chapters and Chiefs of Departments at the national level - up to 15%.

(3) Chapter Presidents - up to 40%.

(4) Secretary General and National Vice-Presidents - up to 40%; The National President - up to 50%. Time-off in excess of this limit may be individually granted to cover increased union-management activities which might occur during a peak period.

(5) Chiefs of Departments at the Chapter level may be granted time-off on an occasional basis as needed.

c. In cases when a union official holds two or more union offices, use of time-off is limited to business of only one office whichever is greater.

d. Union officials will report the need for time-off to supervisors sufficiently in advance to permit rescheduling of work.

e. Time-off limits discussed above do not apply to any time spent in meetings called for matters of only management interest.

f. Time-off for union-management activities described above will not be denied by supervisors except for immediate and temporary reasons of workload urgency for which employee's services are clearly essential. When time-off cannot be agreed to, the employee will be informed when time-off can be granted. Any difference in opinion on workload urgency and use of time-off should be referred through CPO channels to separate command headquarters level for decision.

g. Leave without pay for union officials to serve full-time on union activities will be approved on request of the Union's national office. Full time service with the Union on a leave-without-pay basis will be creditable for reduction in force and step increase purposes. Service credit for severance pay will be recognized for a period of up to 2 years.

Art. 12-Voluntary Dues Allotments. a. The Employer agrees to check-off union dues by payroll deduction subject to provisions of the following paragraphs.

b. Any eligible employee desiring to have his union dues deducted from his pay may, at any time, complete and sign the appropriate portions of the approved form, Request and Authorization for Voluntary Allotment of Compensation Payment of Employee Organization Dues. Such deductions will be effective on the first full pay period following the date that a properly completed allotment form for voluntary deduction is received in the appropriate payroll office.

c. The properly completed form with certifications by the designated officials of the Union will be forwarded or delivered to the Employer's appropriate area civilian personnel office for transmission to the appropriate payroll office. Area civilian personnel offices will assure that completed forms will be transmitted to the appropriate payroll office within one day after receipt.

d. A deduction of one hour's pay in Step D of the pay grade of the employee for each pay period will be made from the pay of an employee who has requested an allotment for dues to the Union, except no deduction for dues will be made by the Employer in any period for which the employee's net earnings, after the other legal and required deductions, are insufficient to cover the full amount of the allotment for dues. Employees paid on a monthly basis (KRE, invited contractors, open messes, and certain Special Services)will have a 13th union dues check-off by deduction from the year-end bonus.

e. A fee of 2 Won per employee per deduction will be charged by the Employer for services rendered in connection with the dues withholding program.

f. The amount of the administrative fee to be retained by the Employer will be deducted from the total dues withheld each pay period and the remaining amount shall be transmitted by the Employer not later than 40 working days after the close of each pay period.

g. The Employer will provide the Union with an initial list in duplicate reflecting the activity name, employee names, individual amount deducted, total amount withheld by the Employer for service fee and the net amount remitted. Each pay period a list of additions or deletions will be provided and annually a revised updated list will be submitted to the Union. The list will be submitted semiannually when mechanization of the payroll function is completed.

h. An employee who authorized the withholding of Union dues may request revocation of such authorization at any time by submitting in duplicate a completed form, Revocation of Voluntary Authorization for Allotment of Compensation for Payment of Employee Organization Dues, or other written request.

i. The Employer will discontinue the withholding of dues from the employees' pay at the beginning of the first full pay period either after 1st March or 1st September of any calendar year, whichever date first occurs after the revocation is received in the appropriate payroll office of the Employer.

j. Any individual allotment for dues withholding will also be terminated automatically upon the employee's separation.

k. The Union will give written notification to the Employer within 10 days after an employee participating in the dues deduction program ceases, for any reason, to be a member in good standing of the Union, i.e., he resigns, has been suspended, or is expelled, in order that the Employer may terminate his allotment of dues.

l. The Union will be responsible for insuring the approved voluntary allotment form is made available to its members and will insure that the forms are properly completed and certified before transmitting them to the Employer.

m. The Union recognizes its responsibility for seeing that its member-employees are fully informed concerning the program for payroll deductions for the Union dues, its voluntary nature and the use and availability of the required form.

n. Changes in the amount of individual employee allotments, by reason of changes in the amount of Union dues, shall not be made more frequently than once a year.

o. The Union shall furnish the Employer, at the earliest practicable date, the name and signature of its representative(s) who are designated to certify the voluntary allotment form. The Union will be responsible for giving the Employer prompt notification of any changes in this designation.

p. The above procedures are applicable also to invited contractors and to KRE. Separate arrangements will be made prior to implementation to meet certain special administrative requirements. Open mess systems and Special Services activities were covered effective 1 July 1968.

CHAPTER II - LABOR-MANAGEMENT RELATIONS

Art. 13-Rights of the Union. a. The Union may at any time request negotiation on policies and procedures relating to personnel policy and working conditions.

b. When such subjects involve possible changes in policy outside the Employer's authority, the Employer will endeavor to obtain higher authority determination without undue delay.

c. Items for negotiation and consultation will include, but not be limited to, such matters as working conditions and facilities, labor-management relations, employee services, disciplinary procedures, methods of adjusting grievances and appeals, granting of leave, promotion plans, demotion practices, internal classification and pay practices, reduction in force procedures, and hours of work.

d. The Union shall present to the Employer, in September - October each year, a request for improvement in employment conditions.

Art. 14-Employer's Rights. a. It is agreed that the customary and usual rights, powers, functions and authority of management are vested in management officials of the Employer.

b. The Employer retains the right in accordance with applicable laws and regulations, to take action in such areas of discretion and policy as mission, budget, security and organization; the technology of performing work; and the determination of schedules of compensation. Also included are: the right to direct the workforce, the right to establish positions, employ, promote, retain, transfer and assign employees; the right to suspend, separate, demote or take other disciplinary action against employees; and the right to relieve employees from duty because of lack of work or in line with para 2, Article XVII, Agreed Minutes, Labor Article, SOFA.

c. The Employer may initiate complaint against the Union following procedures similar to those set forth in Article 15 of this agreement.

d. The Employer shall conduct an annual review on employment conditions within established policy set forth in Article 5 of this Agreement. The Employer will deal with the Union on employment conditions in the course of this review.

Art. 15-Procedures for Labor-Management Relations. In resolving group grievances initiated by the Union, the following procedure will apply:

a. Grievances will first be considered at the Union subchapter and/or local chapter level and at the level of local command and other activities including Invited Contractors. Local chapters of the Union as a minimum will be consulted in advance on reduction in force in organizations where 3 or more incumbent positions are scheduled for cancellation and similarly of significant change to lower grade actions. The local chapters will be advised as to when these RIFs or change to lower grade actions are to be accomplished and the reasons therefor. They will also be provided with information as to offsetting actions which will be taken to assist employees in securing continued employment.

b. Unresolved union grievances at a lower level will be referred for resolution, without delay or without resort to actions not in line with this Agreement, to higher union levels up to the national Union.

c. Unresolved grievances will be referred to the respective headquarters of the Army, Air Force, Navy and KRE, for resolution.

d. Grievances involving overall policy matters not resolved at separate command headquarters levels may be referred by the Union or separate command headquarters for review and further action by Headquarters, USFK.

e. An unresolved grievance of major significance may be referred as a dispute to the Office of Labor Affairs in accordance with para 4, Art. XVII, SOFA Labor Article.

f. Individual employee appeals will be handled in accordance with established policy and procedures.

g. The Union will not recognize or endorse any action disruptive of normal work requirements during the course of these procedures.

Art. 16-<u>Meetings and Other Union Management Activities</u>. Meetings will be held as follows:

a. Each level of command (inclusive of clubs, KRE and invited contractors) and union organization will hold meetings on a periodic basis, with some record maintained of the subjects discussed and agreements, if any, reached.

b. In addition to regularly scheduled meetings, special meetings can be held at the request of either party with appropriate notification of subjects for discussion.

c. Union officials may also participate, upon request, in management activities including attendance at special ceremonies and events.

Labor-Management Agreement (cont'd)

Art. 17-Term of Agreement. The term of this Agreement will be one year from the date of agreement as signed by both parties. The Agreement may be renewed before its expiration date to include any agreed-upon changes. If not renewed it will be extended for three months.

Art. 18-Changes or Supplements to Agreement. a. Any changes or supplements to this Agreement, at the request of either party, will be presented three months prior to the effective date proposed for the change. This time requirement may be waived by the consent of both parties.

b. These changes or supplements will take the form of a supplemental agreement which has equal validity to this Agreement.

c. The supplemental agreement will later be incorporated into this Agreement at the time of renewal, except for a supplement of one-time nature.

Art. 19-Validity of Agreement. a. This Agreement will be effective on the date of signature by both parties, until 20 May 1972.

b. Previous memoranda of understanding or agreements exchanged relating to subjects herein will be superseded by this Agreement.

FOR UNITED STATES FORCES, KOREA:

FREDRIC NEWMAN
Chairman
Joint Labor Affairs Committee

CARL J. BENDER
Executive Secretary
Joint Labor Affairs Committee

FOR FOREIGN ORGANIZATIONS EMPLOYEES UNION:

KANG CHU WON
President

CHANG SU TOK
Secretary General

164

외기노조

71.6.5.

實力行使키로 決議

美大使館不當해고 不容

24日 파업可否投票

쟁의중의 조합원을 집단 해고한 미국대사관측의 부당노동행위에 대한 투쟁대책을 수립하기위하여 6월15일 긴급소집되었던 조합 제2차 중앙위원회는 미국대사관측이 동 부당노동행위를 즉각 철회하지 않을때는 제1차적으로 당사서울지부 6천조합원이 외기노조 전체조직의 지원아래 동정파업을 단행키로했으며 그래도 부당해고가 철회되지 않을때는 제2차적으로 3만전체조합원이 전국적인 동정파업을 감행키로 결의했다.

중앙위원회의 이와같은결의가 있은후 즉시 소집된 동 투쟁위원회 소위원회는 동실력행사를 위하여 오는 6월18일에 서울지부 운영위원회를 개최하고, 22일에는 지부 임시대의원대회를 개최, 법조직적인 투쟁태세를 갖춘다음 24일에는 파업가부투표를 실시키로 결정했다.

미국대사관측이 6월1일 쟁의중인 조합원 92명(모두 10년내지 15년 근속자임) 전원을 해고시킨뒤 조합은 한미우호 관계를 고려하여 되도록 문제를 평화적으로 해결코저 무려15일간에 걸쳐 노동청, 외무부, 미국대사관당국자를과 교섭해 왔고 또한 당사 조합원 92명은 조합에서 4일자의 단식농성 투쟁까지 전개했으나 미국대사관측의 무성의로 문제가 해결되지 않으므로 이와같이 극한투쟁을 결의하게 된것이다.

92명에 대한 사용주인미사절단 후생회의 운영자는 미대사관의 경비업무를 하청하고 있는 업자인 동시에 미8군 영내에서 "크럽"을 운영하고 있는 미국민간인으로 알려지고 있는바 서울시 노동위원회가 작년12월18일 동 쟁의에 대한 적법 판정을 내린 이유도 바로 여기에 근거를 둔것으로 알려지고있다.

지금까지 외기노조는우방외교사절단의 체면을고려하여 온인자중 해왔으나「크럽」을 운영하는 미국 민간인 업자가 외교관 신분으로 치외법권을 주장하는 어처구니없는 태도를 버리지 않고, 또한6월초부터임금및 노동조건을 협의키로 후생회측이 조합에 약속한 기록자서를 이행하지 않으며, 부당 해고를 즉시철회치 않는한 조합은이를끝까지 규탄, 여하한 극한투쟁도 불사할 만반의 태세를 갖추고있다.

또한, 조합은 미사절단후생회가 가령 외교관 신분을 주장할수있는 기관이라고 손치더라도 그들이6월초에 임금 인상문제를 협의키로 자서로서 조합에약속해놓고 이를 이행치않는 배신행위와 전기 임금협상에 앞서 기습적으로 조합원을 전원해고한비신사적인 수법, 그리고 조합원들이담당하던 경비업무를 일시라는구실아래한양건설이란새로운 하청업체에 넘긴 부당노동행위등은 분명히 노조에대한도전행위이며노사분규를 유발한 책임은 사용주측에 있을뿐아니라 설령외교관신분으로 치외법권은누릴수 있다고 하더라도 엄연한 노사관계가 부정될수는 없는 것이므로 조합은 스스로 실력투쟁을 통하여 철회요구를 칭이다。

따라서 조합산하 …

165

미 대사관 경비원 해고와 관련된 문제

(외기노조의 동정 파업)

1971. 6. 21.

1. 문제점

미국 대사관에 종사하던 경비원의 감원문제에 대하여 전국 외국기관 노동조합(외기노조)으로부터 동 조합 산하인 "미 대사관 분회" 경비원 92명 전원에 대한 미 대사관의 해고조치가 경비원의 노동 쟁의에 대한 대사관측의 보복적 행위임을 지적하고, 외기노조원들은 미 대사관 경비원들과 함께 동정파업을 할 기세를 보였다. (투표 결과 부결되었다고 함.)

이러한 외기노조의 행위가 SOFA 의 규정에 위반되느냐? 그 타당성 여부? 노동조합 결성문제와 그 승인문제는?

2. 관계조항

가. SOFA 협정 제17조 4항 (가) :

"고용주와 고용원이나 승인된 고용원 단체간의 쟁의로서, 합중국 군대의 불평처리 또는 노동관계 절차를 통하여 해결할수 없는 것은...

(1) ...노동청에 회부되어야 한다.

166

(2) 그 쟁의가 전기 (1) 에 규정된 절차에 의하여 해결되지 아니한 경우 에는 그 문제는 합동위원회에 회부되며...

(5) ... 합동위원회에 회부된후 적어도 70일의 기간이 경과되지 아니하는 한 정상적인 업무요건을 방해하는 어떠한 행동 에도 종사하여서는 아니된다."

나. 동 17조 4항 (나) :

"고용원 또는 고용원 단체는 노동쟁의가 전기 절차에 의하여 해결되지 아니하는 경우 에는 계속 단체행동권을 가진다. 다만, 합동위원회가 이러한 행동 이 대한민국의 공동 방위를 위한 합중국 군대의 군사 작전을 심히 방해한다고 결정하는 경우 에는 제외 한다."

다. 동 17조 에 대한 합의의사록 5항 :

"조합 또는 기타 고용원 단체는, 그의 목적이 대한민국과 합중국의 공동 이익에 배타되지 아니하는 한, 고용주 에 의하여 승인되어야 한다."

3. 정부측 견해

원칙적으로 고용원과 고용주 간의 쟁의는 한.미 합동위원회에 회부한 이래 70일이 경과한 후 에도 해결책을 발견치 못할 경우 에는 노동쟁의

167

에서 단체권을 행사할수 있게 규정되어 있음. 그러나 이것은 오직 17조 1항 (a) 에 정의한 "고용주" 와 17조 1항 (b) 에 규정된 "고용원"간에만 있을수 있는 일이며, 미 대사관과 외기노조의 경우는 고용주와 고용원의 관계가 아니기 때문에 양자간에는 쟁의란 있을수 없는 일이며, 행여 외기노조가 직접적 관계의 고용관계가 아닌 대사관을 상대해서 쟁의를 감행한다면 이는 미 대사관의 주재국에서의 외교업무 수행에 "심한 방해 행위"라고 간주할수 있다고 사료됨.

동시에 미 대사관의 경비원이 자기들의 분쟁해결 수단으로 미 8군 산하에 고용된 외기노조 조합원들과 함께 단체행동을 감행하는 경우는 합중국 군대의 "군사작전을 심히 방해하는 행위" 라고 추론될수 있음.

끝으로 조합결성을 할수 있느냐 또 승인해야 하느냐 하는 문제에 관해서는 SOFA 협정 제 17조에 대한 합의의사록 5항의 규정에 의해 고용원 단체의 목적이 양국의 공동 이익에 배타되지 아니해야 되고, 또 공동이익의 설정이 양국간에 상치될때 이것은 양국의 합의에 의해 결정되어야 한다는 조건하에서 고용주는 당연히 조합 결성을 승인해야 함. 그러나 구체적으로 대사관 경비원의 경우는 미 대사관 직원들로 구성된 미 대사관 후생회 (U.S. Mission Association) 가 미 대사관의 일부 기관 (An Integral Part) 으로서 국제적 외교 특권을 갖고있는 당사자이기 때문에 동 고용주가 경비원 조합결성을 인정해 주지 않는다면, 비록 경비원

168

들의 조합이 국내 노동법상 인정되는 조합이라 할지라도, 그 단체권 행사에서의 효과면에서는 그 실효성이 없다 할 것임.
미 대사관 경비원을 고용하고 있는 미 대사관 후생회의 법적지위 문제에 관해서는 별첨 참조 하시기 바랍니다.

별첨 : "주한 미 대사관 직원 후생회 경비원의 노동쟁의" 사본 1 부.

169

기 안 용 지

분류기호 문서번호	미일 1453 -	(전화번호)	전결규정 조 항 전결사항
처리기간			
시행일자			
보존년한		차 관	장 관

보조기관	외무부	차관보	
		구미국장	
		북미1과장	
기안책임자		서기관	김봉규 (71. 1. 25)

경 유 수 신 참 조	노 동 청 장	발신	1556

제 목 주한 미대사관 직원 후생회 (U.S. Mission Association) 경비원의 노동쟁의

대 : 노사 1453 - 556 (71. 1. 19.)

대호 문의에 대하여 아래와 같이 회보합니다.

— 아 래 —

1. U.S. Mission Association 의 기구 :

U.S.M.A. 는 미국무성 내규 Foreign Service Act 1946 와 Uniform State / Aid / USIA Regulations 에 의거하여 주한미국사절단 (U.S. Mission : 대사관, USAID 등) 의 직원 후생기관으로 1969. 2. 1. 설치된 것이며 기구 내용의 개략은 아래와 같음.

(1) 조 직 : 구성원은 정회원, 부회원, 임시회원의 3종이 있고, 정회원은 사절단 직원 (외교특권 향유자) 임.

(2) 운 영 : 정규 외교관 3명 (행정담당참사관이 위원장) 으로

공통서식 1-2 (갑) 1967. 4. 4 승인

190mm×268mm 중질지 70g/m²
조 달 청 (500,000매 인쇄)

170

구성된 운영위원회 (Management Board)

에서 모든 운영을 담당함.

(3) 최종감독자: 운영회의 모든 사항은 대사의 최종 결재를 득하게 되어 있음.

2. U.S.M.A. 의 지위 :

가. 법적지위 :

법적으로 볼때 U.S.M.A. 는 국제관례상 일반적으로 인정되고 있는 외교기관은 아니며, ~~따라서~~ 미국대사관의 불가분의 일부 (an integral part) 라고 인정할수 있는 법적 근거는 없음.

나. 사실상의 지위 :

그러나 동 U.S.M.A. ~~의 조직.~~ 운영자와 감독권자가 상기 1항에서 지적한바와 같이 미대사관 직원으로 구성되어 있으므로 ~~대사관 자체의 순수한 후생기관이므로~~ 당자자에 대한 한국 법령의 적용이 사실상 불가능한 지위에 있음.

3. U.S.M.A. 와 경비원과의 관계 :

U.S.M.A. 의 원활한 운영을 위하여 미국대사관은 민간인 (Mr. Herman) 을 1년간 관리자로서 고용 계약 하여 경영하고 있으나 ~~그의 지위는 단순한~~ ~~지위만~~ 미대사관 경비원의 고용자는 U.S.M.A. 인것으로 ~~로서 사실상 미대사관으로 됨.~~ 보임

4. 주한 미대사관 경비원의 노동쟁의에 관한 당부의 의견 :

가. 앞에서 지적한바와 같이 U.S.M.A. 의 실질운영 책임자 당사자가 한국법령의 적용을 받지않는 외교특권을 향유 하고 있으므로 한국법령의 적용이 사실상 불가능 하고,

나. 한.미간의 외교적, 경제적 기타 깊은 유대관계를 감안하여

4471

동 경비원 ▇▇ 권익을 보호함에 있어서는 한국 노동법령의 관계 절차에 따라 실력행사를 함으로서 쟁취하는 ▇▇을 취하기 보다는 상호간 이성있는 원만한 타협이 이루어지는 방향으로 조정함이 가하다고 사료됩니다. ~~이러한 방향에서 해결함에 있어 미대사관측의 부당한 처사가 없도록 하는 필요한 협조는 당부에서 할 것입니다.~~ 끝.

공통서식 1-2 (을)
1967. 4. 4 승인

190mm×268mm 중질지 70g/m²
조 달 청 (500,000매 인쇄)

172

노 동 청

노정 723 7088 27,2557 1971. 7. 5.

수신 외무부장관

참조 구미국장

제목 SOFA노무분과 위원회 한국측 위원명단

1. 미이 723-6233(71. 4. 7)및 노동청 노정 723-3792 (71. 4. 10)과 관련입니다.

2. 변경된 SOFA 노무분과 위원회 한국측 위원명단을 별첨과 같이 통보합니다.

첨부 : SOFA 노무분과위원회 한국측 위원 1부 끝.

노 동 청

173

외 무 부			결재		
접수 일시	197 JUL 71 . 시 분		지시사항		
접수 번호	제27575호				
주무과					
담당자					
귀 순				197 . . .	

노무분과 위원회 한국측위원 명단

직 위	성 명	근 무 처, 직 위	전화번호
위원장	한진희	노동청노정국장	27,2556
간 사	박종관	" 노정담당관	27,2557
위 원	김진경	" 근로지도과장	27,0550
"	이재규	" 직업안정과장	27,2559
"	김대청	중앙노동위원회사무국장	75,7269
"	오자복	중앙병무청 동원소집과장	43,3967
"	김영호	중앙병무청 동원지원과장	43,3983
"	김종환	법무부 법무관	72,8184
"	민석기	" 법무과장	"
"	박용전	치안국정보과장	74,3717
"	김세국	노동청국제노동담담	27,2557

1174

FOREIGN ORGANIZATIONS EMPLOYEES UNION

FOEU#11-212 26 November 1971

SUBJECT: Notification of the Central Executive Council's Resolutions

Commander
United States Forces, Korea
ATTN: Civilian Personnel Director
APO 96301

The FOEU Central Executive Council members in a meeting held on 25 November 1971 reviewed your proposed rate of wage increase by 18% for USFK Korean employees.

Although we appreciate your sincere efforts for improving wages and working conditions of Korean employees based upon friendly labor-management relations, the Council members concluded that an 18% pay increase proposed in your letter of 23 November 1971 was unacceptable. Therefore, in order to push through the finally retreated proposal of 30% pay increase, they resolved to struggle strong as follows:

a. Take a strike vote on 2 and 3 December 1971.

b. When the finally retreated proposal is not accepted, a general strike will be staged for indefinite period of time effective 15 December 1971.

The USFK's counter proposal of an 18% pay increase is not acceptable for reasons:

175

FOEU#11-212 26 November 1971
SUBJECT: Notification of the Central Executive Council's Resolutions

a. That actual increase per year in the cost of staples and other daily necessities exceeded 30% by far.

b. That devaluation in Won by 15% per year occurred already, and labor costs of USFK has decreased by 15% in reality.

c. That USFK Korean employees will be RIFed sooner or later, and their unemployment is at hand. This unstabled employment status has to be carefully considered by management. Only pushing through the finally retreated proposal, recovery from lowered wages to the level of real wages and living wages will be accomplished.

The Council members reaffirmed the importance of classification realignment of KP's grade from KWB-1 to KWB-3. Also, the Council members' discussion included the matter of severance pay computation base using average wages and deterioration in provisions of personnel regulation to make them part of dispute.

We sincerely hope that the finally retreated proposal being resolved by the Central Executive Council be accepted by USFK, and struggle measures stated above will not be needed maintaining peaceful labor-management relations.

An official labor dispute was filed with the Office of Labor Affairs on

2

176

FOEU#11-212 26 November 1971
SUBJECT: Notification of the Central Executive Council's Resolutions

26 November 1971, in accordance with the resolution of the Central Executive Council members.

KANG CHU WON
President

3

177

Office of the Civilian Personnel Director

NOV 27 19..

EACP

Mr. Kang Chu Won
President
Foreign Organizations Employees Union
20, Sokong-dong, Chung-ku
Seoul, Korea

COPY FOR: J-5

Dear Mr. Kang:

Reference our meeting held on 26 November 1971 in which you reported that the FOEU Executive Council approved a strike vote by USFK Korean employees 2-3 December 1971, and that a strike, if finally decided, will occur 15 December protesting the proposal tentative 18% USFK pay increase.

This is to advise you officially that these actions endorsed by FOEU are in violation of the SOFA (Article XVII) and the USFK-FOEU Labor Management Agreement of 20 May 1971 (Article 15, paragraph g). If FOEU implements these actions and refuses to comply with the legal and regulatory requirements prescribed for settling official disputes in a systematic and orderly manner, the USFK will have no alternative but to withdraw its recognition of FOEU as the exclusive representative of USFK Korean employees.

It is sincerely hoped that as National President, FOEU, you will urge the Executive Council to undertake responsible actions which will resolve the dispute in a reasonable prescribed manner.

Truly yours,

FREDRIC NEWMAN
Civilian Personnel Director

Copy furnished:
OLA, ROKG

178

"Come all for Strike Vote to earn wage and ~~life~~ livelihood"

Dear members of the Seoul Chapter, Foreign Organization Employes Union (FOEU)!

On November 23, the United States Forces Korea authority responded with only 18% of wage hike to FOEU's demand of 40% raise issued on October 1.

This is totally a groundless alternative in light of the conditions exist which was resulted from the recent price hike that the central committee, on 25th as it flatly rejected the USFK's alternative plan, has decided to go on a nation-wide strike commencing on December 15, unless 30% of wage hike is adapted.

In due course of this implementation, a pro-and-con strike vote is scheduled to take place during December 2-3. In order to finance this wage struggle, every one is entiled to donate 100 won on vote day.

The authority of finalizing the details of the demand is vested with the board of Chairmen.

Dear Union members!

The wage hike struggle of this year seems to be under a situation that might requires an ~~exteam~~ extreme measure. Thus, every individual is requested to take part in the strike vote to concentrate total effort in gaining our wage hike and ~~life~~. livelihood.

November 28, 1971

Chairman YI Hyo Seung
Seoul Chapter
Foreign Organization Employes Union

179

EACP-C&EM

Mr. Han Chin Hui
Chairman
ROK Component Labor Subcommittee

Dear Mr. Han:

The attached copy of a letter forwarded to Mr. Kang, Chu Won, National President of Forign Organizations Employees Union (FOEU), is transmitted for your information.

I understand that Foreign Organizations Employees Union (FOEU) has filed an official dispute with the Office Labor Affairs, protesting against the proposed tentative 18% USFK pay increase. If USFK withdraws exclusive recognition of FOEU because of its disruptive actions, I wish to remind you that the FOEU dispute may not ~~longer~~ be processed under SOFA procedures. FOEU will no longer have the right to avail itself of the provisions of Article XVII, paragraph 4(a).

I solicit your support in resolving the dispute in a timely and orderly manner as prescribed by the SOFA and current FOEU-USFK Labor Management Agreement.

1 Incl
as

DAVID P. HEEKIN
Colonel, GS
Chairman
US Component Labor Subcommittee

180

" 파업 가부투표에 빠짐없이 참여하여

생활급 임금을 쟁취하자 "

친애하는 서울지부 조합원 동지 여러분 !

우리 외기노조가 지난 10월 1일 임금 40%인상을 미군측에 요구한데 대하여 미군측은 지난 11월 23일 18% 의 인상대안을 제시해 왔읍니다.

이는 최근 물가상승등 요건에 비추어 너무나도 터무니없는 대안임에 지난 25일 개최된 본조합 9차 중앙위원회는 미군측의 대안을 일축하고 최소한 30%의 인상이 아니면 오는 12월 15일을기해 전국 총파업을 단행하기로 결의 하였읍니다.

이에 대비해서 12월 2- 3일, 양일간에 걸처 파업가부투표를 실시하기로 되였으며 또한 금번 임금투쟁을 뒷받침하기 위하여 조합원 1인당 100원씩을 파업가부투표당시 소속 지부에 납부하기로 되였읍니다. 그리고 쟁의에 따르는 부대 요구조건의 결정은 의장단에게 일임키로 되였읍니다.

친애하는 조합원동지 여러분 !

금년도 임금인상 투쟁은 극한투쟁을 전개하지 않으면 안될 실정에 처해 있으니 한분도 빠짐없이 파업가부투표에 참여하여 우리의 생활급 임금을 기여코 쟁취하는데 총력을 다합시다.

1971. 11. 29

전국외국기관노동조합 서울지부

지부장 이 효 승

181

General Strike Set for Dec. 15

SEOUL (Special) — The Foreign Organizations Employees Union (FOEU), representing about 30,000 Korean employes, has officially notified U.S. Forces Korea that it plans a general strike for an indefinite period beginning Dec. 15, civilian personnel officials of USFK said Tuesday.

The strike is planned to protest an offered pay increase of 18% now scheduled for Jan. 1, 1972. Union officials have indicated that a bigger increase is needed to offset a rise in the cost of living and changes in the won-dollar rate.

USFK officials explained that the projected 18% pay increase was determined after evaluation of wages currently paid by 90 reputable Korean enterprises certified by the ROK Office of Labor Affairs. Any further adjustment of the percentage rate would be based on more studies of economic factors that affect employes' living costs, the officials said.

A USFK spokesman said the proposed strike violates the Status of Forces Agreement (SOFA) and the officially signed USFK-FOEU labor management agreement, which require such disputes to be submitted to the ROK Office of Labor Affairs for arbitration.

The spokesman claimed that because FOEU has refused to meet SOFA requirements, its planned strike action is illegal and could result in a USFK withdrawal of its official exclusive recognition of the union.

Since 1967, the wages of the average Korean employe of USFK have increased almost 25% annually to meet the higher cost of living. In addition, employes participate in an escalated plan which provides twice as much severance pay upon termination than that required by ROK labor law, the spokesman said.

Traditionally, USFK meets and in most cases exceeds ROK labor law requirements, the spokesman said. The reputation of USFK as a highly favorable major employer in Korea has been frequently commended by the Office of Labor Affairs, he added.

182

정/리/보/존/문/서/목/록					
기록물종류	문서-일반공문서철	등록번호	25853 7145	등록일자	2006-09-18
분류번호	729.414	국가코드		주제	
문서철명	SOFA-한.미국 합동위원회 노무분과위원회-주한미군과 외기노조간의 노사분규, 1974				
생산과	북미2과	생산년도	1974 - 1974	보존기간	영구
담당과(그룹)	미주	안보	서가번호	--	
참조분류					
권차명					
내용목차	* 외기노조(전국외국기관 노동조합)				

마/이/크/로/필/름/사/항				
촬영연도	*롤 번호	화일 번호	후레임 번호	보관함 번호
2007-09-17	Re-07-08	9	1-67	

결 번

넘버링 오류

결 번

넘버링 오류

관계부처간 실무대책 회의 참석 보고

1. 제 목 : 주한미군의 직속 고용원의 하청 전환 문제에 관한 관계부처간 대책 회의

2. 일시 및 장소 : 74. 4. 22. (월) 14:00 - 15:30
노동청 노정국장실

3. 참석부처 : 외무부, 상공부, 내무부 (치안국), 노동청

4. 당부 참석자 : 북미 2과 사무관 정의용

5. 회의 내용 요지 :

노 동 청 : 가. 73. 11. 1. 주한미군의 직속경비원 47명의 하청 전환 문제에 관한 합동위원회에서의 과제 부여후, 한.미 노무관계 당국간에 11회에 걸친 실무접촉이 있었음.

나. 주한 미군당국은 일단 상기 47명의 해고 통고를 철회하고 별첨과 같은 노무분과위원회의 건의 (안)를 제의하여 왔음.

다. 동 건의 "나"항의"주한 미군이 군사상 필요시 SOFA 제 17조 규정에 의해 고용을 종료시킬수 있다" 는 내용과 "다"항의 하청전환시 고용 조건의 저하등의 문제는 "한국정부의 책임 및 통제하에 있다"는 내용에는 동의할수 없는 것임.

4

예산감소를 위한 하청전환이 "군사상의 필요"로 볼수 있느냐의 문제와 군납업자(용역)들을 한국정부가 통제할수 있느냐의 문제가 있음.

타. 노동청으로서는 일단 47명의 해고를 철회시킨 이상, 동건을 미측 요구대로 조속히 처리할 필요를 느끼고 있지 않으며, 다만 합동위의 과제 부여에 대한 노무분과위의 ~~과제 부여에 대한 노무분과위의~~ 건의 제출 문제를 고려하여 미측 제의를 검토하고 있으나, 미측의 FY74가 끝나는 금년 6월말까지 가능한 한 동 문제 처리를 지연시키고자 함.

상공부 : 가. 동 건의안 "가"항중 "계약체결시 SOFA 규정 16조에 의한다"는 내용은 주한미군이 임의로 모든 직속경비원을 하청전환 시킬수 있다는것으로 해석될수 있으며,

나. "다"항의 계약체결시 "한국정부의 통제"내용은 현재 상무분과위에서 논의되고 있는 군납계약 절차 문제와 관련 군납계약 체결시 한국정부의 간섭을 배제할것을 강력히 요구하고 있는 미측 태도와 상반되는것임.

외무부 : 노무문제에 대한 한국정부의 통제는 군납계약 체결시의 간섭과는 다른 의미로 제의된듯하며, 다만 정부가 용역 군납업자에 대하여 직접 고용시의 고용 조건을 이행토록 할수 있느냐가 의문시됨.

5

노 동 청 : 하청되는 경우 용역업자에 대한 정부의 통제는 사실상 불가능하며, 국가보위법에 의한 단체 행동권의 제약 등으로 인하여 외기 노조의 발언권이 상당히 약화되어 있는 실정임.

외 무 부 : 동건 처리를 지연시키는 것이 아측 입장에 유리하다 하더라도, 미측에 대하여 이러한 인상을 주지않는 것이 좋음. 우리정부도 이 문제 처리에 성의를 갖고 있다는 것을 나타내기 위하여는 미측 제의에 대한 counter - proposal 로서 아측입장(예: 하청전환시 고용 조건의 불변동 보장등)을 반영한 내용의 draft 를 작성하여 미측에 제의하는 것이 좋을것임.

6. 결 론 : 일단 노동청은 미측이 제의한 노무분과위원회의 건의(안)에 대한 한국측 draft 를 작성, 이를 미측에 제의하고, 이에 대한 미측의 반응에 따라 필요시 관계부처간 대책회의 또는 노무분과위원회등을 소집 또는 개최한다.

첨 부 : 미측이 제의한 노무분과위 건의(안)

북미2과	공람	74년 4월 23일	담당	과장	국장	차관보	차관	장관

6

공 란

공 란

공 란

공 란

THE KOREA TIMES,

THURSDAY, SEPTEMBER 26, 1974

Union Asks U.S. Forces To Hike Wages

The Foreign Organizations Employes Union (FOEU) yesterday made a strong demand to the U.S. Forces in Korea to increase the wages of Korean employes at U.S. military units throughout the nation.

The union proposed a meeting today between the union executive committee members and the U.S. Forces authorities.

The union threatened that if the U.S. Forces in Korea does not comply with their demand for wage increases, it would resort to "extreme means," inclding sit-ins, demonstrations and go-slow maneuvers.

Under the current state of national emergency, unionists are banned from staging strikes.

The 20,000-member union said in a statement that its members can hardly manage to eke out their living because of spiralling price increases, if there is no wage hike.

A recent survey by the Korea Development Institute showed that this year's commodity price rises would hit 42.2 percent, the statement said.

The FOEU members had a 17.5 percent wage increase on Jan. 1 this year.

The union said it had completed all proceedings required by law to take extreme measures to push ahead with their wage increase demand.

The union said it submitted a formal request for a wage increase to the U.S. Forces in Korea on March 30 and reported to the Office of Labor Affairs of the initiation of a labor dispute on May 6.

11

Union Asks U.S. Forces To Hike Wages

'74.9.26. K.T

The Foreign Organizations Employes' Union (FOEU) yesterday made a strong demand to the U.S. Forces in Korea to increase the wages of Korean employes at U.S. military units throughout the nation.

The union proposed a meeting today between the union executive committee members and the U.S. Forces authorities.

The union threatened that if the U.S. Forces in Korea does not comply with their demand for wage increases, it would resort to "extreme means," inclding sit-ins, demonstrations and go-slow maneuvers.

Under the current state of national emergency, unionists are banned from staging strikes.

The 20,000-member union said in a statement that its members can hardly manage to eke out their living because of spiralling price increases, if there is no wage hike.

A recent survey by the Korea Development Institute showed that this year's commodity price rises would hit 42.2 percent, the statement said.

The FOEU members had a 17.5 percent wage increase on Jan. 1 this year.

The union said it had completed all proceedings required by law to take extreme measures to push ahead with their wage increase demand.

The union said it submitted a formal request for a wage increase to the U.S. Forces in Korea on March 30 and reported to the Office of Labor Affairs of the initiation of a labor dispute on May 6.

12

74. 10. 14. <S·S>

Korean Union Declines U.S. Pay Offer

SEOUL (S&S) — Members of the Foreign Organizations Employees Union (FOEU) voted Friday overwhelmingly against proposals by U.S. Forces, Korea for wage hikes, paving the way for probable work action in the near future.

More than 21,000 members voted Friday whether to accept USFK offers of 16.4-20 per cent wage increases for Korean national employes at U.S. installations throughout the nation. The union made demands of 40 per cent wage increases for its members in late September.

This demand was made, according to FOEU officials, in the wake of price increases attributed to inflation here.

Union leaders declined to give a specific breakdown on the voting results Friday, but said that the balloting was more than 90 per cent against acceptance of the USFK offers, indicating a future work stoppage if no settlement between USFK and FOEU is reached.

An FOEU official said Friday that union leaders have scheduled a meeting for Wednesday to set a time for a walkout by union members.

The Korean organization made its demands to USFK for wage hikes Sept. 25, adding that "extreme measures" would be taken by FOEU members if their demands were not met. FOEU demanded a 40 percent hike, but officials said they were prepared to accept 30 per cent.

In response to the wage demands, USFK offered union members wage increases of 16.4-20 per cent, according to job scale rating.

If a strike does become a reality after Wednesday, it will be the first work stoppage by a Korean civilian work force at a U.S. military facility since 1970 when the Korea Service Corps staged a walkout at Yongsan Garrison here.

13

노 동 청

노사 1454- 10144 63-8341 1974. 10. 15.

수신 외무부장관

제목 주한 미군내 노사분규 예방 협조 요청

1. 주한 미8군에 종사하는 한국인 근로자로 조직된 외국기관 노동조합은 유류파동후의 물가고를 이유로 4월부터 임금 40%를 인상하여 줄 것을 미8군 당국에 요청하여 왔고 미8군 당국은 임금인상을 하기 위하여 8. 20.- 9. 24.까지 임금 실태조사를 실시한바 있으며,

2. 미8군 당국은 실태조사 결과를 근거로 하여 오는 12월 1일부터 평균 16.4%를 인상하기로 내정하고 10. 10. 그 뜻을 외기노조에 통고한 바 있읍니다.

3. 이에 대하여 외기노조 조합원은 크게 반발하고 인상율 및 인상 시기를 재조정하여 줄 것을 요구하면서 이 요구가 관철되지 않을 경우 단체행동도 불사하겠다고 주장, 쟁의행위 가부 투표를 10. 11. 전국적으로 실시한 결과 98.2%가 찬성 투표 하였읍니다.

4. 노조의 "9월 1일부터 최저 30% 인상" 요청을 현실적으로 실현시키는데 어려움이 있는 것으로 사료되오나 12월부터 16.4%를 인상한다는 미8군 당국의 결정은, 첫째, 작년말 이후의 물가 상승율이 16.4%보다 훨씬 높다는 결과, 둘째, 10월 1일부터 공무원 봉급이 30% 인상된다는 점, 셋째, 금년도 전반기의 임금인상율이 16.4%보다 상회한다는 점 등을 임금인상의 척도로 삼고 있는 근로자들의 불만이 단체행동화될 우려가 농후한 실정임을 알려드리며 아울러 불의에 불상사가 발생할 경우 사전에 예방하는데 적극 협조하여 주시기 바랍니다.

첨부 : 참고자료 1부. 끝.

노 동 청

14

전국 외국기관 노동조합 임금인상 분규에 관한 참고자료

1. 현 황

가. 노조명 및 조합원수

노 조 명 : 전국 외국기관 노동조합

노동조합원수 : 21,200명

나. 현행임금 수준

최 저 : 월 24,257원

최 고 : 월 222,290원

월평균임금 : 93,292원

다. 노동조합 요구사항

임금인상율 : 40%

인상기준일 : 1974. 9. 1.

* 1974. 4월부터 실시한 각 기업체의 임금인상에 자극됨.

라. 사용자측 인상 계획

임금인상율 : 16.4%

인상시기 : 1974. 12. 1.

2. 문제점

가. 사용주측 태도

16.4%는 의외로 저율임을 인정하면서도 임금 실태조사 결과 분석된 숫자이므로 16.4%의 인상율을 변경할 수 없으며, 적용일자도 변경할 수 없음을 주장하고 문제 해결을 위한 재고를 하지 않고 있음.

나. 노조측

사용주측 인상 계획에 크게 반발하고 위장단 회의를 개최하고 10. 11. 전국적으로 파업 가부 투표를 실시하도록 결의하고 현재 투표 실시중이며, 10. 16. 중앙위원회를 소집하고 대책을 협의할 계획임.

美8軍 從業員 賃金引上에따른

勞使紛件對策

16

美8軍從業員賃金引上에따른

勞使紛糾對策

1. 現況

가. 賃金引上適用対象者數 : 22.703名

(勞組員 : 15.800名)

나. 現賃金実態

月額平均 : 72.224원

月平均賃金(賞與金包含) : 93.292 "

다. 賃金引上率決定方法

美公法 92-392号 第53章 第4節에 基한 联邦賃金体制(Fedral Wage System, F.P.M Supplement 532-1)中 陸軍文官規程 P-40에 따라 現地企業体에 勤務하는 同職種勤労者의 平均賃金을 調查하여 그와 同額으로 引上.

17

라. 74年度賃金引上

1) 73. 9 ~ 73. 10 間에 前다항에 依據賃金實態를 調査한后 74. 1. 1부터 12.5%를 引上하였으며

2) 74. 8. 20 ~ 74. 9. 24 間에 다시 實態를 調査한后. 74. 12. 1부터 16.4%를 引上할 計劃임.

마. 74年度(今番)賃金實態調査方法

1) 調査對象業体數 : 111 個業体

2) 調査對象人員 : 總 127.000名中 21.881名

2. 勞使의 主張

가. 使用主側

賃金實態調査結果 集計된 率(平均 16.4%)을 適用하되 本國承認日字를 考慮하여 74.12.1.부터 適用引上한다.

나. 勞組側

18 最少 30%를 9.1부터 引上하되 下厚上薄式으로 調整한다.

3. 労動庁 判断

가. 労組 議長団이 10.10. 争議行為可否投票를 実施할것을 決議하고 10.11. 全国的으로 이를 実施하였는 바

첫째: 美軍当局의 再考促求와

둘째: 傘下 組合員의 反撥에 対한 事前対備策으로 보이며

나. 또한 30% 以上의 引上과 9月1日부터 適用할것을 主張하고는 있으나 『20% 以上』 및 「11月 1日 以前 適用」이 現実化될 경우 이를 받아드릴 態勢인것으로 判断되며

다. 10.16. 中央委員会 召集時 争議行為日字決定이 焦点이 될것이나 争議行為日字를 決定할수도, 아니할수도 없는 立場에 놓이게되어 労動庁의 善後策에만 期待하고 있는것으로 보이며 10月中에 妥結点이 発見되지 않을경우는 争議行為의 効力 如何에 不拘하고 争議行為를 敢行하지 않을수 없다고 생각하고 있는것이 支配的임

19

라. 美軍側은 引上率을 再調整하는것은 美國防省規程上 不可能한것으로 斷定하고 있으며 다만 施行時期에 關하여는 11月 1日로 앞당길수 있는 可能性을 否認하지는 않고 있음으로 보아 本國에 建議하여 11月부터 引上시킬수는 있을것으로 判斷됨.

4. 問題点

가. 美軍側은 特別한 政策的 配慮가 本國에서 이루워지지 않는限 引上率은 不變의 것으로 斷定하고 있는 反面 勞組側은 使用主의 立場 如何는 關係없이 16.4%란 받아드릴수 없는것으로 믿고 있으며 비록 勞組幹部中 一部는 16.4%의 不可變性을 是認하면서도 全体意思의 壓力으로 이를 勞組組合員에게 說得시킬 생각은 하지 못하고 있음

나. 施行期日을 11月 1日以前으로 앞당길 경우도 16.4%가 確定된다면 組合員의 不滿을 除去할수 없는것이 予想됨

20

5. 對策

가. 美軍當局과 交涉하여

1) 16.4%의 引上率에 對한 再考(20%以上)와

2) 11月1日以前 引上을 實現하도록 試圖하되

나. 引上率의 上向調整은 美8軍으로서 單純으로 確答할수 없을것임에 비추어 最惡의 境遇

1) 美8軍은 本國政府에 對하여 20%以上 引上하도록 承認하여줄것을 建議하고

2) 施行日字는 11月1日以前으로 앞당긴

다는것으로 終結하고 美國防省決定에 一任하는 것으로 勞組를 說得하여 紛糾를 終熄 시킨다.

21

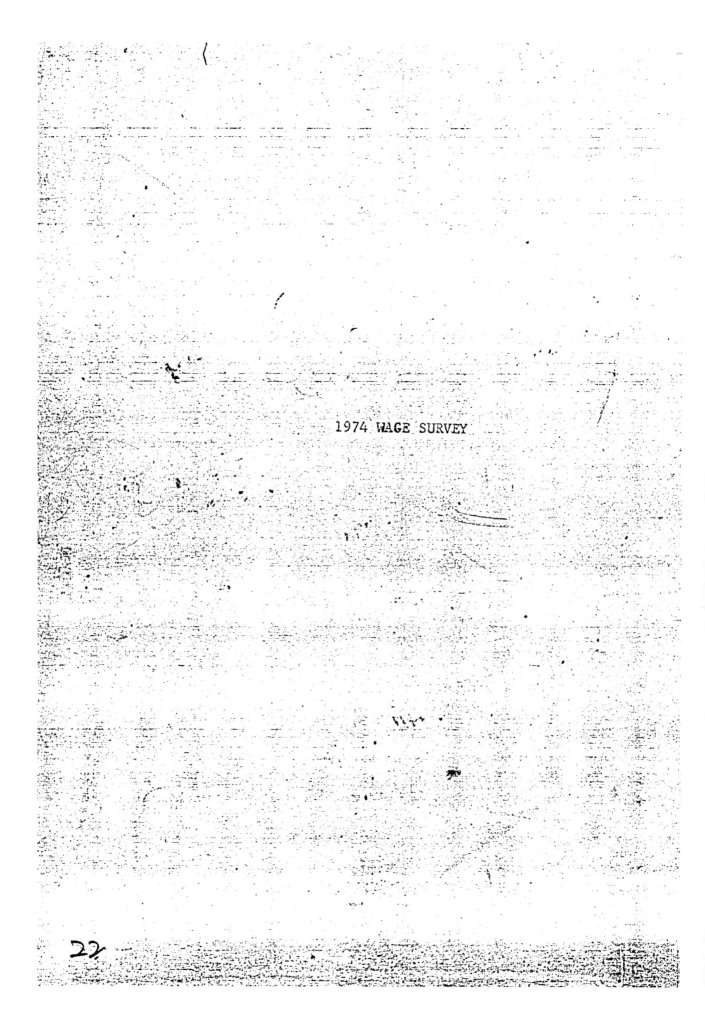

1974 WAGE SURVEY

22

1974 KN WAGE SURVEY

- o Background
- o Percentage Increase
- o Distribution of Increase
- o Effective Date
- o Procedures to Finalize

23

BACKGROUND

o Prevailing Rates & Wage Survey are Prescribed by DoD.

o Industry Sample Broadened

94 Companies in 1973
111 Companies in 1974
38 New companies in Current Survey

127,000 employees in Firms Covered

21,881 Job Matches on 91 Key Jobs

o Survey Started 5 Weeks Early

-- Union & Embassy Pressed

o Collected Data Analyzed by
USARPAC & PACAF Representatives
Navy Rep to Meet with JLAC

24

INCREASES FOR 1974

	Combined
KGS -	18.1
KWB -	15.3
KM -	26.1
All Employees -	16.4

Increase in 1973 -- 17.5%

Average of Increases since 1961 -- 23.4%

EFFECTIVE DATE

o Pay Rates Effective 1 December

- Corresponds to advancement of survey
- Budgets will not support increase
- System does not provide for retroactive payment

25

<u>DISTRIBUTION OF INCREASE</u>

- Increase Spring Bonus to full month and balance in basic salary

- Industry practice supports 4 months bonus payment

  - 111 Companies give 3.98 months pay

  - 127,000 workers average 4.1 months pay

  - 21,800 job matches average 3.86 months pay

- Spring Bonus will require 4.2% of increase

  - 12.2% will apply to basic wages.

26

PROCEDURES TO FINALIZE

- Hold JLAC Meeting
- Consult with Union
- Brief OLA
- Establish Pay Charts
    - Rates/for each step, each schedule
- Forward USFK Recommendations to Joint Labor Policy Committee in Hawaii for approval
    - Amount of base pay increase
    - Amount of bonus increase if any
    - Effective date
    - Authorize use of pay charts

29

USFK Findings on Improvement of Wages and Benefits

1. Wages

Manual			Non-manual			Marine		
Grade	No. of Empl.	% Increase	Grade	No. of Empl.	% Increase	Grade	No. of Empl.	% Increase
WB-1	1,206	19.0	GS-1	1	11.0			26.5
2	963	20.9	2	38	13.2			29.7
3	1,847	17.8	3	1,370	16.3	M-3	40	26.9
4	1,965	15.6	4	2,043	17.3	4	15	27.6
5	2,647	14.3	5	1,652	18.1	5	-	20.1
6	3,631	13.2	6	583	18.6	6	14	19.0
7	1,111	12.4	7	1,142	19.2	7	15	21.5
8	400	12.8	8	137	19.4	8	15	34.2
9	236	13.0	9	756	20.0	9	8	29.1
10	100	15.0	10	161	20.3	10	6	20.4
11	84	16.9	11	405	20.8			
12	11	16.9	12	94	20.8			
13	4	16.9	13	3	20.8			
Total:	14,205			8,385			113	
	Weighted Av. 15.3%			Weighted Av. 18.1%			Weighted Av. 26.1%	

Overall Weighted Average (GS + WB + M) = 16.4%

The above figures of % increase represent total compensation increases including a 50% additional Spring Bonus (which equates to 4.2%).

28

외기노조 노사분규 문제에대한 면담록

면담자 : 이상훈 북미2과장, 클리블랜드 주한미대사관 1등서기관

일시및 장소 : 1974.10.18. 17:00 경제차관보실

면담내용 ;

북미2과장 : 외기노조와 미8군간에 임금인상 교섭이 진행되고 있으나 잘 타결을 짓지 못하고 현재 노동청에서 조정을 시도하고 있다고 듣고있음. 정부로서는 이 문제가 원만히 해결 않되어 외기노조측이 파업을 단행하거나 분규를 자아낼 경우 미칠 영향을 고려하여 이 문제가 조속한 시일내에 타결되기를 바라며 이를 위하여 미정부의 협조를 바라는 바임.

현재 미측이 제시하고 있는 16.4%의 임금 인상율은 경제기획원에서 산출한 22.8%에 훨신 미달하는 것이며 정부 관공리들에 대한 금년도 인상율도 약 34% 이었음을 참고하기 바람.

이와 관련하여 노동청은 외기노조를 납득시키고 조정을 성립시키기 위하여는 다음 사항을 최소한 미측이 양보해 주어야 한다는 바, 이들 조건의 관철을 위하여 협조해 주기 바람.

가. 임금 인상율을 최소한 20%이상으로 할것.

나. 인상 발효기일을 11.1. 이전으로 할것.

다. 인상율 적용을 하후상박으로 하거나 아니면 일률 적용토록 할것

크리브랜드1등서기관 : 잘 알았음. 상부에 보고한 후 회답하겠음.

공람	74년 10월 18일	담당	과장	국장	차관보	차관	장관

미군 종업원 임금 인상에 따른 노사분규 문제

1. 경 위 :

가. 미군 당국은 74. 1. 1.부터 임금 17.5를 인상 함.

나. 외기노조는 유류파동후 물가고를 이유로 74. 4부터 임금 40%인상을 미측에 요구 함.

다. 미측은 74. 8. 20. - 9. 24. 간 자체 조사 방법에 의한 임금 실태 조사후 74. 12. 1.부터 16.4% 인상을 계획하고 10. 10. 이를 노조측에 통고 함.

라. 노조측은 "9. 1.부터 최저 30%인상"을 내세우고 10. 11. 쟁의행위 가부 투표 실시 결과 98.2%가 찬성 함.

마. 10. 16. 14:00시 노조측은 중앙위원회 회의를 개최하고 10. 29. 파업 결의 함. 미측도 미군참모장 맥클라우드 소장 주재하에 회의를 개최 하고 인상률에는 변동이 있을수 없다는 방침을 굳힌것으로 알려짐.

바. 10. 17. 09:00시 한.미 간에 확대 노사회의가 개최된바, 미측은 노조측에 대하여 노동청과 우선 협의할것을 종용 함.

2. 노동청 판단 :

가. " 20% 이상 11. 1. 이전 적용 " 이 현실화될 경우 노조측이

30

발아드릴것으로 보임.

나. 노조측은 10. 16.자 중앙위원회 회의 결정대로 10.29. 파업에 돌입할 것으로 보임.

다. 현행 보위법상 단체 행동이 금지되어 있으나 만약 노조측이 단체 행동을 강행하게 되는경우 한.미 양국 관계나 국내정치에 미치는 영향이 심대할것임.

라. 미측이 이문제를 SOFA 합동위에 회부하는경우 SOFA 제 17조에 의거 70일간의 유예기간이 생기므로 노조측으로서는 생계 문제와 관련, 사태가 더욱 악화될 우려가 있음.

3. 대 책 :

가. SOFA 합동위원회 회부 문제

현 상황하에서 70일간의 유예기간등 불리점이 있으므로, 미측이 제기하여 오는 경우 현재 노동청이 중재중에 있으므로 제 17조 4항 규정을 들어 우선 그 결과를 기다려야 할것임을 내세워 합동위회부를 지연시킴.

31

나. 노동청 조정안 :

다음 노동청 조정안을 적절한 시기에 미 대사관측에 제시하고 협조를 요청 함.

(1) 73. 8.30. - 74.8.30. 기간중 경제기획원 .. 물가 상승률이 27.2%이며 74. 1. 1. - 8. 30. 간 노동청 조사, 국내임금 인상율이 22.8%임을 들어, "최소한 20%를 11. 1. 이전에 적용해줄 것을 요청하거나,

(2) 미측이 정한 인상율(16.4%)을 규정상 변경할수 없다고 할경우에는 현재 상후하박으로되어 있는 인상폭을 하후상박으로하거나 또는 16.4% 일제 인상으로하되, 인상시기를 10.1.(늦어도 10. 15.)로 할것을 요청 함.

(3) 상기 (1), (2)안이 받아들여지지 않을경우 미측이 본국 정부에 (1)안 또는 (2)안을 건의할것을 요청함.

32

4. 참 고:

74. 10. 16 13 : 30 - 14 : 00 미주국장과 노동청 노정국장간에 협의를 가짐.

북미2과	공람	74년 10월 16일	담당	과장	국장	차관보	차관	장관
			[signature]	[signature]	[signature]	[signature]		

33

保衛法해제등 6個項을決議

勞總대의원대회

74년도 한국노총전국대의원대회가 18일오전10시 서울 龍山구鐵友회관에서 열려 노동자의 기본권리를 규제하고 있는 국가보위법을 해제할것 등 6개항의 노동기본권보장에관한 결의문을 채택했다.

대의원 2백33명과 일반근로자등 1천여명이 참석한대회에선 ①근로자집단 감원에 대한항의 ②세제개선 ③임금및근로조건개선 ④현대조선의 반성및 관리개선 ⑤주한미군 종업원의 임금및 근로조건개선등을 촉구하는 결의문도아울러 채택했다.

74. 10. 19. 조선.

34

긴급

기 안 용 지

분류기호 문서번호	미이 723 -595	(전화번호)	전결규정 조항 국장 전결사항
처리기간			
시행일자	1974. 10. 23.		
보존년한		국 장	
보조기관	과 장		협조
기안책임자	양세훈	북미2과	

경유		발송	검열 1974.10.23 통제관
수신	노동청장	1974.10.23 외무부	
참조	노정국장		
제목	외기노조 노사분규 문제		

~~1.~~ 현재 귀청이 조정중에 있는 외기노조와 주한미군 당국간의 임금 인상문제로 인한 노사분규에 대하여 미군당국은 이 문제가 조속히 해결되지 않고 노조측에 의하여 방위목적을 저해하는 행위가 발생하는 경우 별첨 내용과 같이 이 문제를 SOFA 합동위원회에 회부할 예정임을 통고하여 왔음을 알립니다.

~~2. 당부는 74.10.18. 주한미대사관 관계관을 초치하여 귀청이 조정안으로 제시하고 있는 "최소한 20%, 11.1. 이전 인상"을 미측에 강력히 촉구한 바 있읍니다.~~

첨 부 : 미측이 합동위에 회부코저하는 내용. 끝.

정서
관인
발송

35

0201-1-8A (갑)
1969. 11. 10 승인

190mm×268mm(특급인쇄용지40g/m²)
조 달 청 (1,000,000매 인 쇄)

공　　　란

공 란

공 란

공 란

공 란

공 란

공　　　　란

공　　　란

공　　　란

공 란

공 란

공 란

공 란

공 란

공 란

공 란

공　　　란

공 란

공　　란

공 란

공 란

공 란

지급

기 안 용 지

분류기호 문서번호	미이 723-	(전화번호)	전결규정 조 항 전결사항
처리기간			
시행일자	1974.10.23.		
보존년한		국 장	
보조기관	과 장		협조
기안책임자	유광석	북미2과	
경유 수신 참조	노동청장 노정국장	발신 1974.10.23 외무부	통제 10.23
제 목	외기노조 노사분규 문제		

연 : 미이 723-595 (74.10.23.)

1. 주한 미군당국은 한미합동위원회 미측대표 명의의 별첨 서한으로 주둔군지위협정 17조 4항 (가)(2)의 규정에따라, 임금인상을 둘러싼 노사분규 문제를 합동위원회에 회부할것을 통보해옴과 동시에 74.10.25. 10시 미군 SOFA 회의실이나 기타 원하는 장소에서 동 문제를 검토하기위한 특별위원회 회의를 개최할것을 제의하여왔음을 통고합니다.

2. 상기 특별위원회 미측 위원은 노무분과위원회 위원및 주한미군 감독관, 주한미 해군대표로 구성될 것이라함을 첨언합니다.

첨 부 : 합동위원회 미측대표 서한 사본 1부.

정서 | 관인 | 발송

58

0201-1-8A (갑) 1969.11.10 승인

190mm×268mm(두급인쇄용지40g/m²) 조 달 청 (1,000,000매 인 쇄)

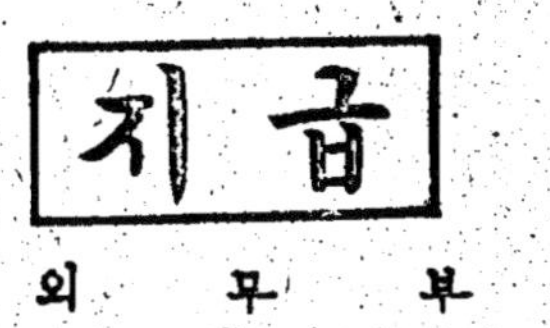

외 무 부

미이 723- (70-2324) 1974.10.23.

수 신 : 노동청장

참 조 : 노정국장

제 목 : 외기노조 노사분규 문제

1. 주한 미군당국은 한미 합동위원회 미측대표 명의의 별첨 서한으로 주둔군지위협정 17조 4항 (가)(2)의 규정에따라, 임금인상을 둘러싼 노사분규 문제를 합동위원회에 회부할 것을 통보해옴과 동시에 74.10.25. 10시 미군 SOFA 회의실이나 기타 원하는 장소에서 동 문제를 검토하기위한 특별위원회 회의를 개최할 것을 제의하여 왔음을 통고합니다.

2. 상기 특별위원회 미측위원은 노무분과위원회 위원및 주한 미군 감독관, 주한미군 감독관, 주한 미해군 대표로 구성될 것이라 함을 첨언합니다.

첨 부 : 합동위원회 미측대표 서한 사본 1부. 끝.

외 무 부 장 관

5P

공 란

공 란

공 란

공　　란

공 란

공 란

공 란

공 란

정/리/보/존/문/서/목/록					
기록물종류	문서-일반공문서철		27458	등록일자	2007-07-25
분류번호	729.414	국가코드		주제	
문서철명	SOFA 한.미국 합동위원회 노무분과위원회, 1979				
생산과	안보담당관실	생산년도	1979 - 1979	보존기간	영구
담당과(그룹)	미주	안보	서가번호	--	
참조분류					
권차명					
내용목차	* 주한미군 한국인 근로자 문제 - 비세출 자금기관 한국인고용원에 대한 퇴직금 - 통신업무 하청 전환 - 해고				

마/이/크/로/필/름/사/항

촬영연도	*롤 번호	화일 번호	후레임 번호	보관함 번호

면 담 록

1. 일 시 : 79. 1. 24. 10:30-11:00

2. 면 담 자 : 민 병 석 안보문제담당관
   R.A. Kinney SOFA 미측간사
   (배석 : 윤 병 세 사무관)

3. 제 목 : 미군 통신업무의 하청업자로의 전환 문제

4. 내 용 :

가. 미측 설명

- 작년 표제건에 대한 노조 및 한국정부의 요청과 관련, 주한미군 당국은 통신업무의 한국 하청업자로의 전환 및 이에 따른 인력 감축 조치를 잠정적으로 유예한 바 있음.

- 미국방성은 그간 이와 관련된 제반 검토를 완료했는 바, 이에 의하면 주한미군 통신업무를 하청업자에게 전환하는 것을 더 이상 지연시킬수 없게 된 것으로 봄. (해당 근로자는 약 240명 정도, 실시시기는 4. 1. 부터)

- 현재 주한미군 당국은 노동청 및 국방부등 한국 정부 관계요로의 협조를 구하고 있는 중이며, 1. 25. SOFA 합동위 회의 직전, SOFA 미측 대표가 한국측 대표에게도 이에 대한 미측의 입장을 설명하기를 희망함.

나. 아측 설명

- 본건은 가능한한 현상을 계속 유지하는 것이 바람직함.

- 이와 관련한 노사간의 사전 충분한 협의와 이해가 선결되어야 할것이며, 작년처럼 일방적인 감원 통고는 문제 해결을 어렵게 할 것임.

- 노동청등 관계부처와 충분히 협의후 신중한 검토있기를 희망함.

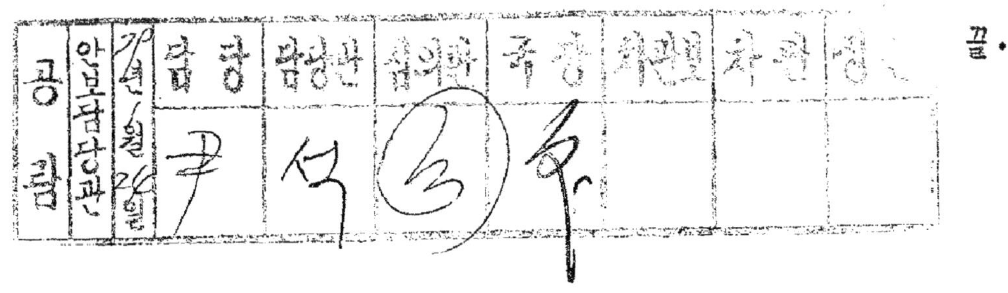

끝.

- 2 -

3

공 란

LABOR-MANAGEMENT AGREEMENT

BETWEEN

UNITED STATES FORCES, KOREA

AND

FOREIGN ORGANIZATIONS EMPLOYEES UNION

CONTENTS

6

Article 1. General Objectives and Policies.

a. This agreement is made by and between the United States Forces, Korea (USFK), hereinafter referred to as the "Employer" and the Foreign Organizations Employees Union (FOEU), hereinafter referred to as the "Union." The parties to this agreement recognize that they have a mutual and cooperative interest in the effective accomplishment of the assigned responsibilities of the USFK, better employee-management communications and improved working conditions. Their mutual interests will be furthered by the establishment and maintenance of employee-management cooperation pursuant to the Labor Article, US-ROK Status of Forces Agreement (SOFA) or such directives as may become applicable.

b. This agreement and such amendments and supplementary agreements as may be agreed upon hereunder from time to time will constitute a Labor Management Agreement between the Employer and the Union. Both the Employer and the Union will undertake necessary actions to assure compliance with this Agreement. In instances of non-compliance both parties will take immediate steps to assure compliance with this Agreement, and for continued constructive labor-management relations.

Article 2. Definitions.

For the purpose of this Agreement, the following definitions apply unless otherwise specified:

a. The Employer. USFK and its Army, Air Force and Navy components at all levels of command (including KRE, and other non-appropriated fund activities) and activities associated with or under the jurisdiction of the USFK or one of its military components. Included are those organizations and persons (including invited contractors) designated under paragraph 1a of Article XVII of the US-ROK Status of Forces Agreement.

b. The Employee. Korean national employees assigned to USFK components and activities identified under paragraph a above.

c. The Union. An organized Korean employee group (Foreign Organizations Employees Union) which represents the employees of the Employer cited above.

Article 3. Controlling Authority.

In the administration of all matters covered by this agreement, the Employer and the Union shall be governed by the US-ROK SOFA, current and future supplementary agreements, memoranda, amendments and agreed official minutes of US-ROK SOFA; prevailing laws and regulations of higher authority (such as US Civil Service Commission, Office of Management and Budget, Department of Defense, Departments of Army, Air Force, and Navy, Pacific Area Command, etc.)

7

including USFK policies and regulations in existence at the time of this agreement and any future policies and regulations required by SOFA and higher authority. Where there is any conflict between the provisions of this Agreement and the provisions of the US-ROK SOFA, and laws and regulations of higher authority, the provisions of SOFA and the laws and regulations will prevail.

Article 4. Matters Subject to Consultation and Negotiation.

a. It is agreed that matters appropriate for consultation and negotiation include personnel policies, practices and working conditions which fall within the scope of authority of the Employer. However, no obligation exists to consult or negotiate with respect to such areas as mission and function of the Employer; its budget; its organization; number, types, and grades of positions or employees; work project or tour of duty; the technology of performing its work; its internal security practices; or those matters which are outside of the Employer's authority. The Employer will inform the Union as early as possible and when security considerations permit any planned change which is anticipated to affect the Employees and their employment conditions. Included are changes in organization, changes in number and type of employees, reduction in force, and changes in technology of performing work.

b. When Union requests are appropriate and require change in policy outside the Employer's authority, the Employer will endeavor to obtain higher authority determination without undue delay.

Article 5. Exclusive Recognition of the Union.

The Employer recognizes the Foreign Organizations Employees Union as the exclusive representative of the employees of the Employer provided the following requirements are met:

a. A copy of the Union's constitution, by laws, and a statement of objectives are presented to the Employer.

b. A current roster of the Union's officers and representatives is furnished the Employer. The roster of Union's officers will include name, union status, office term, and the employing organization.

c. The Union has a membership of not less than 50 percent of the employees of the Employer.

d. Requirements of Republic of Korea labor laws pertaining to union certification and union activities are met.

e. Chapters and subchapters of the Foreign Organizations Employees Union will automatically be recognized upon formal notification by the national Union provided that the Chapter has a membership of more than 50 percent of the employees the Chapter represents. Such Chapters and Subchapters shall be established for organizations which will ensure a clear and identifiable community of interest among the employees concerned and will promote effective dealings and efficiency of the operations.

f. The union represents the interest of all employees covered by this Agreement without discrimination and without regard to the union membership.

Article 6. Effective Date and Terms of Agreement.

a. The effective date of this agreement shall be the date of signature by both parties. It will remain in effect for one year from the effective date.

b. Previous memoranda of understanding or agreements exchanged relating to subjects herein shall be superseded by this Agreement.

c. Proposals for the new agreement will be presented to other party at least 30 days before the expiration date.

d. If a new agreement is not agreed upon at the expiration date of this agreement, this agreement will remain effective for 3 months from the date of expiration.

Article 7. Amendment and Renewal of Agreement.

The parties may mutually effect amendments of, or supplements to, this Agreement before the expiration date if such action is necessary to reflect legal or regulatory changes. For other than legal or regulatory changes either party may, 90 days after renewal of this agreement, and no more often thereafter than each succeeding 90 day period during the life of the Agreement, give written notice to the other party of its intention to reopen negotiations for the purpose of amending the agreement or to negotiate any supplement thereto. Amendment is defined as the adding of a new article to the Agreement. It is understood by both parties that introductions of amendments to the Agreement does not contemplate and is not intended to mean complete or even substantive revision of the approved Agreement. Any request to reopen the Agreement to amend same, or to negotiate a supplement thereto, shall be in writing, and must include a summary of the amendment or supplement proposed and the reasons therefore. All meetings to consider a proposed amendment or supplement will be conducted within a reasonable time after receipt by either of the parties of the other party's desire to amend or supplement the Agreement, and in no case be later than 30 calendar days after receipt of the written request.

Article 8. Rights of Employer.

The Employer retains the right, in accordance with applicable laws and regulations (1) to direct employees of the units covered by this agreement, (2) to hire, promote, transfer, assign and retain employees within the units covered by this agreement, and to suspend, demote, discharge, or take other disciplinary action against employees, (3) to relieve employees from duties because of lack of work or for other legitimate reasons, (4) to maintain the efficiency and security of the US Government operations, (5) to determine the methods and personnel by which such operations are to be conducted and (6) to take whatever actions may be necessary to carry out the mission of the Employer during emergency such as war, hostilities, or where war or hostilities may be imminent, or natural catastrophe.

Article 9. Rights of the Union.

a. The Union shall have the right to request for consultation or negotiation and to present its views either orally or in writing to the Employer with respect to personnel policies, procedures and working conditions affecting employees insofar as appropriate under Article 3, Controlling Authority and Article 4, Matters Subject to Consultation and Negotiation. Matters for consultation and negotiation will include, but not be limited to, working conditions and facilities, labor-management relations, employee services, disciplinary procedures, methods of adjusting grievances and appeals, granting of leave, promotion plans, demotion practices, classification and pay practices, reduction in force procedures, and hours of work.

b. The Union has the right, upon its request, to be present at formal discussions, hearings, or meetings between the Employer and employees concerning grievances and appeals unless the employee concerned specifically requested that the union official be excluded. During the meeting or hearing, the Union may present information on behalf of the employee. The Employer, in turn, may also request information from the Union during adjudication of the grievances or appeals. No more than one (1) union official will present information or represent the employee.

Article 10. Rights of Employees.

a. Employees have the right, freely and without fear of penalty or reprisal, to organize or join, or to refrain from joining, any lawful employee organization.

b. Employees have the right to designate Union representatives for the purpose of consulting with management officials on individual grievances and appeals or to handle their own grievances and appeals, and to choose their own representatives in accordance with applicable regulations. The Employer will not discipline or otherwise discriminate against any employee because he has filed a grievance, testified at a grievance hearing, or designated a Union official as his representative on individual grievances and appeals.

Article 11. Eligibility for Union Membership and Office.

a. In the interest of effective and efficient operation of the US Forces, Korea, the Employer recognizes the right of all employees represented by this Agreement to join any lawful union or to refrain from such activity, and to exercise these rights freely and without fear of penalty or reprisal.

b. Except as provided in para c below, the right to join and assist a lawful union shall extend to participation in its management and to acting as an official union representative.

c. The following individuals may join the Union but may not act as a representative or participate in the management of the Union:

(1) Management Officials: An employee with or without supervisory responsibilities whose authority includes recommendation of or participation in the: (a) Planning and revising organizational structure; (b) Planning, evaluating and revising program, including development of policies and regulations; (c) Coordinating program; (d) Planning general work flow and methods; (e) Deciding overall goals and standards; (f) Budgeting and accounting procurement, contracting and property disposal; (g) Exercising fiscal control; (h) Determining program and organizational needs for space, personnel and equipment; and (i) Investigating and inspecting programs, and directing corrective actions.

(2) Supervisors: An employee having authority, in the interest of a command or activity, to hire, transfer, suspend, lay off, recall, promote, discharge, assign, reward, or discipline other employees, or responsibly to direct them, or to adjust their grievances, or effectively to recommend such action, if in connection with the foregoing the exercise of authority is not of a merely routine or clerical nature, but requires the use of independent judgment (Exclusions: Up to Level II Supervisor as defined under Appendix A, EA CPP 690-2 and up to Foreman Level as defined under Appendix B, EA CPP 690-2).

(3) Employees engaged in personnel work in other than purely clerical capacity.

d. In those cases not specifically covered by the above criteria, final determination of eligibility for union official will be made in accordance with the duties and responsibilities officially assigned by the Employer.

e. No employee shall carry on any activities as an officer, agent or member of the Union which will conflict or give the appearance of conflicting with the proper exercise of, or be incompatible with his official duties and responsibilities. In the event such a conflict arises, the Employer will notify the Union and employee concerned who will be provided at least 30 calendar days to correct his performance.

f. Union officials who are promoted and/or reassigned into positions where they are not eligible to hold union office under the preceding criteri will be permitted to serve as Union officials until their current term of office expires. These employees will not be eligible to run for another term of office unless they request to be relieved of their supervisory or managerial responsibilities.

Article 12. Status of Union Officials.

a. As long as the Union is accorded by the Employer the exclusive recognition, any person who is elected or appointed to a union office in accordance with this Agreement and the Union constitution will be recognized by the Employer as a representative of the Union. However, the recognition as a representative of the Union will be granted only upon formal notification to OCPD by the President of the national FOEU or, in the case of the President of the National FOEU, by the Chairman of the FOEU national convention.

b. No union official acting in an official capacity will be discriminated against for his acts as a union official so long as such acts are in accordance with this Agreement, the Labor Article of the SOFA, and ROK Labor Laws nor will there be any discrimination against any employee because of his authorized union activities.

c. The Union will not undertake any action intended to hinder any supervisor or employee in the discharge of his official duties.

d. The Employer will consult with the Union before taking adverse personnel actions affecting union officials who are elected to an office in accordance with the Union constitution and this agreement.

Article 13. Use of Official Time.

a. Accredited union officials are authorized to use official time without charge to annual leave or loss of pay to attend union-management meetings, to participate in official union-management activities, to participate in formal grievance and appeal hearings, and to attend the FOEU Central Committee meeting which is limited to once a month and to the FOEU Central Committee members, When consistent with the best interest of the Employer and the Employees, exceptions to the above may be authorized by the immediate supervisor of the union official on a case by case basis upon request in advance by the union officials to visit ROK government offices or Federation of Korean Trade Unions.

b. The following criteria on use of official time-off without charge to annual leave or loss of pay for the activities specified above, including exceptions, will apply:

(1) The National President and Secretary General - up to 60%.

(2) Vice-Presidents at national level and Chapter Presidents - up to 50%.

(3) Subchapter Presidents, Vice-Presidents of Chapters and Chiefs of Departments at the national level - up to 25%.

(4) Subchapter Vice-Presidents - up to 20% of the regularly scheduled tour of duty during a pay period (limited to two vice-presidents per subchapter).

(5) Chiefs of Departments at the Chapter level may be granted time off on an occasional basis as needed, but normally not to exceed 15%.

c. Time-off in excess of the above limits may be individually granted by the Employer to cover increased union-management activities which might abnormally occur during a peak period. Such approvals must be consistent with prevailing workload and mission-support needs.

d. In cases when a union official holds two or more union offices, use of time-off is limited to business of only one office whichever is authorized greater amount of time-off.

e. Union officials will request time-off with adequate justification sufficiently in advance to his immediate supervisor, or if the immediate supervisor is not available to the next higher level supervisor to permit rescheduling of work. Time-off described above will not be denied by supervisors except for immediate and temporary reasons of urgent workload for which employees' services are clearly essential. When time-off cannot be granted, the employee will be informed when an alternate time-off period can be granted.

f. Upon completion of the union-management business, the union official will immediately report back to work and furnish his supervisor a report of the total official duty time utilized to conduct the business. The report will be submitted on the Standard Form 71, Application for Leave. Such leave will be categorized as "Other Leave (Administrative Leave)" and be clarified under remarks column showing time and place of the union-management meeting, joint activity, or grievance and appeal hearings held. Such leave must be so annotated on employee time and attendance report and supported by the completed SF 71.

g. Leave without pay for union officials to serve full-time on union activities may be approved on request of the Union's national office. Full time service with the Union on a leave-without-pay basis will be creditable for reduction in force and step increase purposes. Service credit for severance pay will be recognized for a period of up to two (2) years.

h. The Union will submit a complete roster to the Employer identifying Union officials by union status. Once, the complete roster is submitted, the union will inform the Employer any of change to the roster within 14 calendar days from the date the change officially took place.

Article 14. Limitations on Use of Official Time.

a. Activities identified solely or predominantly with internal union affairs such as planning and conducting union national and chapter conventions and meetings, conduct of union officer elections and similar activities will be conducted during off-duty hours and off-post.

b. Distribution of union literature and solicitation of membership will not be conducted during regular working hours, but may be conducted outside of regular working hours such as lunch periods on-post, so long as such activities do not involve union or group meetings.

Article 15. Use of Official Facilities.

Material submitted by the Union for posting on bulletin boards may be posted at designated locations only after obtaining consent of the appropriate commander or his official representative.

Article 16. Voluntary Union Dues Allotment.

a. The Employer agrees to check-off dues by payroll deduction subject to provisions of the following paragraphs.

b. Any employee desiring to have his union dues deducted from his pay may, at any time, complete and sign the appropriate portions of the approved form, Request and Authorization for Voluntary Allotment of Compensation for Payment of Employee Organization Dues. Such deductions will be effective on the first full pay period following the date that a properly completed allotment form for voluntary deduction is received in the appropriate payroll office.

c. The properly completed form with certifications by the designated officials of the Union will be forwarded or delivered to the Employer's appropriate servicing area civilian personnel office for transmission to the appropriate payroll office. Area civilian personnel officers will assure that completed forms are transmitted to the appropriate payroll office within one day after receipt.

d. A deduction of one hour's base pay in Step J of the pay grade of the employee for each four-week pay period will be made from the pay of an employee who has requested an allotment for dues to the Union, except no deduction for dues will be made by the Employer in any period for which the employee's net earnings, after the other legal and required deductions, are insufficient to cover the full amount of the allotment for dues. Employees paid on a monthly or bi-monthly basis (invited contractors, open messes, and certain Recreation Services) will have a 13th union dues check-off by deduction from the year-end bonus. Employees paid more frequently than every four weeks, e.g., weekly or bi-weekly, will have their union dues checked off from every fourth week pay to have a total of 13 deductions a year.

e. A fee of 5 Won per deduction per each pay period will be charged by the Employer for administrative services rendered in connection with the dues withholding program.

f. The amount of the administrative fee to be retained by the Employer will be deducted from the total dues withheld each pay period and the remaining amount will be transmitted by the Employer to the Union not later than 40 working days from the close of each pay period.

g. The Employer will provide the Union with an initial list in duplicate reflecting the activity name, employee's name, individual amount deducted, total amount withheld by the Employer for service fee and the net amount remitted to the Union. Each pay period a list of additions or deletions will be provided and a revised updated list will be submitted at least semi-annually to the Union.

h. An employee who authorizes withholding of union dues may request revocation of withholding at any time by submitting completed forms (JK Form 76) or other written request. The request will be prepared in triplicate and submitted to the civilian personnel office by the employee. The civilian personnel office will transmit the first two copies of the revocation request to the appropriate payroll office, and the third copy to the union within one work day.

i. The Employer will discontinue the withholding of dues from the employee's pay at the beginning of the first full pay period either after 1st March or 1st September of any calendar year, whichever date first occurs after the revocation is received in the appropriate payroll office of the Employer either by 1 March or 1 September.

j. Any individual allotment for dues withholding will also be terminated automatically upon the employee's separation.

k. The Union will give written notification to the Employer within 10 days after an employee participating in the dues deduction program ceases, for any reason, to be a member in good standing of the Union, i.e., he resigns, has been suspended, or is expelled, in order that the Employer may terminate his allotment of dues.

l. The Union will be responsible for insuring the approved voluntary allotment form is made available to its members and will insure that the forms are properly completed and certified before transmitting them to the Employer.

m. The Union recognizes its responsibility for seeing that its member-employees are fully informed about the program for payroll deductions for Union dues, its voluntary nature and the use and availability of the required forms.

n. Changes in the amount of individual employee allotments, by reason of changes in the amount of Union dues, shall not be made more frequently than once a year.

o. The Union shall furnish the Employer, at the earliest practicable date, the name and signature of its representative(s) who is designated to certify the voluntary allotment form. The Union will be responsible for giving the Employer prompt notification of any changes in this designation.

p. The above procedures are applicable also to invited contractors, NAF activities, and to KRE. Separate arrangements may be made prior to implementation to meet certain special administrative requirements.

Article 17. Grievance Procedures.

a. The grievance procedures under this Article are exclusively for resolving grievances which are limited to the interpretation and application of this Agreement. Individual employee appeals and grievances are specifically excluded from this Article. Such individual grievances and appeals will be handled in accordance with established separate policies and procedures of the Employer.

b. Grievances will first be considered at the Union subchapter or local chapter level at the local command and on-site activities including invited contractors.

c. Unresolved grievances between local Employer and Union elements will be referred for resolution, without delay and without resort to actions not in line with this Agreement, to the next higher level employer and/or union up to the respective headquarters of the Army, Air Force, Navy, or KRE and the national union.

d. Grievances not resolved at separate component command headquarters level will be referred by the national union or separate command headquarters for review and further action by Headquarters, USFK.

e. The Union will prohibit and, if necessary, eliminate any action disruptive to Employer's normal work requirements during the course of settlement procedures.

Article 18. Meetings and Other Union-Management Activities.

a. The Employer and the Union agree to meet at reasonable times and confer in good faith with respect to personnel policies and practices and matters affecting working conditions, so far as may be appropriate under applicable laws and regulations and under Article 4 hereof.

b. The Employer (inclusive of clubs, KRE and invited contractor) and recognized union element will hold meetings on a periodic basis, with records maintained of the subjects discussed and agreements reached, if any. In addition to regularly scheduled meetings, special meetings may be held at the request of either party with appropriate notification sufficiently in advance.

c. Subjects for discussion in the regular and special meetings shall be exchanged sufficiently in advance to permit preparations. Discussions will normally be restricted to the subjects thus exchanged in advance.

d. As a rule, labor-management meetings will be held among the minimum and equal number of representatives from both parties. Representation from either party shall normally consist of three or less representatives, one of which shall be designated as the spokesman.

e. Subject to Employer's approval, Union officials may request participation in management activities including attendance at special ceremonies, events and conferences pertaining the Union members.

FOR UNITED STATES FORCES, KOREA:

GEORGE A BLAKESLEE
Chairman
Joint Labor Affairs Committee

FOR FOREIGN ORGANIZATIONS EMPLOYEES UNION:

HWANG KYU MU
President

28 NOV 1978
(Date)

MEMORANDUM OF UNDERSTANDING

In order to avoid confusion in the interpretation and application of the Labor-Management Agreement and to insure effective communications in labor-management relations, it is agreed that the following terms and corresponding definitions apply to the USFK-FOEU labor relations program.

Inform: To make known; to communicate knowledge; to give information; to tell.

Consult: To deliberate together; to ask advice of; seek the opinion of; to discuss or consider. To exchange opinions through discussion in resolving a problem. (NOTE: To reach a mutual agreement or to obtain the other's consent is not required.)

Negotiate: To meet and confer with another so as to arrive through discussion at some kind of agreement or compromise about something; come to terms by meetings and discussions. (NOTE: Normally, a mutual agreement or consent of the other party follows a negotiation.)

FOR UNITED STATES FORCES, KOREA:

GEORGE A. BLAKESLEE
Chairman
Joint Labor Affairs Committee

FOR FOREIGN ORGANIZATIONS EMPLOYEES UNION:

HWANG KYU MU
President

28 NOV 1978

Appendix A

18

통 화 록

1979. 3. 2.

제 목 : 주한 미군통신여단 근로자의 하청전환 문제

통화자 : 노동청 노정계장 고인내

안보문제담당관실 윤병세

내 용 :

2. 28. 주한미군 인사처장은 노동청관계자에게 다음과 같이 통보하여 옴. (구두)

1. 주한 미군 통신여단에 근무하는 한국인 근로자를 하청업자에게 전환하는 문제는 무기한 거론 않겠음.

2. 이는 Vessey 사령관의 특별조치에 의한 것 임.

* 참 고 : Kinney SOFA 미측 간사도 3. 2. 당부 내방시 상기 취지를 통보하여온 바 있음.

끝.

공람	안보담당관	79년 3월 2일	담당	담당관	심의관	국장	차관보	차관	장관
						보고필			

19

노동청 노정과장 안보담당관실 방문

1979. 4. 6.

제목 : 주한 미군 근로자 퇴직금 지급 문제

참석자 : 안보담당관
노정과장
외기노조 위원장, 사무국장

일시 : 79. 4. 6. 15:00

장소 : 안보문제담당관실

외 무 부 : 동 퇴직금 지불이 일시에 인출되는 경우, 물가에 영향을 줄 수 있으므로 재무부에 의견을 구해야 할 것임.

노 동 청 : - 동 퇴직금을 근로자들이 한꺼번에 인출하지 않을 것이므로(약600억 : $1.2억) 문제가없을 것임.
- 주한 미군 근로자는 외기노조와 미군과의 합의로 퇴직금을 받는 것으로 알고 있으므로, 동 문제의 지연은 근로자 동요의 우려가 있음.

외기노조 : - 동 합의각서는 근로자에 유리한것 임
- 동 퇴직금에 관한 근로자의 인출 및 사용에관해 표본조사를 실시, 자료제출(국장 오찬시)

外務部

勞總建議事項 措置計劃 報告.

< · · 部 · · · 局 · · · 課 電話: >

建議事項	措置計劃	備考
< · · · 勞組>		
1.	1.	
가.	가.	
나.	나.	
다.	다.	
2.	2.	
가.	가.	
나.	나.	
⁓	⁓	

註 : ①. 1979.3.22 12:00 까지 行政調整室(第1行政調整官 210号 70-2011)로 提出.

②. 勞動庁 勞政局 勞動組合課 (63-9973) ‥ 金事務官.

* 勞總 事務局 企劃室 (782-3884) ‥ 金部長.

21

勞組別 當面 建議事項

外務部

建議	内容要旨	所管部處	備考
<韓國勞動組合總聯盟>			
1. "愛國勤勞者"塔 建設 計劃	◦ 抗日獨立과 反共 建國運動者像 그리고 經濟建設과 國家 安保役軍을 表象 ◦ 各界代表(勞·使·政等)로 委員會를 構成 ◦ 國·公立 公園內 200餘坪 敷地에 建立 ◦ 約 2億원 所要	勞動廳	
2. 勞動界人物의 勞動行政 및 勞動政策分野 要職 登用	◦ 前職 및 現職의 有能한 勞動運動 出身者들에게 各政策 機構 또는 諮問機構 進出, 또는 實務擔當 公務員으로 登用	保社部 勞動廳 總務處	

2

外務部

建議	內容要旨	所管部處	備考
	• 船員携帶品의 通關規定 補完…… 稅關裁量制로 因해 被害船員이 허다하므로 所持品 限度規定의 制定 必要.		
<全國外技勞動組合> 1. 駐韓美軍部隊 所屬 勤勞者들의 離韓對策 (職)	~~駐韓美軍部隊 所屬 勤勞者들의 離職 對策 講究~~ ① 各種 技術訓練의 支援 ② 個人택시, 自動車 運輸事業 免許의 取得	保社部 勞動庁 ~~交通部~~ ~~建設部~~ 外務部	

행정조정실

23

3

建議	內容要旨	所管部處	備考
	② 外國人專用 觀光째의 運營權 賦與.		
	③ 技能職 勤勞者의 經歷認定		
	④ 海外就業의 積極推進.		
	⑤ 國內就業의 積極斡旋.		
	⑥ 海外移民의 積極支援.		
	⑦ 住宅資金 및 事業資金의 支援.		
	⑧ 離職對策 協議機構의 設置		

협정조정실.

24

12

當面問題에 관한 建議事項

1 9 7 9. 3. 8

韓國勞動組合總聯盟

25

韓国労動組合総聯盟

1. 「愛国勤労者」塔 建設計劃

①趣旨── 抗日独立과 反共建国運動者像 그리고 経済建設과 国家安保 役軍을 표상한다.

②各界代表(労·使·政등)로 委員会를 構成한다.

(労総 ── 実務委員会)

③国·公立公園内 200여평 敷地에 建立한다.

④소요자금── 약 2億원

2. 労動界人物의 労動行政 및 労動政策分野 要職登用

前職 및 現職의 有能한 労動運動 出身者들에게 各政策審議機構 또는 諮問機構進出, 保障 및 政府, 立法府要職(別定職) 또는 実務担当公務員으로 登用

>6

全国纖維労動組合

1. 労動政策의 基調転換

勤労者들의 生計保障과 権益向上을 위한 果敢한 政策과 行政指導의 強化

2. 労動行政의 改善

①調整決定된 団体協約의 不履行에 대한 強硬措置

②労動行政体系의 合理化

③不当労動行為에 대한 迅速処理

④新規組織課程에 대한 行政上의 矛盾是正

3. 79년도 賃金引上要求의 貫徹

①最低生計費의 絶対保障

②賃金隔差의 解消

③賃金의 物価運動制 실시

4. 国際紡織 労使紛糾의 収拾

①労組活動에 대한 会社側介入배제

②組合員 意思에 따른 執行部구성

③不当労動行為로 희생된 11名 組合員의 救済

5. 合同紡織의 運営 正常化

①老朽施設의 과감한 代替

②保有施設의 全面 稼動으로 失職防止

全国公務員労動組合協議会(鉄道・逓信・専売労組)

1. 超過勤務手当単価의 現実化

時間外 勤務는 平常勤務時間当 単価보다 1.5倍를 더 주는 것이 原則인데도 勤労基準法上의 通常賃金을 適用하지 않고 公務員報酬中 (通常賃金)本俸으로만 時間当単価를 算定함으로써 超過勤務가 平常勤務時間当 単価보다 도리어 적어지는 矛盾을 内包하고있어 이의 是正을 要望함.

2. 79年度 技能職公務員의 俸給調整에 대한 問題点 是正

①技能職公務員의 俸給引上을 下厚上薄型으로 是正

※ 79년도 技能職公務員의 俸給引上率이 8等級이상은 15% 内外이나 9等級은 11.61%, 10等級은 10.35%(9.10等級이 全体技能職 公務員의 63.66%차지)로 최악의 下薄引上을 하였음.

②이는 俸給調整課程에서 技能職을 除外하고 行政職만을 基準하는데서 問題点을 招来하였음

③技能公務員의 上位等級拡大(昇進의 길을 열어줄 것)

※ 6・7・8等級등 上位等級의 定員을 拡大 調整하여 9・10等級등 下位等級의 長期勤続滞症을 解除하고 財源配分比率에 있어서도 최소한 職務級 45%, 勤続給 55%의 比率이 成立되도록 要望함.

-3-

全国海員労動組合

1. 船員関税事犯에 대한 赦免者 行政制裁해제

제9대 大統領就任계기로 大赦免된 船員들이 総理訓令 제114호(一定期間 乘船資格제한)로 就業못해 家計難(総理室과 海運港湾庁에 文書建議中)

2. 船員法개정

78년도 国会上程이 保留되었던 船員法改正案의 79년중 実現苦待.

①賃金条項의 語句解釈上의 紛争要因배제

②勤労基準法 未達条項의 是正

3. 船員処遇의 正常化対策

危険度, 労動強度, 家族離散등의 特殊性으로 보아 外国에서는 船員대 陸上의 賃金比가 1.5 : 1로 되어있는 点을 감안하여 処遇의 正常化 誘導희망

4. 水産業 共済制度

零細船主의 支払能力이 脆弱하여 船員賃金 또는 沈没, 破船등 事故로 인한 災害補償의 不能事例가 許多하므로 共済加入強制化 시급.

5. 入港船当直者의 家族面会方案

入国碇泊船員中 当直者는 帰家不能이며 家族은 非船員으로 乘船이 不許되어 相逢이 不可한 바 船員의 士気昂揚을 위해

人道的 措置必要

6. 宿願事業의 支援

①船員綜合病院건립 ···· 建坪 2.000 坪 이상을 計劃中임. 国·公有地占用과 財源補助기대

②仁川 시멘즈 크라브 (Seamen Club) 建立 ····組合保有敷地 1.000 坪에 現代式施設計劃中임. 公益性 堪案한 財源補助기대.

③各港口船員待機所 설치 ····通船業者의 出沒등 收益者負担原則으로 自進參与기대

④浦項製鉄正門의 船員出入허용 ····保安上理由로 出入不許되어 10分 經路를 2 時間 海上迂廻시키는 現状임. 早速是正요망

⑤船員携帯品의 通関規定보완 ···· 稅関裁量制로 인해 被害船員이 허다하므로 所持品 限度規定의 制定이 必要함.

-5-

30

全国外機労動組合

1. 駐韓美軍部隊소속 勤労者들의 離職対策

① 각종 技術訓練의 支援

② 개인택시, 自動車運転事業免許의 取得

③ 外国人専用 관광택시의 運営権부여

④ 技能職 勤労者의 経歴認定

⑤ 海外就業의 積極推進

⑥ 国内就業의 積極알선

⑦ 海外移民의 積極支援

⑧ 住宅資金 및 事業資金의 支援

⑨ 離職対策 協議機構의 設置

全国聯合労勳組合

1. 退職雑給職員에 대한 退職金의 早速支給

①法務部는 법무810-42132 호(78. 12. 26)로 雜給職員에도 勤労基準法上의 退職金을 支給해야 한다고 有權解釈을 내렸음.

②서울특별市庁支部에 소속했던 200여명의 退職者에게는 79年 2月10日경부터 退職金을 支給하고 있으나 釜山直轄市庁支部에 소속했던 80명의 退職者에게는 상금껏 支給하지않고 있음.

③釜山直轄市庁支部에 소속했던 退職組合員들의 怨声이 자자하며 国家를 相対로 退職金請求訴訟을 提起할 움직임마저 보이고 있어 退職金의 早速支給이 요망됨.

2. 雜給職 清掃員에 대한 精勤手当支給

大統領令 제9295호로 改正된 雜給職員規程 제8조3항은 精勤手当을 規定하고있으나 本組合산하의 1萬 2천여 雜給職 清掃組合員에게 精勤手当을 전혀 支給하지 않고있어 이의 是正을 要望함.

32

當面問題에 관한 建議事項

1979. 3. 8

韓國勞動組合總聯盟

33

韓国労動組合総聯盟

1. 「愛国勤労者」塔 建設計劃

①趣旨── 抗日独立과 反共建国運動者像 그리고 経済建設과 国家安保 役軍을 표상한다.

②各界代表(労・使・政등)로 委員会를 構成한다.

(労総 ── 実務委員会)

③国・公立公園内 200여평 敷地에 建立한다.

④소요자금── 약 2億원

2. 労動界人物의 労動行政 및 労動政策分野 要職登用

前職 및 現職의 有能한 労動運動 出身者들에게 各政策審議機構 또는 諮問機構進出, 保障 및 政府, 立法府要職(別定職) 또는 実務担当公務員으로 登用

-1-

34

全国聯合労動組合

1. 退職雑給職員에 대한 退職金의 早速支給

①法務部는 법무 810-42132 호 (78. 12. 26) 로 雜給職員에도 勤労基準法上의 退職金을 支給해야 한다고 有權解釈을 내렸음.

②서울특별市庁支部에 소속했던 200여명의 退職者에게는 79年 2月 10日경부터 退職金을 支給하고 있으나 釜山直轄市庁支部에 소속했던 80명의 退職者에게는 상금껏 支給하지않고 있음.

③釜山直轄市庁支部에 소속했던 退職組合員들의 怨声이 자자하며 国家를 相対로 退職金請求訴訟을 提起할 움직임마저 보이고 있어 退職金의 早速支給이 요망됨.

2. 雜給職 清掃員에 대한 精勤手当支給

大統領令 제 9295 호로 改正된 雜給職員規程 제 8 조 3 항은 精勤手当을 規定하고있으나 本 組合산하의 1萬 2천여 雜給職 清掃組合員에게 精勤手当을 전혀 支給하지 않고있어 이의 是正을 要望함.

미 주 국

197 9 . 4 . 4 .

공람미파	담 당	과 장	심의관	국 장	차관보	차 관	장 관
	유	(서명)		(서명)			

제 목 : 주한미군 근로자 퇴직금에 관한 주한 미군사령부와 전국외국기관 노동조합간 합의 각서

요 약

1. 1979. 4. 30.까지 퇴직금을 산출, 주한미군은 1979.5.31. 까지 퇴직금의 은행예치를 완료하고, 각종업원은 예치된 금액을 인출하거나 예치하거나 선택권을 갖음.

2. 1979년 4월30일 이후의 퇴직금은 매년 각 종업원의 개인 구좌에 예치한다.

3. 현존 퇴직금 규정은 효력이 소멸되고 이 합의각서의 규정으로 대체

* 동 합의 각서는 SOFA 합동위에 회부될 것 임.

조치사항

36

기 안 용 지

분류기호 문서번호	미안 723-	(전화번호)	전결규정 조 항 전결사항
처리기간			국 장
시행일자	1979. 4. 10.		
보존년한			

보조기관	심의관		협조	15118
	담당관			
기안책임자	유창현	안보문제담당관실		

경유 수신 참조	수신처참조	발신		통제	1979. 4. 10

제 목	주한 미군 퇴직금 지불관련 자료 송부

79. 1. 24. SOFA 합동위의 퇴직금 지불문제를 노무분과위에 과제위촉에 따라 주한 미군과 외기노조는 별첨과 같이 합의한 바, 퇴직금 지불에 관한 자료를 송부하오니 업무에 참고하시기바랍니다.

첨부 : 1. 동 합의각서 (세출 기관, 비세출 기관)

2 인사규정 (발췌)

수신처 : 재무부장관 (이재국장)

경제기획원장관(기획국장)

법무부장관 (법무실장)

끝.

정서 / 관인 / 발송

0201-1-8A (갑)
1969. 11. 10승 인

190mm×268mm(2급인쇄용지60g/m²)
조 달 청 (1,500,000매 인 쇄)

37

V

주한미군 근로자 퇴직금 지급문제협의기록

79. 4. 10.

주한 미군 근로자의 퇴직금에 관한 미군과 외기노조간의 합의사항(78. 4. 3.) 검토를 위한 관계부처간의 회의를 79. 4. 10. 프라자 호텔에서 개최하였는바, 그 주요내용은 다음과 같음.

일 시 : 79. 4. 10. (화) 12:00 - 13:45

장 소 : Plaza 호텔 도원 (봉황실)

참석자 : 외무부 - 미주국장. 안보문제담당관
경제기획원 - 투자4과장 (표세진)
재무부 - 금융정책과 (정건용)
법무부 - 법무과장 (황길수)
노동청 - 노정국장 (한진희)
노정과장 (윤석춘)

주요발언요지 :

(외무부)

4. 3.자 미군 - 외기노조간의 합의내용을 검토해본 결과 한국고용원의 이익 반영문제, 법적측면에서의 문제점 및 국내경제문제와의 관계등 관계전문기관의 검토가 필요한 것으로 사료됨.

38

(노동청)

노무분과위원회에 이관되어온 동 문제는 원칙적으로 미군과 한국고용원간의 문제로 사료 되어 노동청은 동 양자간의 협의를 우선적으로 추진 하였던것이며 특히 한국고용원을 대표하는 외기노조는 직접 당사자임으로 최대의 자기이익을 가장 잘 반영할 수 있는 기관으로 생각되어 동 합의가 나오게 된 것 임.

(경기원)

동 합의 내용은 미측의 퇴직금 증가율 부담을 경감시키는 반면 한국고용원의 퇴직금 이율적용문제에 불리한 면이 있음.

(법무부)

차후 퇴직금은 매년 퇴직후 재 고용이라는 변칙적 방법이 적용되고 있는바, 이문제는 근로기준법 위반 가능성이 있음으로 검토되어야 할 것임.

(재무부)

약600억에 해당되는 동 퇴직금이 일시에 풀릴경우, 국내물가에 영향이 있음으로 일시에 풀리는것은 바람직하지 않음.

3P

결 론 :

사안의 성격상 오래 지연시킬수 없는 문제임으로 약 1주일의 여유를 두고 각 관계부처는 다음 사항을 연구하여 정부의 안을 작성함.

(노동청) : 노동자의 복지에 관련한 문제

(법무부) : 노동법규와 관련한 국내법규와의 관계

(재무부) : 최대의 은행이자 신설적용 가능성 검토

끝.

- 3 -

40

주한 미군 근로자 퇴직금 지급문제 협의 오찬

1. 일 시 : 79. 4. 10. (화) 12:00

2. 장 소 : Plaza 호텔 3층, 도원(봉황실)

3. 참석자 :

경제기획원	투자4과장	(표 세진)
재무부	금융정책과장	(김중웅)
노동청	노정국장	(한진희)
	노정과장	(윤 석춘)

끝.

41

주한 미군 근로자 퇴직금 지급 문제

1. 문제 제기

주한 미군과 전국 외기노조간에 합의된 주한 미군 세출기관 한국인 종업원 퇴직금 지불에 관한 양해각서(79. 4. 3.)는 주한 미군이 1979. 4. 30.까지의 퇴직금을 은행에 예치하고, 종업원은 동 퇴직금을 은행에 예치를 계속하거나 인출할 수 있으므로 약600억원($1.2억)이 일시에 풀릴경우 물가 및 금융에 미치는 영향을 고려할 필요가 있음.

2. 동 각서의 교섭 경위 및 내용

1) 경 위

- 78. 9. 26. SOFA 합동위 미측간사Kinney, 한국정부가 미국정부로 부터 퇴직금 전액을 이수할것을 제의
- 79. 1. 24. SOFA 합동위는 퇴직금 지불문제를 노무분과위에 과제 위촉
- 79. 2. 13. 노무분과위 한.미 양위원장은 동 문제를 주한 미군과 외기노조가 협의할 것에 합의
- 79. 4. 3. 주한 미군과 외기노조는 동각서에 합의를 봄

참 고 : 비 세출기관 종업원(약6,000명)의 퇴직금 문제는 제123차 합동위원회(77. 12. 6.)

42

첨부물 제32호 '비 세출자금 기관 근로자의
퇴직금 문제는 외기노조와 주한 미군간에
계속 협의하여 해결한다는 합의각서에 따라
78. 4. 1. 합의(인사규정 690-11) 로
해결됨.

2) 합의 각서 내용

- 1979. 4. 30. 까지의 퇴직금올 미측은 79. 5. 31. 까지
은행예치, 각 종업원은 인출하거나 예치하는 선택권
을 갖음
- 79. 4. 30. 이후의 퇴직금율은 1 년 근무, 1개월분의
급여율로 함.
- 동 합의 각서의퇴직금제도는 전 세출기관, 초청계약자
의 한국인 종업원과 노무단 단원에게 적용함
- 모든 현존 퇴직금 규정은 효력이 소멸되며 이 합의
각서의 규정으로 대체됨
- 본 합의각서의 시행은 미국방성 및 SOFA 합동위원회
의 승인을 조건으로 함.

* 세출기관 고용원	:	16,400명
노무단 단원	:	3,300명
초청계약자 한국인 고용원	:	600명

43

3. 동 문제에 대한 경기원. 재무부 반응

경 기 원 (자금기획과)	:	동 금액이 동시에 시중으로 유출될 경우 문제가 있음.
재 무 부	:	이재국(금융정책과) : 통화정책에 영향을 줄 것 임. 외환국(외환정책과) : $1.2억의 유입은 별 문제 없음
노 동 청 (노정과)	:	퇴직금 문제 지연은 근로자 동요의 우려가 있음. (4. 6. 노정과장 내방)
외기노조	:	동 퇴직금을 근로자들이 일시에 인출하지 않을 것으로 보임 (동 퇴직금에 관한 근로자의 인출여부 및 사용용도에 관해 표본조사를 실시, 자료 제출할 것임.) (4. 6. 외기노조 위원장, 사무국장 내방)

첨 부 : 1. 동합의각서

2. 인사규정 (발췌)

3. 비세출자금기관 근로자 퇴직금 지불에 관한 합의각서

44

4. 건 의

가. 동 퇴직금이 일시에 풀려도 국내 경제에 커다란 지장이 없는경우 외기노조 - 주한 미군 과의합의내용을 양해한다.

나. 국내 경제에 영향이 있는 경우 노무분과위에서의 서명 이전에 다음 조치를 취한다.

- 재무부와 노동청과 협의하여 외기노조를 설득한다.
  - ㅇ 시차별 지급 (예 : 분기별)
  - ㅇ 특별사유가 있는 경우에만 일시 지급
- 예치된 금액에 대하여는 법정 최고 이자를 지불한다.
- 외기노조 설득 기간중 국내 경제에 영향이 없는 범위에서 최대 금액을 우선 지급한다.
  - ㅇ 적정 최고 금액은 재무부와 노동청과 협의 결정
- 외기노조의 설득이 용이하지 않는 경우 취급 은행을 설득하여 일시 지불을 위한 예치 요청에 응하지 않도록 한다.
- 만족할 만한 합의 또는 기간이 경과한후 노무분과위원회 절차를 취한다.

끝.

45

미국장 차관보 차관

보 고 서

감 관 4/16

제 목 주한미군 근로자 퇴직금 지불 문제

보고자, 직책 사무관 성명 정 건 용

일 시 1979. 4. 16.

1. 내용

주한 미군과 전국 외기노조간에 합의된 주한 미군에 근무하는 한국인 근로자에게 대한 퇴직금 지급에 관한 내용임.

< 퇴직금 산정 방법 >

- 79년 4월 30일 전원 퇴직한 것으로 간주하여 퇴직금 지급 (약 120 백만불)

- 79년 5월 이후 퇴직시까지의 퇴직금은 1년 마다 1개월 급여분 만큼 추가 지급

※ 근로자의 재산증식 목적과 미군의 부담경감 목적이 합치

< 대 상 인 원 >

16,400 명

2. 그간의 경위

가. 78.9월 SOFA 합동위 미측 간사 Kinney가 퇴직금 전액을 한국정부가 인수할 것을 제의.

나. 79.2월 노무분과위의 한.미 양 위원장은 이를 미군과 외기노조가 협의할 것에 합의.

재 무 부

46

다. 79. 4. 3일 주한 미군과 외기노조 동 각서 합의.

라. 현재 노무분과위 한국측 위원장 (노동청 노정국장) 서명 보류중 (재무부측 의견 요구)

마. 향후 한국측 위원장 서명후 SOFA 합동 위원회 승인요

3. 문제점

〈 현재 합의 각서 내용 〉

미군은 5. 30일 까지 근로자가 원하는 은행에 예치 통장으로 지급
(근로자는 하시라도 인출 가능)

〈 문 제 점 〉

지급되는 퇴직금이 일시에 지급되는 경우 일시에 해외부문을 통한 통화 증발 (약 600 억원)

4. 처리 의견

- 퇴직금 지급에 따라 일시에 600 억원의 통화 증발이 예상되어 동 자금의 동결내지 사용 제한등의 조치를 강구할 필요는 있으나
  - ○ 퇴직금 지불 문제는 이미 노사간에 합의 되었으며
  - ○ 퇴직금 사용은 근로자의 고유 권리이고
  - ○ 한편으로 국제수지 개선 효과도 있으며
  - ○ 과거에도 약 147 억원 가량이 이러한 방식으로 지급 되었고
  - ○ 제한을 가할 경우 근로자들의 소요가 예상되므로 노동청및 노조를 통하여 적극적인 홍보 활동을 하여 최대한 저축으로 흡수 유도하는 것이 좋겠음.

(통화 관리에 정책적인 참고)

47

4. 20.
노동관리장으로부터 入手

退職金算定比較表

例示 : 木工 WB 6 - 10号 (15年勤続勤労者)

年度別 \ 區分	累進制適用時 (現行制度)	79.4.30退職金受領時 (改正制度)	差額
79	5.273.905 원	5.349.246 원	75.341 원
80	6.411.545 〃	6.955.334 〃	543.789 〃
81	7.672.164 〃	8.651.712 〃	979.548 〃
82	9.395.888 〃	10.733.817 〃	1.337.929 〃
83	11.200.577 〃	13.285.891 〃	2.085.314 〃

算出内訳

現行制度 : 基本給에 累進率을 乘하여 計算
賃金은 每年 15% 引上된것으로 推定하여 計算

改正制度 :
- 基本給에 累進率을 乘하여 計算
- 利子는 特別家計 定期預金 年利子 20.1%로 計算
- 解雇手当은 基本賃金 1個月分
- 年未滿 勤続期間은 月割 計算 (平均 15日分 賃金)
- 病假는 15日分의 賃金으로 計算

評價

現行制度 : 基本給에 累進率만을 乘하여 支給

改正制度
- 79. 4. 30로 退職金을 受領時에는 現行制度의 退職金外에 解雇手当, 病假手当, 年未滿月割計算등의 特惠가 있으며,
- 前記 特惠外에 高率의 銀行利子로 因하여 81年度 退職時는 979,548원, 83年度退職時는 2,085,314원의 勤労者 実利益이 있음.
- 따라서 改正制度에 依한 退職金 支給이 勤労者에게 有利하다고 判断됨.

48

計算根拠

例示 : 木工 WB 6-10号 (15年勤續者)

基本賃金 : 150.683 원

平均賃金 : 235.626 〃

1. 累進制를 適用할時 (現行制度)

79年 150.683 원 × 35個月 = 5.273.905원

80 〃 173.285 〃 × 37 〃 = 6.411.545 〃

81 〃 199.277 〃 × 38½ 〃 = 7.672.164 〃

82 〃 229.168 〃 × 41 〃 = 9.395.888 〃

83 〃 263.543 〃 × 42½ 〃 = 11.200.577 〃

2. 合議覚書에 依해 79. 4. 30 受領後退職時

79 〃 150,683 원 * 35 個月 + 75.341원 = 5.349.246원
(基本賃金) (年未満月割)

80 〃 5.349.246원 + 1.075.192원 + 270.969원 + 86.642원 + 173.285원
(利子) (平均賃金) (病假左) (減員手当)
= 6.355.334원

81 〃 6.695.407원 + 1.345.776원 + 311.614원 + 99.638원 + 199.277원
(利子) (平均賃金) (病假左) (減員手当)
= 8.651.712원

82 〃 8.352.797원 + 1.678.912원 + 358.356원 + 114.584원 + 229.168원
(利子) (平均賃金)? (病假左) (減員手当)
= 10.733.817원

83 〃 10.390.065원 + 2.088.403원 + 412.109원 + 131.771원 + 263.543원
(利子) (平均賃金) (病假左) (減員手当)
= 13.285.891원

49

주한 미군 근로자 퇴직금 문제 회의요지

일 시 : 79. 4. 23. (월) 16:30 - 18:00

장 소 : 경제기획원 투자4과

참석자 :

경기원	:	투자4과장	(표 세진)
재무부	:	금융정책과	(정 건용)
노동청	:	노정과장	(윤 석춘)
외무부	:	안보문제담당관실	(유 창현)

요 지 :

재무부 - 통화정책을 세우는데 이번 퇴직금 지급을 고려하겠음.

- 현 단계에서는 저축을 장려하는 것이 좋음.

경기원 - 동 퇴직금이 소비자금화 할 경우 물가를 교란하는 요소로 작용할수 있음.
이를 막기위해 단계적인출, 금융 incentive 를 생각할수 있으나 이는 현실적으로 어려움

- 퇴직금에 관한 합의각서상 총 임금은 기본급 이외에 수당등 근로자에 지급액을 합산하는 것으로 명확히 할 필요가 있음.

- 감원시 1개월분의 평상임금 지급 규정중 감원시를 퇴직시로 하는 것이 바람직함.

공람	안보담당관	79년 8월 24일	담당	담당관	심의관	국장	차관보	차관	장관
			유	석		(서명)			

50

노동청 - 동 퇴직금 지급은 미측, 근로자 양측에 이익이고, 퇴직금문제 지연은 근로자 동요의 우려가 있으므로 동 퇴직금 문제는 합의 각서대로 시행하는것이 바람직함.

- 동 합의각서 수정에관해 미측은 응하지 않을 것으로 보임.

결 론 : 동 퇴직금 문제는 정부가 개입할 여지가 적으므로 저축을 장려하고 동 합의각서를 시행하는것이 바람직함.

건 의 : 동 결론을 경제기획원장관의 승인을 얻은후, 명일(4. 24.) 경기원에서 노동청이 통고하여 처리하도록 함.

51

< 内部 報告 ; 79. 4. 23 >

주한미군부대근무 한국인 종업원 퇴직금 지급문제

정기원

1. 현퇴직금 규정 및 적립현황

- 1954년 부터 주한미군과 한국인 종업원 (전국외국기관 노동조합) 은 근속년수의 증대에 따라 누진율을 적용하는 퇴직금 협정을 맺고 퇴직금을 적립함.
- 현재 대상종업원은 16,400명, 퇴직금적립액은 약600억원 (120백만불) 임.

2. 개정(안)의 내용

- 기적립된 퇴직금은 77. 4월 30일을 기준으로 현퇴직금규정에 의해 일시 지급
- 향후는 매년 퇴직금의 법정한도인 30일분을 지급

3. 고섭의 배경

가. 미군측

- 퇴직금의 누진으로 앞으로 퇴직금 적립부담의증대

나. 외기노조측

- 퇴직전에 지금까지의 퇴직적립금의 일시 수령 — 앞으로 미군철수와 관련하여 예상되는 감원에 대비하여 자활책 강구
- 자진 이직할 경우 현퇴직금 규정은 비자진 이직의 경우에 비하여 퇴직금율이 불리
- 현급여제도가 시간급이므로 본합의가 이루어지지 않을 경우 근로 시간수의 감소우려
- 미군측의 퇴직금 적립부담 경감으로 근로자의 후생복지혜택 (교육, 후생비등) 가능

52

4. 추진경위

- '78. 9. 26 : 한미행협 합동위 미측 간사가 한국정부가 미국정부로 부터 퇴직금 잔액을 인수 할 것을 제의

- '79. 1. 24 : 합동위에서 퇴직금 지불문제를 동 합동위 노무분과 위원회 (위원장 : 노동청 노정국장)에서 검토하도록 위촉

- '79. 2. 13 : 노무분과위 한.미양 위원장은 동 문제를 주한미군과 외기노조가 협의할것에 합의

- '79. 4. 3 : 주한 미군과 외기노조간 협의를 거쳐 합의 각서에 서명

- '79. 5. 10 : 본합의내용의 승인을 위한 한미합동위 개최 예정

5. 문제점 및 건의

가. 문제점

0 퇴직금 수령액의 감소

본직의 근속년한에 따른 누진율의 적용이 배제됨으로 퇴직금의 누적적 증대효과가 상실됨

(그러나 일시금으로 지급받는 금액을 년20% 이자율로 활용하면 양자가 비슷한 수준임)

0 퇴직금의 일시인출에 따른 통화팽창

나. 건 의

0 주한미군측과 외기노조간에 합의가 되었고 특히 외기노조측에서 시행되기를 적극적으로 희망함으로 한미행협 한미합동회의에서 승인을 보류케 할 필요는 없을것임.

0 일시에 지급될 퇴직금 약 600억원이 한꺼번에 인출될 경우 통화에 미치는 영향이 클것이므로 이를 장기간 은행에 예치시킬 수 있는 유인 조치의 강구가 있어야 할 것임.(재무부에서 방안 검토중)

53

" 참 고 "

< 주한미군과 외기노조간 합의각서내용 >

(1) 기적립퇴직금의 일시지급

- 1979. 4. 30 까지의 퇴직금은 79. 5. 31 까지 종업원이 선정하는 은행의 각자 개별구좌에 예치하고 예치금은 종업원의 의사에 따라 전액 또는 일부인출가능 - 사실상의 지급임.

- 퇴직금 산정은 현행 퇴직금지급규정대로 산정
다음 2방법중 높은 액수로 결정

1. 79. 3. 20 이전 최근 24개월중 최고 계속 3개월동안의 평상임금 (기본급)월평균액을 기초로 비자발적 퇴직금율 적용

2. 79. 3. 20 이전 최근 12개월중 최고 계속 3개월의 총임금 월평균액 (수당, 상여금포함)을 기초로 1년 근무에 1개월분의 비율 적용

(2) 79. 4. 30 이후의 퇴직금

- 현재의 누진제를 없애고 1년 근무에 대하여 1개월분의 급여율로 함.

- 산출기초는 12개월동안의 최고 계속 3개월간의 총임금 (수당, 상여금포함)월평균액으로 함.

(3) 기타 특전의 규정

- 해고수당의 신설
감원되었을 때는 1개월분의 평상임금추가 지급 (1년 미만 근무자 제외)

- 병가기간의 근무기간 합산

(4) 적용범위 : 16,4?? 명

- 세출예산 근로자 (12,500 명)

- 한국근로단 단원 (3,?00 명)

54

(5) 퇴직금규정의 효력

- 모든 현존퇴직금 규정은 본 합의 각서의 효력발생과 동시에 소멸

(6) 시행조건

- 본 합의각서의 시행은 미국방성 및 한미행협 합동위원회의 승인을 조건으로 함.

(현 퇴직금 제도)

근무 년수	퇴직금 지급 월수		근 무 년 수	퇴직금 지급 월수	
	자 원	비 자 원		자 원	비 자 원
1	1	1	14	24	32
2	2	2	15	26.5	35
3	3	4	16	29	37
4	4	5	17	31.5	38
5	5.5	7.5	18	34	41
6	7.5	10	19	37	42.5
7	9.5	12.5	20	40	43.5
8	11.5	15	21	42	45
9	13.5	17.5	22	44	46
10	15.5	20	23	46	47.5
11	17.5	23	24	48	48.5
12	19.5	26	25	50	50
13	21.5	29			

56

(현행 및 개정규정상의 퇴직금 비교예시)

(천 원)

현근속 년수	퇴직년도	현규정상 퇴직금(A)		개정규정의퇴직금(B)	B - A	
		자 원	비자원	공 통	자 원	비자원
5 년 96,000 원	1년후	540	720	680	140	△ 40
				(770)	(230)	(50)
	3년후	1,192	1,555	1,035	△157	△ 520
				(1,441)	(249)	(△114)
10 년 160,000 원	1년후	2,100	2,760	2,384	284	△ 376
				(2,784)	(684)	(24)
	3년후	3,715	5,011	2,975	△ 740	△2,036
				(4,562)	(847)	(△449)
16 년 224,000 원	1년후	5,292	6,468	5,718	426	△ 750
				(6,754)	(1,462)	(286)
	3년후	8,951	10,282	6,546	△2,405	△3,736
				(10,499)	(1,548)	(217)
22 년 288,000 원	1년후	9,936	10,260	8,971	△ 965	△1,289
				(10,627)	(691)	(367)
	3년후	15,552	15,552	10,036	△5,516	△5,516
				(16,298)	(746)	(746)

주 : ( ) 내는 퇴직금 수령액에 대하여 년 20% 이자 포함할 경우임.

57

駐韓美軍의 종업원
退職金 支給問題에
関한 副總理 報告内容
이오니 参照하시기 바랍니다.

58

〈最終 報告 ; 79.4.30〉

주한 미군부대근무 한국인 종업원 퇴직금지급문제에 대한 협의결과

1. 근로기준법 저촉여부 문제

   - 취업상태를 사실상 계속하면서 일정시점에서 기히 적립된 퇴직금을 일시에 지급하고 향후는 해마다 1년분을 지급하는 것은 근로기준법 제28조에서 규정하는 퇴직금 지급제도의 취지에 비추어볼때 문제점이 있다고 하겠으나

   - 동사안의 경우는 노사간의 완전합의에 의하여 퇴직금 지급규정을 개정 (법정하한선인 " 근속년수 1년에 대하여 30일분이상의 평균임금" 조건을 충족) 하고 이에 따른 퇴직금을 선지급하는 형식이 되는 것이므로 엄격하게 법에 저촉된다고 볼 수는없음.

   * 근로기준법 제 28조 (퇴직금 제도)

     사용자는 계속 근속년수 1 년에 대하여 30일분 이상의 평균임금을 퇴직금으로서 퇴직하는 근로자에게 지급할 수 있는 제도를 설정하여야 한다. 다만, 근로년수가 1년미만인 경우에는 그러하지 아니하다.

2. 타 국내기업과 노조에의 파급문제

   퇴직금 지급 규정의 개정은 노사간의 합의를 전제로 하는데 주한미군과 외기노조간의 경우는 노사간에 완전합의가 이루어진 것이나, 국내 타 기업의 경우는 사용자측에서는 퇴직금 일시 지불에 따르는 부담이 과중하기 때문에 중도 일시지불에 합의하기가 어려울 것이며 근로자측에서는 퇴직전에 퇴직금 일시지급을 강력히 주장할 수 있는 법적근거가 없기 때문에 노사간 합의가 이루어지기 어려울 것이므로 타 국내기업과 노조에의 파급은 없을 것으로 판단됨.

59

3. 통화관리면에서의 문제

- 재무부에서는 600억원의 퇴직금 지불이 공무원 1회 상여금 지급액 약 1,000억원에 미달되는 것이로 통화관리면에서 커다란 교란요인으로는 판단하지 아니하고 전체적인 통화관리운용을 통하여 흡수 가능한 것으로 판단

- 퇴직금 지급을 2 - 3차에 걸친 단계적으로 실시하도록 하는것은 한국인 종업원의 입장에서는 현시점에서 일시에 목돈을 지급받기를 희망하는 것이므로 반대하고 있으며, 또 은행에 예치해두고 분할 인출토록 하는것은 법이 정한 임금 지급원칙상의 "전액불" 원칙에 위배되므로 정부가 강제할 수는 없음.

4. 결론

- 외기노조와 주한 미군 사이에 이미 합의된 것이므로 이를 승인함이 타당한 것으로 사료됨.

- 통화관리면에서 동퇴직금 지급의 새로운 요인을 감안하여 운용토록 하고 외기노조를 통하여 은행에 장기 예치하거나 회사채 매입등을 적극 권장토록 함.

60

기 안 용 지

분류기호 문서번호	미안 723-	(전화번호)	전결규정 조 항 전결사항
처리기간		국 장	
시행일자	1979. 5. 7.		
보존년한			
보조기관 심의관			협조
담당관			
기안책임자	유창현	안보문제담당관실	
경유 수신 참조	경제기획원(기획국장), 재무부(이재국장) 법무부(법무실장)	1979. 5. 7 외무부	통제 1979. 5. 7
제 목	주한 미군종업원 퇴직금 가지급 합의각서 시행		

연 : 미안 723- 15118 (79. 4. 10.)

1. 주한 미군 종업원 퇴직금지급 문제와 관련, 그간 79.4.10.및 79.4.23.(경기원) 관련부처와 협의를 한바 있읍니다.

2. 노무분과위원회는 주한 미군 한국인 세출기관 종업원 퇴직금 가지급합의 각서를 금번 SOFA 합동위원회 (79.5.10. 개최)에 회부한바, 별첨 동 합의각서를 참고하시고, 동 합의각서 시행에 이견 여부를 지급 회보 바랍니다.

첨부 : 동 합의각서 1부. 끝.

정서 / 관인 / 발송

0201-1-8A (갑)
1969. 11. 10 승인

190mm×268mm (2급인쇄용지60g/m²)
조 달 청 (1,000,000매 인쇄)

61

미 주 국

1979. 5. 8.

총무미과	담 당	과 장	심의관	국 장	차관보	차 관	장 관

제 목　주한미군 종업원 퇴직금 지급합의각서 이행 협조 요청

요 약

한국노조는 79. 5. 1. 공문을 통해 동 합의각서의 조속 이행을 위한 협조를 요청함.

동 합의 각서 이행시

- 미8군의 예산 절감을 이유로한 평균 임금의 감축을방지할 수 있으며,
- 외화 획득의 이점이 있으며,
- 주한 미군 철수 계획에 대비, 자영 및 공동 사업자금의 확보의 이점이 있음.

끝.

조치사항

62

미주과

韓 國 勞 動 組 合 總 聯 盟

서울特別市永登浦區汝矣島洞1番地117號

FEDERATION OF KOREAN TRADE UNIONS

電話 (782) 3884-7

DATE 1979. 5. 1.

노총법규 제446호

수 신 외무부 장관

제 목 미8군 한국인 종업원에대한 퇴직금지급 합의각서 이행협조요청

당연맹 산하 외국기관노동조합 보고에 의하면 주한미군에 고용되고 있는 한국인 종업원의 퇴직금제도는 "79년 10월로써 종료됨에 따라 전종업원의 퇴직금을 (약 600억추산) 1973. 4. 30 까지 종업원이 원하는 국내은행에 개인구좌로 예치하는 절차를 거쳐 일시지급하는 방향에서 미8군과 합의각서를 교환한바 있으나 한미합동위원회의 한국측은 국내 "인플레이션"을 우려하여 합의각서의 이행을 보류하고 있다는바, 은행에 예치하게 됨으로 저축증대에 기여할수 있을뿐 아니라 노사관계로 인한 임금지불을 정부가 억제조치함은 부당하며 근로자의 경제적 지위향상을 초래 한다는점을 고려하여 합의각서에 대한 조속한 이행을 위하여 적극협조하여 주시기 바랍니다.

"참고사항"

1) 미8군은 예산절감을 이유로 매년 근로시간을 단축시키고 있음을 고려할때 (시간당 임금체계) 퇴직금산출에 기초가 되는 근로시간의 감축을 방지하여 수억원의 손실을 방지할수 있으며

2) 미군철수 계획으로 인한 종업원의 심리적 불안이 고조되고 있는 현실에서 퇴직금을 8군이 관리하고 있는것보다 국내은행에 개인구좌로 예치하므로써 심리적 불안의 해소와 은행이자의 수입은 종업원의 경제적 향상을 초래할수 있으며

발송 No. 1979. 5. 2 한국노동조합총연맹

63

결재	외 무 부		지시사항	
	접수	제 16425 호		안
주무과	접수일시			
담당자	회람		197 년 까지 처리할것	

미 64

3) 국가적으로는 7—9%의 이자를 지불하면서 외환을 차관하고 있는 현실을 감안할때 무이자의 막대한 외화가 획득될수 있다는 잇점이 있으며

4) 주한미군의 철수계획으로 오는 대량실업사태에 대비하여 자영및 공동사업자금의 확보등 잇점이 있읍니다.

원래 퇴직금은 임금의 후불적 성격으로 이들 종업원은 대부분이 반평생을 미8군의 작전업무 수행에 투신하여온 댓가로써 지급되는 금번의 합의각서가 종업원의 경제적 이익과 생활안정에 기여할수 있다는 점을 고려할때 국민의 재산을 보호하여야 할 정부의 위치에서는 당연히 승인하여야 할 문제라고 사료되어 조속한 처리를 요청하는 바입니다.

유첨: (1) 합의각서 1부.

(2) 종업원 퇴직금 임시지급으로 인한 혜택금액 명세 1부. 끝.

한국노동조합총연맹

위원장 정

65

[illegible] 수행시 혜택금액

[illegible]계산으로 인한 혜택금액

1개월작업시간 [illegible]

1시간당 평균임금 $2.75

1개월임금합계 $484.00

16,400명 x $484 x 6/12 = $3,968,800.00

$3,968,800.00 x 500 = 1984[illegible]원

약 20억원

2. [illegible] 계산하여 [illegible]

보는 금액 1인당 843 시간

843 시간은 5/12 개월의 근무월임

16,400 x (484 x 5/12) = $3,307,060.00

$3,307,060 x 500 = 1,653[illegible] 만원

약 16억5천만원

3. 감원시 평상임금 1개월분 추가지급으로 인한 혜택금액

1개월 작업시간 176

1시간당 평균임금 $2.75

1개월평상임금 $290.40

1개월평균임금 $484.00

-12-

66

16,400 × $290.40 = $4,762,560.00

$4,762,560.00 × 500 = 2,381,28 만원

약 24 억

월별 계산해직금 20억

병가 〃 15억 5천만원

감원시 1개월분 해직금 24억

합계 59억 5천만원

- 13 -

駐韓美軍直屬從業員

退職金引出交涉經緯

全國外國機關勞動組合

68

駐韓美軍勤勞者退職金支給

1. 對象人員 : 16.400名
   - ○ 歲出豫算勤勞者 : 12.500名
   - ○ 韓國勞務團(KSC) : 3.300名
   - ○ 招請契約勤勞者 : 600名

2. 支給豫想額 : 約 600 億원

3. 支給 經緯

1979년 1월 24일자 한-미 행협 합동위원회가 노사분과 위원회에 분임한 과제와 이과제 이행에 관한 1979 2월 13일 노사분과 위원회 한-미 양 위원장의 합의에 따라 주한미군과 전국외국기관 노동조합은 동문제를 협의하여 1979. 4. 3일 합의 각서에 서명하였음

- 1 -

69

주한 미군 직속종업원 퇴직금 교섭행위

현 주한미군 한인종업원의 퇴직금제도는 54년에 시작 79년 10월 이면 끝나게 되어있음

외기노조는 지난 78. 5. 22일 주한미군당국에 현행 퇴직금 제도의 모순점을 들어 개선요청하였으나 이를 시정치 않았으며 주한 미군당국은 78년말부터 퇴직금 지급의도를 비추었으나 조합은 전략적으로 인출의사를 밝히지 않았음. 급기야 지난 79. 2. 4일 고용주측은 조합이 요구치도 않은 직속종업원 퇴직금 지급안을 제시해왔으나 너무나 성의없는 대안임으로 조합대안(79. 2. 20)을 제시케 되었으며 노사간 수차에 걸친 협의끝에 대다수 종업원들이 인출을 원함으로 79. 4 3 일 노사 쌍방 합의각서에 서명케 이르렀음.

그간 경위는 다음과 같음

78 5 22 : 주한미군 종업원 퇴직금제도 개선요청

1) 주한미군 퇴직금제도 54년시작 79년 10월이면 끝나게 되어있음

2) 이원화제도 폐지 일률적 고율지급.

3) 15년이상 장기근속 높은 누진율 실시할것.

2

70

4) 새로운 누진율을적용 15년부터 45년까지 근속자는 매년 3개월분을 증가할것.

1. 주한미군 퇴직금 지급안 (2월 14일)

(1) 종업원 앞으로 은행예치

(2) 은행선택 종업원에 일임

(3) 이자율 안전보호 여점

(4) 예치금액 4년후 인출

(5) 종업원 은행구좌에 1년에 한번 정기적납입.

(6) 79년 3월 1일 효력발생 이날이후 은행구좌에 퇴직금납입

2. 외기노조 1차대안 (2월 20 일)

(1) 본인의견에 의해 일시불로 인출

(2) 근무중 제일 금액이 많은 3개월분 평균 고율지급

(3) 적치휴가 현금지급

(4) 적치병가 현금지급

(5) 지급후 고용조건 변화없음

(6) 계산시 일자 모자랄시 월별수 가산지급

(7) 누진율 가산지급

(8) 조합 퇴직금 개선안 79년 3월말까지 협의결정

(9) KRE·NAF 종업원 직속종업원과 동일

3. 주한미군 2차대안 (2월 23일)

(1) 현재까지 퇴직금 각종업원 은행구좌에 예치
전액·일부·계속 종업원선택

(2) 고율, 12개월동안 가장 높은 계속 3개월 평균

(3) 만기에 모자라는 기간 월할지급 이후 매년 지급
퇴직금 월할지급

(4) 감원 우선결정 및 휴가관련 취업일 가산현행대로

(5) 2율 퇴직금율폐지 시행일로부터 매년근무에 대해
1개월의 퇴직금지급

(6) 시행일이후 감원 평상임금 추가지급

(7) 매년 지급 퇴직금 은행구좌에 예치

4. 외기노조 2차대안 (2월 26일)

(1) 현재까지 퇴직금 각종업원에 지급

(2) 계산고율, 24개월동안 가장 높은 계속 3개월평균

(3) 만기에 모자라는 기간 월할지급 이후 매년 지급
퇴직금도 월할지급

(4) 감원 우선결정 및 휴가에 관련한 취업일 가산
현행대로

-4-

72

(5) 지급후 새로 누진율 적용

(6) 시행일이후 잔여 1개월 해당금액 추가지급

(7) 적치한 연가 현금

(8) 적치한 병가 현금

(9) 협정일부터 30일이내 지급

(10) NAF. KOAX 종업원 직속종업원과 동일

(11) 79년 7월1일 임금인상시 해당 인상율 가산지급

5. 주한미군 3차대안(3월8일)

(1) 79년 4월 30일 기산일까지 종업원이 선정한 은행구좌에 예치 기산일인 79년 4월30일부터 30일이내 예치완료

인출 자유선택

(2) 4월30일 기산일까지 퇴직금산출은 다음과 같이 하다

ㄱ. 79년 3월31일이전 24개월중 최고 계속 3개월 평균산출 고율 또는

ㄴ. 79년 3월31일 이전 12개월중 최고 계속 3개월 평균 산출 만1년 근무 1개월분의 비율 대수중 높은 액

73

(3) 79년 4월30일 기산일 수권만기간 못미치는 기간 월할지급

7. 매만1개월 근무기간에 대해 연누진액의 12분의1

(4) 휴가취득 및 감원 우선순위 근무년월일 변동없이 계속 유효

(5) 79년 4월30일 마감일이후 1년근무 1개월 급여일로 하되 산출매년 마감일직전 90일동안 받는 급여의 총액

월평균이금액 각구좌에예치 마감일 30일전 예치완료

(6) 해직당시 1년미만 월할지급

(7) 감원 1개월분 평상임금 추가지급

(8) 자진사직 및 귀책해직을 제외한 해직시 축적병가 퇴직금 산출 근무기간 간주.

(9) 위각항 완료후 퇴직금 전의무완료

6. 외기노조 3차대안 (3월14일)

(1) 79년 4월30일 기산일까지 전종업원 의사집약하며 지역선정 은행구좌에 개인명의로 예치

은행예치 기산일인 4월30일부터 5월20일까지 완료후 1주일내 본인통장을 예출 인출선택 자유의사

(2) 4월30일 기산일까지 퇴직금산출

- 6 -

74

ㄱ. 3월 31 일이전 24개월중 최고 계속 3개월 월

평균산출 고율에 의한 액수 또는

ㄴ. 3월 31 일 이전 12개월중 최고계속 3개월 월

평균산출 기초 1년근무 1개월분비율 액수중 높은액

(3) 79년 4월 30 일 기산일기해 만기에 못미칠시

월할지급

ㄱ. 만 1개월 근무기간 누진액의 6분의 1 해당금액

ㄴ. 79년 3월 31 일 이전 90일간 월평균 12분의

1 해당금액월할

(4) 근무년월일 계속유효

(5) 79년 4월 30 일 마감일이후 1년근무 1개월급

여율로 하되 산출 매년 마감일 직전 최고 3개월

급여 월평균

(6) 해직당시 1년미만 월할지급 90 일 1/12 해당금액

(7) 감원 9개월분 평상임금 추가지급

(8) 자진사직 귀책사유 8군안과 동일

7. 주한미군 최종안 (3월 16 일)

(1) 79년 4월 30 일 기산일까지 퇴직금은 국내모든

동의 은행중 종업원 선정은행 개인구좌에 예치

조합은 예금접수 동의은행과 별도 협약 교섭약정

-7-

75

조합은 은행약정 내용을 종업원들이 선정에 참고토록 할수 있다

은행예치 기산일 4월 30일부터 늦어도 30일이내 완료한다. 산출자유선택 · 은행예치절차는 조합과 협의작성

(2) 4월 30일 기산일까지 퇴직금산출

ㄱ. 3월 31일 이전 24개월중 최고 계속 3개월 월평균 산출 고율에 의한 액수 또는

ㄴ. 79년 3월 31일 이전 12개월중 최고 계속 3개월의 총임금 월평균액(보나스 년총액 월균할)산출 기초 1년근무 1개월분 비율 액수중 높은액

(3) 79년 4월 30일 기산일 만기에 못미칠시 월할지급

ㄱ. 매만 1개월 근무 년누진액 1/12 또는 8개월 누진경우 1/6 해당금액

근무기간 현재와 동일

(4) 79년 4월 30일 이후율은 1년근무 1개월급여로 하되 산출기초는 매해 3월 31일을 기해 이날직전 12개월동안 최고3개월의 총임금(보너스 년총액월균할) 월평균액으로 한다 매년 3월 30일기해 30일이내 은행 예치완료.

-8-

76

(5) 해직당시 1년미만 월활지급

(6) 감원시 1개월분 추가지급 1년미만 제외

(7) 자진사직, 귀책사유 전항동일

(8) 위각항 완료후 퇴직금 지급이행 완료

8. 외기노조 최종안(3월 20일)

(1) 은행예치 4월 30일부터 늦어도 5월20일이내 예치완료

10일이내 개인통장지급 예치금 인출 자유의사

은행예치절차 외기노조와 협의작성

(2) 4월30일 가산일까지 퇴직금산출(전항동일)

(3) 4월30일 기산일 만기에 기해 미달 근무월활 지급

ㄱ. 매만1개월 1/12 또는 6개월 누진경우 1/6 해당 금액

ㄴ. 퇴직금 산출시 1개월근무 79년 3월31일이전 12개월동안 최고계속 3개월중임금 평균 1/12금액 월활.

(4) 전항동일

단, 법정퇴직금 미달시 추가지급

(5) 전항동일

-9-

77

해직전 1년중 금액높은 계속 3개월동안 총급여 월평균 1/12 해당금액

(6) 전항동일 (감원시 추가지급)

(7) 자진사직 병가삭제 (전항동일)

- 10 -

78

주한미군사 종업원 퇴직금 지불사례

퇴직금인출부서	지급년도	인원	금액	비고
경비원 및 정비공	72. 7. 15	1,200	약 50억	10호봉에서 5호봉으로 떨어짐 직급 1급강등
인텡교	73. 10. 1	130	2억	병가 이월 못함
초청업체	75. 10. 1	2.500	60억	변화없음
교역처	77. 4	1,899	50억	누진제없음 감원시 1개월 평상임금 추가, 법정퇴직금지급
비충당	78. 3. 15	2.000	30억	누진제없음 감원시 1개월 추가지급 NAF. KOAX 은행장기저축 2년후 인출합의
충당	79. 5	16.400	600억	(2) 병가 현금지급 (3) 감원시 1개월추가지급 (1) 월할계산

-11-

7P

직속 종업원 퇴직금 수령시 혜택금액

1. 월별계산으로 인하여 혜택금액

1개월작업시간 176

1시간당 평균임금 $ 2.75

1개월 임금합계 $ 484.00

16.400명 × (484 × 6/12) = $ 3.968.800.00

$ 3.968.800.00 × 500 = 1.984.40만원

약 20억임

2. 병가를 퇴직시 근무년한으로 계정하여 지불시 혜택보는 금액 1인당평균 843 시간

843 시간은 5/12 개월의 근무일임

16.400 × (484 × 5/12) = $ 3.307.060.00

$ 3.307.060 × 500 = 1.653.53 만원

약 15억원5천만원

3. 감원시 평상임금 1개월분 추가지급으로 인한 혜택금액

1개월 작업시간 176

1시간당 평균임금 $ 2.75

1개월평상임금 $ 290.40

1개월평균임금 $ 484.00

16.400 × $290.40 = $4.762.560.00

4.762.560.00 × 500 = 2.381.28 만원

약 24 억

월별 계산혜택금 20억

병가 〃 15억 5천만원

감원시 1개월분혜택금 24억

합계 59 억 5천만원

- 13 -

현퇴직금제도

근무년한	자원	비자원	비고
1	1	1	법정퇴직금 지급제도가 있음
1 1/2	2	2	기본금 :
2	2	2	제수당 : } 포함됨
2 1/2	3	3	상여금 :
3	3	4	
3 1/2	4	5	법정=누진 (감원서)
4	4	5	
4 1/2	5	6	
5	5 1/2	7 1/2	
5 1/2	6 1/2	9	
6	7 1/2	10	
6 1/2	8 1/2	11 1/2	
7	9 1/2	12 1/2	
7 1/2	10 1/2	14	
8	11 1/2	15	
8 1/2	12 1/2	16 1/2	
9	13 1/2	17 1/2	
9 1/2	14 1/2	19	

-14-

근무년한	자 원	비자원	비 고
10	15 1/2	20	
10 1/2	16 1/2	22	
11	17 1/2	23	
11 1/2	18 1/2	25	법정 = 누진 (자원 11년까지)
12	19 1/2	26	10년부터 ~ 15 년까지
12 1/2	20 1/2	28	매년 3개월부씩 누진됨
13	21 1/2	29	
13 1/2	22 1/2	31	
14	24	32	
14 1/2	25	34	
15	26 1/2	35	
16	29	37	
17	31 1/2	38 1/2	매년 1개월 ~1 개월반씩 누진됨
18	34	41	법정퇴직금율 미달
19	37	42 1/2	예) 기본금 100
20	40	43 1/2	수당및 상여금 60% 가됨
21	42	45	
22	44	46	
23	46	47 1/2	
24	48	48 1/2	
25	50	50	기본 法定퇴직금기준 50 = 30 (法定)

- 15 -

83

1. 퇴직금 제도 3가지구분

1) 법정퇴직금 미달시 기본급, 제수당 상여금포함

예, 6년근무자

식당요원 WB-15호봉
기본 월급여 수령액 52.529원
기본 상여금 수당포함 89.095원

법정년한시 6년 × 89.095 = 534.570

누진율 10년 × 52.595 = 525.920

2) 자원사직 (본인자의) : 기본봉급계산

3) 비자원퇴직 (감원 및 정년퇴직) : 기본봉급계산

2. 퇴직금 누진율 모순점

1) 1-15년사이 매년 누진율 3개월

2) 15-25년사이 매년 누진율 1개월-1개월반

예. 기본 봉급 100%

수당 (상여금포함) 60%

계 160%

3) 종업원 평균년령 48세 근무기간 평균 16년
법정퇴직금 미달 누진율 적용

3. 자원 퇴직과 비자원 퇴직금제도로 인해 78년도에 945명 자원퇴직 막대한 퇴직금 손실 봄.

-16-

114

예. 목공 WB - 6 - 10 호봉

기본봉급 매월 150,683

기본및 상여금 수당 235,626

15년 근속자

자원시 누진율 26 1/2 × 150,683 = 3,993,099

비자원시 누진율 35 × 150,683 = 5,273,905

손실액 1,280,806

1,280,806 × 945 = 1,210,361,670

78년도 자원퇴직으로

945명 12억 1천만원 손실봄 (국가적손실)

4. 자원 퇴직시와 법정퇴직금 기간의 차이많음 (누진율 혜택 적음)

예 현장반장 WB - 11. 5호봉

기본금 (매월) 221,959

기본수당, 상여금포함 346,865

11년근속자

자원 기본급여액 221,959 × 17.5 = 3,884,181

법정 기본 상여금 수당 346,865 × 11년 = 3,815,515

5. 주한미군 단계적철군 78년 12월부터 실시 1개대대 전투병력 철군완료 앞으로 4-5년 완전철수예정

6. 외기노조는 철군으로 인해 발생되는 이직대책안을 77년 7월에 작성 정부관계요로에 제출함 현재 이무런 대책이 없음.

-17-

85

7. 이직대책 일환으로 고율의 누진율인 퇴직금 수령하는데 수개월의 노사교섭끝에 합의함

8. 외기노조는 종업원들이 반평생을 받쳐 모아둔 전재산을 소홀히 다루지 못하게 하기위해 사후관리에도 역점을 두어 장기저축에 최대의 역점을 두었음

9. 금번 퇴직금은 중간 청산이라고 간주되기 때문에 현재까지 퇴직금을 청산하고 앞으로의 퇴직금제도는 근로기준법 위배되지 않는 범위내에서 현재의 고율의 누진율을 활용하여 주기바람

10. 주한미군은 매년 임금인상을 실시하는데 퇴직금 자동인상으로 예산을 확보치 못하여 매우 저조한 인상을 하고 있다

11. 예산문제로 의료보험제도도 실시를 하지 못하고 있음

12. 간접혜택

1) 철군으로 우려되는 실직사태를 대비 자영및 집단사업자금화 할수 있다

2) 미군기관의 시간급제도로 인하여 계속 시간감축등으로 퇴직금액 감축을 막을 수 있다.

3) 매년 근로자의 임금인상으로 늘어가는 퇴직금 누진은 은행이자로 보존될 수 있다

4) 주택이 없거나 빚을지고 있어 고액의 접세또는 이자를 물고 있는 근로자를 도울 수 있다

5) 국가적으로는 7-9% 더이자를 물면서 도입하는 차관을 비교할때 무이자로 외화를 일시에 획득하는 조치이나 정부에서는 크나큰 국가 이익이라 사료됨.

駐韓美軍直屬從業員

退職金引出交涉經緯

全國外國機關勞動組合

駐韓美軍勤勞者退職金支給

1. 對象人員 : 16.400名
   - ○ 歲出豫算勤勞者 : 12.500名
   - ○ 韓國勞務團(KSC) : 3.300名
   - ○ 招請契約勤勞者 : 600名

2. 支給豫想額 : 約 600 億원

3. 支給 經緯

1979년 1월 24일자 한-미 행협 합동위원회가 노사분과 위원회에 분임한 과제와 이과제 이행에 관한 1979 2월 13일 노사분과 위원회 한-미 양 위원장의 합의에 따라 주한미군과 전국외국기관 노동조합은 동문제를 협의하여 1979. 4. 3일 합의 각서에 서명하였음

-1-

7. 이직대책 일환으로 고율의 누진율인 퇴직금 수령하는데 수개월의 노사교섭끝에 합의함

8 외기노조는 종업원들이 반평생을 받쳐 모아둔 전재산을 소홀히 다루지 못하게 하기위해 사후관리에도 역점을 두어 장기저축에 최대의 역점을 두겠음

9 금번 퇴직금은 중간 청산이라고 간주되기 때문에 현재까지 퇴직금을 청산하고 앞으로의 퇴직금제도는 근로기준법 위배되지 않은 범위내에서 현재의 고율의 누진율을 활용하여 주기바람

10 주한미군은 매년 임금인상을 실시하는데 퇴직금 자동인상으로 예산을 확보치 못하여 매우 저조한 인상을 하고 있다

11 예산문제로 의료보험제도도 실시를 하지 못하고 있음

12 간접혜택

1) 철군으로 우려되는 실직사태를 대비 자영및 집단 사업자금화 할수 있다

2) 미군기관의 시간급제도로 인하여 계속 시간감축등으로 퇴직금액 감축을 막을 수 있다

3) 매년 근로자의 임금인상으로 늘어나는 퇴직금 누진은 은행이자로 보존될 수 있다

4) 주택이 없거나 빚을지고 있어 고액의 집세또는 이자를 물고 있는 근로자를 도울 수 있다

5) 국가적으로는 7-9% 더이자를 물면서 도입하는 차관을 비교할때 무이자로 외화를 일시에 획득하는 조치이니 정부에서는 크나큰 국가 이익이라 사료됨.

- 18 -

경 제 기 획 원

투사 316-209 (70-4171) 1979. 5. 8.

수신 외무부장관

제목 주한미군 종업원 퇴직금 지급 합의각서에 대한 의견회시

미안 723-19184 (79. 5. 7)로 조회하신 주한 미군 한국인종업원 퇴직금 지급 합의각서 시행에 관한 당원의 의견을 다음과 같이 통보합니다.

다 음

1. 동 퇴직금 문제는 당사자인 주한미군과 외기노조간에 합의가 된 것이므로 그 시행에는 이견이 없음

2. 다만 동퇴직금의 일시 인출시 통화에 미치는 영향을 고려하여 장기 은행예치를 적극 권장토록 하여야 할것임. 끝.

경 제 기 획 원 장 관

정부공문서 규정 제27조 제2항의 규정에 의하여 기획국장 김재익 전결

에너지는 국력이다 아껴써서 애국하자

90

결재	외무부			지시사항	
	접수번호		제 165[illegible] 호		
주무과	접수일자		[illegible] 5. 8		
	처리근거				
담당자				197 . . . 까지 처리할것	

미주국

재 무 부

금정 1221 - 　　　　70-4705　　　　1979. 5. 12.

수신 외무부 장관

제목 주한 미군 종업원퇴직금 가지급 합의각서 시행에 대한 의견

1. 미안 723 - 19184(79. 5. 7)과 관련입니다.

2. 동 합의각서가 시행될때 퇴직금 일시 지급에 따라 통화증대 가능성에 따른 통화 정책면에서 대책 강구가 요구되나, 동 자금이 근로자의 노임적 성격이라는 점을 감안할 때 합의 각서 내용대로 시행하는 것은 불가피 하다고 사료됩니다.

3. 이에 부수하여 통화 정책면에서 참조하여 저축증대등의 방법을 적극 추진할 것임. 끝.

재 무 부 장 관

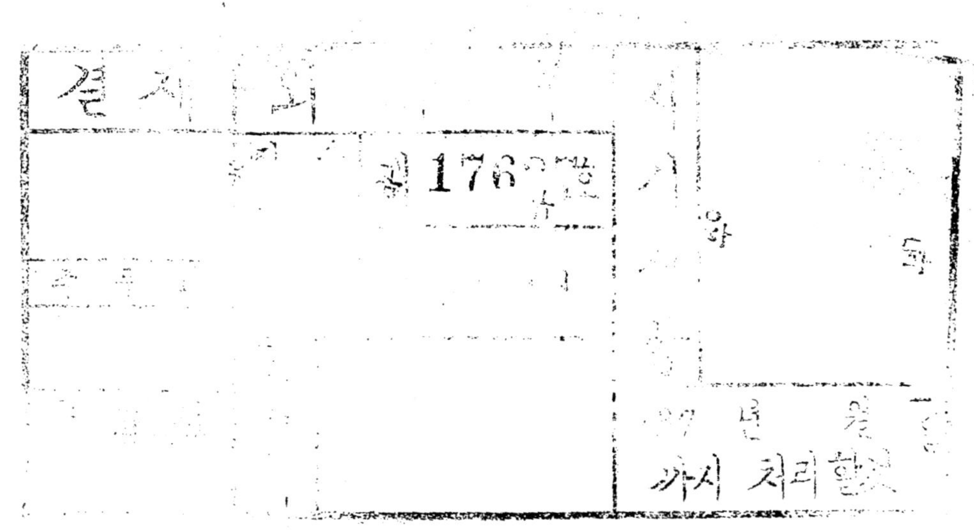

주한 미군 한국인 세출기관 종업원 퇴직금 가지급 합의각서

1979. 5. 23.
안보문제담당관실

1. SOFA 합동위 한.미양국대표 동합의각서에 서명

- 주한 미군 한국종업원 퇴직금 지급문제와 관련, 동 퇴직금 지불시(약600억원) 통화에 미치는 영향등을 그간 관련부처와 협의한 바, 동 합의각서 시행에 이의가 없다는 통보를 받았음.
- 주한 미군측은 동 합의각서 시행에 관해 미국방성의 승인을 받았음.
- 따라서 제131차 SOFA 합동위(79.5.10. 개최)에서 한.미 양국 정부의 승인후, 동 각서에 서명할 것에 동의한바에 따라 SOFA 합동위 한.미양측 대표는 79. 5.중 동 합의각서에 서명할 예정임.

2. 동 합의각서의 내용

- 동 합의각서 적용대상 인원 : 16,400명
  (세출기관 근로자 : 12,500명, 한국노무단 : 3,300명, 초청계약자 한국인 근로자 : 600명)
- 퇴직금 예상액 : 약 600억원 ($ 1.2억)
- 1979. 4. 30. 까지 퇴직금을 산출, 주한 미군은 79. 6. 11. 까지 예금통장을 각 종업원이 수령할 수 있도록 퇴직금의 은행예치를 완료하고, 각 종업원은 예치된 금액을 인출하거나 예치하거나 선택권을 갖음.
- 1979. 4. 30. 이후의 퇴직금은 1년 1개월분의 비율로 매년 각 종업원의 개인구좌에 예치함.
- 현존 퇴직금 규정은 효력이 소멸되고 이 합의각서의 규정으로 대체됨.

앙고재	안보담당관	79년 5월 23일	담당	담당관	심의관	국장	차관보	차관	장관
			유	석	(서명)				

94

- 동 합의각서의 시행은 미국방성 및 한.미합동위의 승인을 조건으로 함.

3. 교섭 경위

78.5.22. 외기노조는 주한 미군당국에 퇴직금제도 개선을 요청함.

78.9.26. SOFA 합동위 미측간사 Kinney 는 한국정부가 미국정부로 부터 퇴직금 전액을 인수할것을 제의

79.1.24. SOFA 합동위는 퇴직금 지불문제를 노무분과위에 과제위촉

79.2.13. 노무분과위 한.미양위원장은 동문제를 주한 미군과 외기노조가 협의할 것에 합의

79. 4. 3. 주한 미군과 외기노조는 동각서에 합의를 봄

79. 5. 4. 노무분과위 한.미양위원장, 동 합의각서에 서명

79. 5.10. 제131차 SOFA 합동위에서 양측대표는 한.미양국 정부의 승인 즉시 동 각서에 서명할 것에 동의함.

4. 관련 부처의 의견

경제기획원 : ○ 동 합의각서 시행에 이견이 없음.
○ 다만 동퇴직금의 일시 인출시 통화에 미치는 영향을 고려, 장기 은행 예치를 적극 권장하도록 해야 할 것임.

재 무 부 : ○ 동 합의각서의 시행은 불가피 함.
○ 이에 부수하여 통화 정책면에서 참조, 저축 증대의 방법을 추진할 것임.

끝.

95

주한 미군 한국인 세출기관 종업원 퇴직금 가지급 합의각서

1979. 5. 23.
안보문제담당관실

1. 고섭 경위

78. 5. 22. 외기노조는 주한 미군당국에 퇴직금제도 개선을 요청함.

78. 9. 26. SOFA 합동위 미측 간사 Kinney, 한국정부가 미국정부로부터 퇴직금 전액을 인수할 것을 제의

79. 1. 24. SOFA 합동위는 퇴직금 지불문제를 노무분과위에 과제 위촉

79. 2. 13. 노무분과위 한.미양위원장은 동 문제를 주한 미군과 외기노조가 협의할 것에 합의

79. 4. 3. 주한 미군과 외기노조는 동 각서에 합의를 봄
79. 5. 4. 노무분과위 한.미양위원장 동 합의각서에 서명
79. 5. 10. 제131차 SOFA 합동위에서 양측 대표는 한.미양국 정부의 승인 즉시 동 각서에 서명할것에 동의 함.

2. 동 합의 각서의 내용

- 동 합의각서 적용대상 인원 : 16,400명
(세출기관 근로자 : 12,500명, 한국노무단 : 3,300명, 초청계약자 한국인 근로자 : 600명)

- 퇴직금 예상액 : 약 600억원 ($1.2억)

- 1979. 4. 30. 까지 퇴직금을 산출, 주한 미군은 79. 6. 11. 까지 예금통장을 각 종업원이 수령할 수 있도록 퇴직금의 은행예치를 완료하고, 각 종업원은 예치된 금액을 인출하거나 예치하거나 선택권을 갖음.

96

- 1979. 4. 30. 이후의 퇴직금은 1년 1개월분의 비율로 매년 각 종업원의 개인구좌에 예치함.
- 현존 퇴직금 규정은 효력이 소멸되고 이 합의각서의 규정으로 대체됨.
- 동 합의각서의 시행은 미국방성 및 한.미합동위의 승인을 조건으로 함.

3. 관련부처의 의견

경제기획원 : ○ 동 합의각서 시행에 이견이 없음.

○ 다만 동 퇴직금의 일시인출시 통화에 미치는 영향을 고려, 장기은행예치를 적극 권장토록 해야할것 임.

(투사 316-209, 79. 5. 8.)

재 무 부 : ○ 동 합의각서의 시행은 불가피 함.

○ 이에 부수하여 통화 정책면에서 참조, 저축증대등의 방법을 추진할 것임.

(금정 1221- 641, 79. 5. 12.)

97

공 란

MEMORANDUM OF UNDERSTANDING

SUBJECT: Advance Severance Payment Procedures for Korean National Appropriated Fund Employees of the US Forces, Korea

1. In accordance with the ROK-US Joint Committee task assigned to the Labor Subcommittee on an exigent basis on 24 January 1979 and the agreement between the US and ROK Component Chairmen of the Labor Subcommittee on 13 February 1979 for carrying out the task, the US Forces, Korea and the Foreign Organizations Employees Union now agree as follows:

a. Payment will be made in advance of actual separation for all severance pay credit accumulated to employees as of 30 April 1979 and will be placed in individual employee bank accounts in a bank selected by the employee from all of those banks which have agreed to participate in the plan. The union may negotiate depositor services directly with those banks if they agree. The union may publicize the services agreed to by the banks to the employees for their consideration in bank selection; however, the individual employees selection remains optional. The USFK will complete the deposits at the earliest possible date so that the bank books are made available for pick up by the employees before 11 June 1979. In those few cases with advance severance pay computation difficulties, the bank book pick up date may be delayed but those delays should not exceed 10 days. Employees will have the option of withdrawing the money from the bank, in full or in part, or leaving the entire amount on deposit. Agreements with the banks on deposit procedures will be formulated in consultation with the union.

b. The advance severance pay for services up to the cut off date, 30 April 1979, will be calculated: (1) At the Schedule II (High Line) rate based on the average of the highest three consecutive months of normal wages received in the 24 months prior to the last day of the pay period ending before 20 March 1979; or (2) at the rate of one month's total wage for each one year of service based upon the average of total wages received for the highest three consecutive months during the 12 months prior to the last day of the pay period ending before 20 March 1979 with bonus payments prorated over the entire 12 months, whichever is greater.

c. Advance severance pay for services of less than one full credit period up to the cut off date, 30 April 1979, will be prorated to the last full month of service. The proration will be: (1) 1/12th of the increment between full-year credits, or 1/6th of the increment between half-year credits, for each full month of service; or (2) 1/12th of one month's total wage for each one full month of service based upon the average of total

99

wages received for the highest three consecutive months during the 12 months prior to the last day of the pay period ending before 20 March 1979 with bonus payments prorated, if the basic advance severance pay computation is based upon 1b(2) above.

d. There will be no change in Service Computation Date (SCD) for leave accrual or Reduction-in-Force retention priority purposes.

e. The rate of severance pay for services after the cut off date, 30 April 1979, will be one month's average of the total wages received during the highest three consecutive months during the 12 months immediately preceding the last day of the pay period ending before 31 March of each successive year with bonus payments prorated over the entire 12 months. This amount will be placed in the employees' bank accounts annually. The deposits will be completed not later than 30 days after the annual cut off date.

f. Upon separation, the service period for which severance pay has not been deposited in the employees' accounts will be prorated to the last full month of service. The proration will be 1/12th of the average one month of total wages received during the period since the last cut off date immediately preceding the separation with bonus payments received during the previous 12 months prorated for each full month of service since the last annual cut off date.

g. In cases of separation due to Reduction-in-Force, one additional month's normal wage will be paid, provided 1 full year of service has been completed.

h. The service credit for severance pay purposes, at the time of separation by other than resignation or separation for cause, will be extended for a period equal to the total number of hours of unused sick leave accumulated by the employee.

i. A deposit of severance pay in an individual's bank as provided herein, and provision, where applicable, of the additional benefits contemplated herein shall fully discharge the entire US Forces, Korea severance pay obligation for the services for which the severance pay deposits have been made, and shall preclude any further claim for severance pay or related additional benefits by an employee or his representative based upon services for which the deposit has been made. Individual employees will execute an affidavit to this effect at the time of bank selection.

0015 100

j. This revised plan will be applicable to all full-time Korean employees of Appropriated Fund activities, invited contractors, and members of the Korean Service Corps.

k. This Memorandum of Understanding, when approved in accordance with paragraph 2, below, shall supersede and replace all existing plans applicable to the employees specified in paragraph j above.

2. Implementation of this Memorandum of Understanding is subject to the prior approval of the US Department of Defense and the ROK-US Joint Committee.

FOR THE US FORCES, KOREA:

George A. Blakeslee

GEORGE A. BLAKESLEE
Civilian Personnel Director
Chairman
Joint Labor Affairs Committee

FOR THE FOREIGN ORGANIZATIONS EMPLOYEES UNION:

HWANG, KYU MU
President

4 May 1979
Date

3

101

합 의 각 서

제목: 주한 미군 한국인 세출 기관 종업원 퇴직금 가 지급

1. 1979년 1월 24일자 한-미 행협 합동 위원회가 노사 분과 위원회에 분임한 과제와 이 과제 이행에 관한 1979년 2월 13일 노사 분과 위원회 한-미 양 위원장의 합의에 따라, 주한 미군과 전국 외국 기관 노동 조합은 동 문제를 협의, 이제 다음과 같이 합의한다.

a. 1979년 4월 30일로 정하는 기산일 까지 축적된 각 종업원의 퇴직금은 가 지급 국내 모든 은행중 예금 접수에 동의하는 은행중에서 각 종업원이 선정한 은행 개인 구좌에 예치한다. 노동 조합은 예금 접수에 동의하는 은행과 써비스 관리 규정을 별도 교섭 약정하여 이를 각 종업원에게 주지 시켜 각자의 은행 선정에 참고가 되도록 할 수 있으나 은행 선정은 어디 까지나 각자 종업원의 의사에 맡긴다. 주한 미군은 1979년 6 월11일 까지 예금 통장을 각 종업원이 수령 할 수 있도록 가능한 한 빠른 시일내에 은행 예치를 완료한다. 퇴직금 가 지급액 산정상의 문제가 있는 소수의 경우 통장 수령 기한일을 10일간 연장 할 수 있다. 각 종업원은 예치된 금액을 전액 또는 일부를 인출하거나, 또는 예치를 계속하는 선택권을 갖는다. 은행과의 예치 절차는 외기 노조와 협의 작성한다.

b. 1979년 4월 30일 기산일 까지의 퇴직금 가 지급액 산출은 다음과 같이 한다. (1) 1979년 3월 20일 이전에 끝난 봉급 기간 최종일 이전 24개월 기간중 종업원이 받은 최고 계속 3개월 동안의 평상 임금 월 평균액을 산출 기초로하여 제 II 율표 (고율) 에의한 액수, 또는 (2) 1979년 3월 20일 이전에 끝난 봉급 기간 최종일 이전 12개월 기간중 종업원이 받은 최고 계속 3개월의 총 임금 월 평균액 (보나스는 년 총액을 월 균할) 을 산출 기초로한 1년 근무에 1개월분의 비율에 의한 액수중 높은액으로 한다.

c. 1979년 4월 30일 기산일을 기하여 퇴직금 가 지급액 수령 만기에 미달되는 근무 기간은 월할 지급한다. 월할은 다음과 같이한다. (1) 매 만 1개월의 근무 기간마다 년 누진액의 12분의 1, 또는 6개월 누진의 경우 그 누진액의 6분의 1, 에 해당되는 금액, 또는 (2) 위 제 1b(2) 항 규정에

102

따라 퇴직금 가 지급액이 산출 되었을때 매 만 1개월의 근무 기간마다 1979년 3월 20일 이전에 끝난 봉급기간 최종일 이전 12개월 동안에 종업원이 받은 최고 계속 3개월의 총 임금 (보나스는 년 총액을 월 균활) 월 평균액의 12분의 1에 해당하는 금액으로 월활한다.

d. 휴가 취득 및 감원 우선 순위에대한 근무 기간 기산 일자 (SCD) 는 현재와 동일하게 변동없이 계속한다.

e. 1979년 4월 30일 이후의 퇴직금율은 1년 근무에 대하여 1개월분의 급여율로하되 그 산출 기초는 매해 3월 31일 이전에 끝난 봉급 기간 최종일을 기하여 이날 직전 12개월 동안에 종업원이 받은 최고 계속 3개월의 총 임금 (보나스 는 년 총액을 월 균활) 월 평균액으로 한다. 앞으로 이 금액은 매년 각 종업원의 은행 구좌에 예치하며 산출 기산일인 4월 30일을 기하여 늦어도 30일 이내에 은행에 예치 완료한다.

f. 해직 당시 만 1년이 미달되어 은행에 미 예치된 부분에 대하여는 월활 지급한다. 월활은 매 만 1개월의 근무 기간으로하며 그 산출 기초는 마지막 은행 예치 기산일과 해직일 사이 기간에 받은 총 급여의 (보나스는 년 총액을 월 균활) 월 평균의 12분의 1에 해당되는 금액으로 한다.

g. 감원이 되었을때는 1개월분의 평상 임금을 추가 지급한다. 단 총 근무 기간이 1년이 미달되는 자는 제외 한다.

h. 자진 사직 및 귀책 사유로 인한 해직을 제외한 퇴직 경우, 퇴직 당시 까지 종업원이 축적하여둔 병가에 대하여는 그 시간에 해당되는 기간 만큼 근무 기간으로 간주 연장하여 퇴직금 산출 근무 기간으로 한다.

j. 본 합의 각서에 정한 퇴직금은 각자의 은행에 예치와 본 합의 각서에 정한 해당 추가 혜택을 지급 완료 함으로서 주한 미군은 은행 예치 완료된 해당 기간의 근무에 대한 퇴직금 지급 의무를 전부 그리고 완전히 이행 완료 하며 종업원 또는 그의 대리인으로부터 은행 예치 완료된 해당 기간의 근무에대한 퇴직금및 해당 혜택에대한 추가 청구의 대상이 되지 않는다. 각 종업원은 이를 확인하는 서약서를 은행 선정 통고시 작성 제출한다.

103

j. 이 합의 각서에 명기된 퇴직금 제도는 전 세출 기관, 초청 청부 업체 한국인 종업원과 한국 근로단 단원에게 적용한다.

k. 본 합의 각서가 아래 제 2항의 규정에 의하여 승인됨과 동시 위 j 항에 명시된 신분의 종업원에게 적용되는 모든 현존 퇴직금 규정은 효력이 소멸되며 이 합의 각서의 규정으로 대체된다.

2. 본 합의 각서의 시행은 미 국방성 및 한 미 행협 합동 위원회의 승인을 조건으로 한다.

주한 미군을 위하여:

George H Blakeslee

죠지 에이. 브랙스리
인사 처장
주한 미군 합동 노무 위원회
의장

전국 외국 기관 노동 조합을 위하여:

[signature]

황 규 무
위 원 장

1979. 5. 4
일 자

AP 15-24 (2)

104

합 의 각 서

제목: 주한 미군 한국인 세출 기관 종업원 퇴직금 1979.5.1

1. 1979년 1월 24일자 한·미 행정 합동 위원회가 노사 분과 위원회에 부여한 과제와 이 과제 이행에 관한 1979년 2월 13일 노사 분과 위원회 한·미 양 위원장의 합의에 따라, 주한 미군과 전국 외국 기관 노동 조합은 동 문제를 협의, 이제 다음과 같이 합의한다.

a. 1979년 4월 30일로 정하는 기산일 까지의 각 종업원의 퇴직금은 국내 모든 은행중 예금 접수에 동의하는 은행중에서 각 종업원이 선정한 은행 개인 구좌에 예치한다. 노동 조합은 예금 접수에 동의하는 은행과 서비스 관계규정을 별도 교섭 약정하여 이를 각 종업원에게 주지 시켜 각자의 은행 선정에 참고가 되도록 할 수 있으나 은행 선정은 어디 까지나 각자 종업원의 의사에 달린다. 주한 미군은 1979년 5월 31일 까지 예금 통장을 각 종업원이 수령 할 수 있도록 가능한 한 빠른 시일 내에 은행 예치를 완료 한다. 퇴직금 산정상의 문제가 있는 소수의 경우 통장 수령 기한일은 10일간 연장 할 수 있다. 각 종업원은 예치된 금액을 전액 또는 일부를 인출하거나, 또는 예치를 계속하는 선택권을 갖는다. 은행측의 예치 절차는 미군 노조와 협의 실행한다.

b. 1979년 4월 30일 기산일 까지의 퇴직금 산출은 다음과 같이 한다. (1) 1979년 3월 20일 이전에 끝난 봉급 기간 최종인 이전 24개월 기간중 종업원이 받은 최고 계속 3개월 동안의 평상 임금 월 평균액을 산출 기초로 하여 제표준표 (고용)에 의한 액수, 또는 (2) 1979년 3월 20일 이전에 끝난 봉급 기간 최종일 이전 12개월 기간중 종업원이 받은 최고 계속 3개월의 총 임금 월 평균액 (보나스는 년 총액을 월 균할)을 산출 기초로한 1년 근무에 1개월분의 비율에 의한 액수중 높은액으로 한다.

c. 1979년 4월 30일 기산일을 기하여 퇴직금 수령 만기에 미달되는 근무 기간은 월할 지급한다. 월할은 다음과 같이한다. (1) 매 만 1개월의 근무기간마다 년 누진액의 12분의 1, 또는 6개월 누진의 경우 그 누진액의 6분의 1. 에 해당되는 금액, 또는 (2) 위 제1b(2)항 규정에 따라 퇴직금에

MP15-25

105 ~~103~~

산출 되었을때는 매 만 1개월의 근무 기간마다 1979년 3월 20일 이전에 끝난 봉급기간 최종일 이전 12개월 동안에 종업원이 받은 최고 계속 3개월의 총 임금 (보나스는 년 총액을 월 균할) 월 평균액의 12분의 1에 해당하는 금액으로 월할한다.

d. 휴가 취득 및 감원 우선 순위에대한 근무 기간 기산 일자 (SCD)는 현재와 동일하게 변동없이 계속한다.

e. 1979년 4월 30일 이후의 퇴직금율은 1년 근무에 대하여 1개월분의 급여율로하되 그 산출 기초는 매해 3월 31일 이전에 끝난 봉급 기간 최종일을 기하여 이날 직전 12개월 동안에 종업원이 받은 최고 3개월의 총 임금 (보나스는 년 총액을 월 균할) 월 평균액으로 한다. 앞으로 이 금액은 매년 각 종업원의 은행 구좌에 예치하며 산출 기산일인 4월 30일을 기하여 늦어도 30일 이내에 은행에 예치 완료한다.

f. 해직 당시 만 1년이 미달되어 은행에 미 예치된 부분에 대하여는 월할 지급한다. 월할은 매 만 1개월의 근무 기간으로마다 그 산출 기초는 마지막 은행 예치 기산일과 해직일 사이 기간에받은 총 급여의 (보나스는 년 총액을 월 균할) 월 평균의 12분의 1에 해당되는 금액으로 한다.

g. 감원이 되었을때는 1개월분의 평상 임금을 추가 지급한다. 단 총 근무 기간이 1년이 미달되는자는 제외 한다.

h. 자진 사직 및 귀책 사유로 인한 해직을 제외한 퇴직 경우, 퇴직 당시 까지 종업원이 축적하여둔 병가에 대하여는 그 시간에 해당되는 기간만큼 근무 기간으로 간주 연장하여 퇴직금 산출 근무 기간으로 한다.

i. 본 합의 각서에 정한 퇴직금은 각자의 은행에 예치와 본 합의 각서에 정한 해당 추가 혜택을 지급 완료 함으로서 주한 미군은 은행 예치 완료된 해당 기간의 근무에 대한 퇴직금 지급 의무를 전부 그리고 완전히 이행 완료하며 종업원 또는 그의 대리인으로부터 은행 예치 완료된 해당 기간의 근무에대한 퇴직금및 해당 혜택에 대한 추가 청구의 대상이되지 않는다. 각 종업원은 이를 확인하는 서약서를 은행 신청 반드시 작성제출 한다.

j. 이 합의 각서에 명기된 퇴직금 제도는 전 세출 기관, 초청 계약자의 한국인 종업원과 한국 근로단 단원에게 적용한다.

K. 본 합의 각서가 아래 제 2항의 규정에 의하여 승인됨과 동시 위 J 항에 명시된 신분의 종업원에게 적용되는 모든 현존 복리금 규정은 효력이 소멸되며 이 합의 각서의 규정으로 대체된다.

2. 본 합의 각서의 시행은 미 국방성 및 한 미 행정 합동 위원회의 승인을 조건으로 한다.

주한 미군을 위하여:	전국 외국 기관 노동 조합을 위하여:
조지 에이. 브릭스미	황 규 무
인사 처장	위원장
주한 미군 합동 노무 위원회	
의장	

1979. 4. 3
일자

LABOR STANDARD ACT

Law No. 286, Promulgated on 15 May, 1953
Amended by Law No. 791, December 4, 1961
Amended by Law No. 2708, December 24, 1974

CHAPTER I. General Provisions

ARTICLE 1. (Purpose) The purpose of this Act is to stipulate the standard of labor conditions in conformity with the Constitution, whereby the minimum level of laborer's living may be secured and advanced, and the balanced development of national economy may be achieved.

ARTICLE 2. (Standard of Labor Conditions) The labor conditions as stipulated in this Act shall be of the lowest level, and no person, a party to a labor contract, shall be authorized to drop down a labor condition to a lower degree for the reason of above-mentioned standard.

ARTICLE 3. (Determination of Labor Conditions) Labor conditions shall be determined by free will of the employer and employee on equal footing.

ARTICLE 4. (Observance of Labor Conditions) Both employee and employer shall comply with collective bargaining agreements, labor service regulations and terms of labor contracts and shall keep faith and credit in its practice.

ARTICLE 5. (Equal Treatment) No employer shall discriminate against employees by distinction of sex, nor may he include any discrimination in the terms of labor conditions because of nationality, religion, or social status.

ARTICLE 6. (Ban on Forced Labor) No employer shall demand such a labor service as may conflict with free will of the employee concerned by violence, intimidation, wrongful confinement or any other mental or physical coercion.

ARTICLE 7. (Ban on Violence) No employer shall inflict an assault or a battery upon an employee in an accident or for any other reason.

ARTICLE 8. (Elimination of Intermediary Exploitation) No person shall be justified except by law, to intervence with the employment of another person for profit-making purpose, nor act as a middleman or broker for profit making purpose.

ARTICLE 9. (Guarantee for Exercise of Civil Rights) No employer may be allowed to reject the reguest of an employee for his hours of lease in the course of duty hours necessary for exercise of his franchise, other civil rights or civil duties. Provided, however, that an employer may change the requested hour, unless such change impedes the exercise of the said rights or performance of the said civil duties.

ARTICLE 10. (Scope of Application) This Act shall apply to all enterprises, or workshops, except for an enterprise or workshop where only the relatives living in the same household are employed, or domestic servants, or such an enterprise of workship as may be provided by a Presidential decree.

ARTICLE 11. (Ditto) This Act, and Presidential decree pursuant thereto, shall equally apply to the government, Seoul Special City, Busan City, province, city, county, town, township or other equivalent thereto.

ARTICLE 12. (Duty of Reporting) An Employer or employee shall, if requested by the Labor Committee under the Director General of the Office of Labor or the Labor Inspector, without delay file a report on the matters necessary for the

enforcement of th
ARTICLE 13. (
formed of the gis
gulations, which s
(2) The employe
and dormitory re
shall keep employ
ARTICLE 14. (
means a person er
or workshop (her
ARTICLE 15. (
means the owner
the owner so far
ARTICLE 16. (
involve mental la
ARTICLE 17. (
this Act means a
and the employer
ARTICLE 18.
all the money an
labor service.
ARTICLE 19.
in this Act mean
three months pri
number of total
even when less t
service.
(2) If the amou
the ordinary wag
be the average v

ARTICLE 20.
been made with
only such unsatis
(2) Such potion
paragraph shall
ARTICLE 21.
year, except wh
completion of a
ARTICLE 22.
show the employ
conclusion of lat
ARTICLE 23.
expressly shown
shall be entitled
or may effect i

enforcement of this Act, or shall present himself at a place as designated.

ARTICLE 13. (Posting of Regulations) (1) The employer shall keep employees informed of the gist of this Act or Presidential decree pursuant thereto, or of labor regulations, which shall be posted up or placed at the workshop at any time.

(2) The employer shall post up or keep the provisions relative to dormitory house and dormitory regulations at the dormitory house in the decree of paragraph 1 and shall keep employees informed thereof.

ARTICLE 14. (Definition of Employee) The term "employee" as used in this Act means a person engaged in whatever occupation offering labor service at an enterprise or workshop (hereafter referred to as "enterprise") for the purpose of earning a wage.

ARTICLE 15. (Definition of Employer) The "employer" referred to in this Act means the owner or manager of an enterprise, or other person who acts on behalf of the owner so far as matters relative to employees are concerned.

ARTICLE 16. (Definition of Labor) The term "labor" as used in this Act shall involve mental labor and physical labor.

ARTICLE 17. (Definition of Labor Contract) The term "labor contract" as used in this Act means an agreement with the aim that employees shall offer a labor service and the employer shall pay its corresponding wages.

ARTICLE 18. (Definition of Wage) The term "wage" as used in this Act means all the money and goods, paid to the employee by the employer in consideration for labor service.

ARTICLE 19. (Definition of Average Wage) (1) The term, "average wage" as used in this Act means the total amount of wage paid to employee during the period of three months prior to occurrence of its reason for computation of wage divided by the number of total days during the said period, this rule, shall apply *mutatis mutandis*, even when less than three months have passed after commencement of a said labor service.

(2) If the amount computed pursuant to the provisions of paragraph 1 is lower than the ordinary wage of the worker concerned, the amount of the ordinary wage shall be the average wage.

CHAPTER II. Labor Contracts

ARTICLE 20. (Labor Contracts Violating this Act) (1) When a labor contract has been made with such a labor condition as may not satisfy requirements under this Act, only such unsatisfactory portion of the said contract shall be null and void.

(2) Such potion as invalidated in accordance with the provision of the preceding paragraph shall be governed by the standard specified by this Act.

ARTICLE 21. (Duration) The duration of a labor contract shall not exceed one year, except when there is no term specified or when a certain term is specified for completion of a certain labor service.

ARTICLE 22. (Clear Statement of Labor Conditions) The employer shall clearly show the employee the wage, working hours and other labor conditions at the time of conclusion of labor contract.

ARTICLE 23. (Violation of Labor Condition) (1) If any of the labor conditions expressly shown under Article 22 be inconsistent with the reality the said employee shall be entitled to claim for damages resulting from breach of agreed labor condition, or may effect immedidiate dissolution of the said contract.

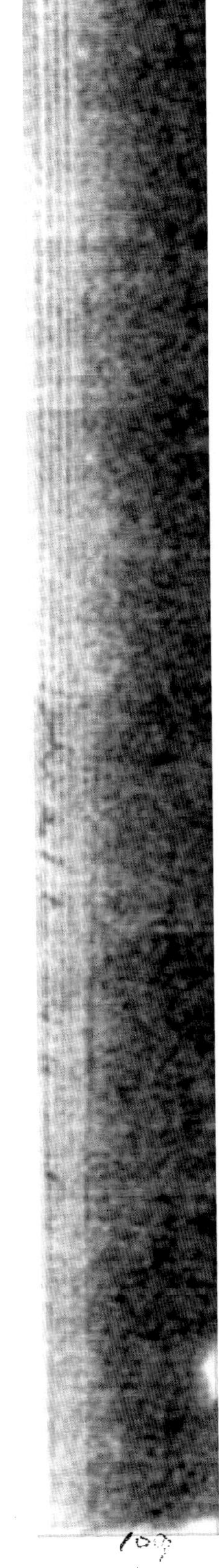

(2) If the employee is to demand compensation for damages in accordance with paragraph 1, he may do so through the Labor Committee, and if the labor contract has been dissolved, the employer concerned shall pay the employee concerned travel expenses to go back home, if he has to change his place of living for the purpose of securing employment.

ARTICLE 24. (Ban on Establishing Penalty for Non-Performance) No employer shall make any contract establishing rules providing for a penalty or amount of damages for non-performance of a said contract.

ARTICLE 25. (Ban on Set-off) No employer shall set off an advance or other claim secured by offering labor service against the prospective wages.

ARTICLE 26. (Ban on Involuntary Saving) (1) No employer shall make a contract providing for any involuntary saving deposit or custody of deposited money incidental to a principal labor contract.

(2) When an employer needs to hold custody of the money deposited by his employee, the said employer shall be bound to obtain an approval from the Director General of the Office of Labor by showing the means of its custody and of repayment.

ARTICLE 27. (Restriction of Dismissal, etc.) (1) No employer shall put any employee to dismissal, temporary retirement, suspension, transfer, reduction of wage, or other punitive damages without justifiable reason.

(2) No employer shall be authorized to dismissal any employee during the course of temporary retirement due to recuperation from an occupational injury or disease and the immediately following thirty days; nor any female employee before and after childbirth be dismissal during the period of a temporary retirement as stipulated in this Act and of the immediately following thirty days; however, an exception shall be allowed, when employer has paid the lump sum compensation under Article 84 or when a disaster or calamity or any other unavoidable reason may prevent continuance of the same enterprise.

(3) In the case of the latter part of the proviso of paragraph 2 the said employer shall obtain verification from the Director General of the Office of Labor in that connection.

ARTICLE 27-II (Prior Notice of Dismissal) (1) If an employer desires to dismiss an employee he shall give the employee such warning at least 30 days in advance. If a warning was not given 30 days in advance, the ordinary wage for not less than 30 days shall be paid to the employee dismissed. Provided, however, that this shall not apply in case it is impossible to continue business on account of natural calamity, incident or any other unavoidable circumstance and the Minister of Health and Social Affairs recognized the situation, or if the employee is dismissed because of his own responsibility.

(2) Concerning the proviso of paragraph 1, the determination that an employee was dismissed because of his own responsibility shall be subject to the approval of the Labor Committee.

ARTICLE 28. (Retirement Allowance Plan) An employer shall establish a plan by which not less than 30 days average wage per year for each consecutive year employed shall be paid as retirement allowance to the retired employee. Provided, however, that this shall not apply in cases where the number of years employed is less than 1 year.

ARTICLE 29. (Exception to Application of Prior Notice of Dismissal) The provisions of Article 27-II shall not apply to any of the following labor employees:

1. Daily employe
2. Employees wh
3. Monthly paid
4. Employee whc
work.
5. Employees wh
ARTICLE 30. (L
following death or
up his wages, co
there-from, provide
extended by agreer
ARTICLE 30-2.
wance, accident co
entitled to be paid
for public purpose,
ARTICLE 31. (C
after termination
describing the tern
matters by stating
(2) A certificate
what has been rec
(3) No employer
intent to obstruct
ARTICLE 32. (l
ployees for each
any other items a
(2) Whener alter
the corresponding
ARTICLE 33. (l
employees and esse

ARTICLE 34. (
if necessary, fix t
or occupation.
(2) If the Direct
under paragraph
ARTICLE 35. (
has been fixed, th
said amount, exce
1. When an au
obtained in or
due to mental
2. When a labo
account of an
3. When an au
obtained in or

1. Daily employed employee who has failed to work for three consecutive months.
2. Employees who are employed for a period not exceeding two months.
3. Monthly paid employee who has not yet worked for six months.
4. Employee who is employed for a period not exceeding six months in a seasonable work.
5. Employees who have been under probational employment.

ARTICLE 30. (Liquidation) Upon request of the rightful person for liquidation following death or retirement of an employee, the employer shall be bound to deliver up his wages, compensation or all other money and goods not later than 14 days there-from, provided, however, that under a specific circumstance the period may be extended by agreement of both parities.

ARTICLE 30-2. (Priority of Claim for Payment of Wage) Wage, retirement allowance, accident compensation and other claims arising from labor relations shall be entitled to be paid prior to other claims except pledge, mortgage, tax and payments for public purpose, from the total amount of employers property.

ARTICLE 31. (Certificate) (1) Whenever an employee requests of his employer after termination of conract, the said employer shall immediately issue a certificate describing the term of employment, classification of work, title and wage or any other matters by stating true facts.

(2) A certificate as mentioned in paragraph 1 shall contain nothing other than what has been required by the said employee.

(3) No employer shall use any secret sign nor conduct a fraudulent act, with an intent to obstruct employment of the said employee wilfully.

ARTICLE 32. (List of Employees) (1) An employer shall draw up a list of employees for each workshop, containing name, birth date, personal background and any other items as specified by a Presidential decree.

(2) Whener alteration takes place in the items to be entered under paragaph 1, the corresponding correction shall follow without delay.

ARTICLE 33. (Preservance of Documents) The employer shall preserve the list of employees and essential documents concerning the labor contract for three years.

CHAPTER III. Wage

ARTICLE 34. (Minimum Wage) (1) The Direct General of the Office of Labor may, if necessary, fix the minimum wage for employees engaged in a particular enterprise or occupation.

(2) If the Director General of the Office of Labor desires to fix the minimum wage under paragraph 1, the concurrence of Labor Committee shall be required.

ARTICLE 35. (Exception to Application of Minimum Wage) If the minimum wgae has been fixed, the employer shall not employ employees for a wage falling short of said amount, except in one of the following cases:

1. When an authorization of the Director General of the Office of Labor has been obtained in order to employ an employee whose labor effciency was diminished due to mental or physical handicap.
2. When a labor service has failed to continue during the required working hours on account of an individual impediment of employee.
3. When an authorization of the Director General of the Office of Labor has been obtained in order to employ an employee who is on probational employment, or whose

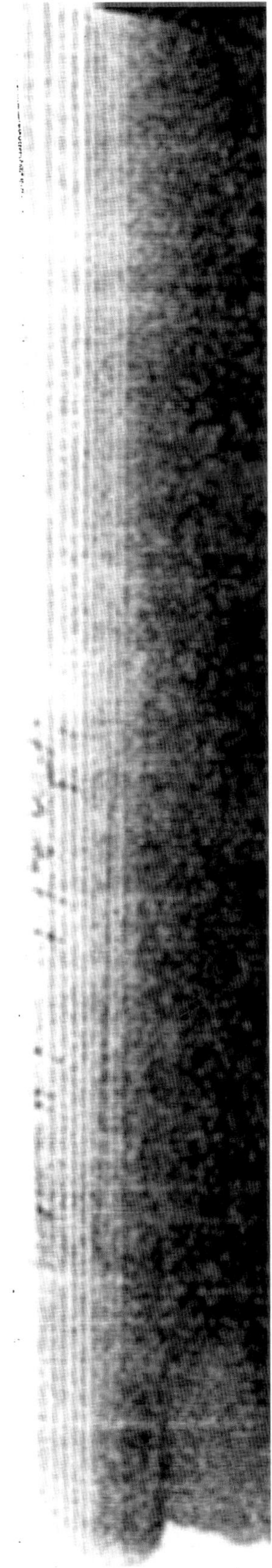

111

labor service is required to be performed for particularly short working hours.

ARTICLE 36. (Payment of Wage). (1) Payment of wage shall be made in its full amount to employee immediately in legal tender; Provided, however, that the wage may partially be deducted or payment other than by means of cash be made, if otherwise stipulated by legal provisions or collective bargaining agreement.

(2) The wage shall be paid once or more per month at a prescribed date; an exception shall, however, be found for the case of extraordinary wage, allowance or any other payment or such other wage as may be specified by a Presidential decree.

ARTICLE 37. (Emergency Payment) Employer shall be bound to advance a partial payment in proportion to the labor service so far offered even prior to its payment date, whenever any employee may request it, in order to apply for an extraordinary expense necessitated by childbirth, disease, disaster or any other case of emergency as may specified by a presideutial decree.

ARTICLE 38. (Payment during Interruption of Labor Service) When a temporary interruption of labor service has been caused by such a reason as may be ascribable to the employer, the said employee shall be entitled to an allowance not less than 60% of his or her average wage during the period of labor interruption; Provided, however, that this shall not apply in cases where continuance of business is impossible due to unavoidable circumstances and the Labor Committee has recognized such situation.

ARTICLE 39. (Contract Work) The Employer shall be bound to secure payment of a reasonable wage in proportion to working hours, in case of contract work or any other similar one.

ARTICLE 40. (Wage Ledger) Employers shall draw up a wage ledger for each workshop and enter the items for basis of account, amount of wage and others as specified by a Presidential decree at the time of each payment.

ARTICLE 41. (Precription) Claim for payment of wage under the provisions of this Act shall be extinguished by prescription, if not exercised for three years.

CHAPTER IV. Working Hours and Recess

ARTICLE 42. (Working Hours) (1) The standard of working hours shall be eight hours per day and forty eight hours per week excluding recess hours; provided, however that the limit of working hours may be extended to sixty hours a week as maximum by a mutual agreement.

(2) In case of a particular circumstance, the time limit under paragraph 1, may be extended by an authoriztion of the Director General of the of Labor. If there is not enough time to proceed for an authorization due to an imminent situation, however, an *ex post facto* approval shall be obtained without delay.

(3) Whenever it is regarded as inadequate to extend working hours under paragraph 2, the Director General of the Office of Labor shall have authority to instruct allowance of reasonable length of recess or day off in proportion to the above-mentioned extended working hours.

ARTICLE 43. (Harmful or Dangerous Work) Underground work or other harmful or dangerous work prescribed by a Presidential decree shall be subject to standard limit of six daily working hours and thirty-six weekly working hours. However, with an approval of the Director General of the Office of Labor it may be extended 2 hours per day and 12 hours per week.

ARTICLE 44. (Recess) (1) Employers shall allow a recess of not shorter than thirty

minutes for every 1
hours during the c
(2) The recess ho
ARTICLE 45. (D
off per week on th
ARTICLE 46. (O
dinary hourly wage
ertime work pursua
(work between 22:
ARTICLE 47. (M
pay for each mont
(2) The paid leave
at his discretion ei
ARTICLE 47-2. (
or managing a busi
for the purpose of
of Health and Socia
within the limits o
42, or to more tha
pursuant to the prc
the provisions of A
1. Transportation
business;
2. Motion picture
and research, a
3. Medical and sa
and beauty parl
4. Any other bus
be necessary.
ARTICLE 48. (A
with pay for one y
90% of a year's att
(2) An employer sl
in the foregoing par
have worked more
number of days of
wage or grant the p
(3) The employer
when the employee
other rules or the a
the period may be a
carrying out the en
(4) The period of
injury or disease, o
under Article 60, s
interruption in the
ARTICLE 49. (E

minutes for every four working hours and not shorter than one hour for every eight hours during the course of labor work.

(2) The recess hours may be used at the option of employee.

ARTICLE 45. (Day Off) Employers shall be bound to allow one or more paid day off per week on the average for his employees.

ARTICLE 46. (Overtime, Night and Holiday Work) An employer shall pay the ordinary hourly wage plus 50% or more thereof for each hour of over time work (overtime work pursuant to the provisions of Articles 42 and 43) and night-time work (work between 22:00 hours and 06:00 hours) or holiday work.

ARTICLE 47. (Monther Paid Leave) (1) The employer shall allow one day off with pay for each month.

(2) The paid leave pursuant to the provisions of paragraph 1 may be used by a worker at his discretion either by accumulating or dividing his leave within one year.

ARTICLE 47-2. (Exception to Work Hour and Rest Hours) Any employer, owning or managing a business falling under one of the following sub-sections. if necessary for the purpose of national defense, may, after obtaining the approval of the Minister of Health and Social Affairs extend the work day to more than 8 hours per day within the limits of the 48 hours work week, pursuant to the provision of Article 42, or to more than 6 hours per day with the limit of the 36 hours work week pursuant to the provisions of Article 43, and may alter the rest hour pursuant to the provisions of Article 44:

1. Transportation business, sale and storage business, financial and insurance business;
2. Motion picture production and show business, press agency, educational study and research, and advertising business;
3. Medical and sanitary practice, entertainment, incineration and scavengery, barber and beauty parlor;
4. Any other business considered by the Minister of Health and Social Affairs to be necessary.

ARTICLE 48. (Annual Paid Leave) (1) The employer shall allow eight holidays with pay for one year attendance without absence and three holidays with pay for 90% of a year's attendance without absence.

(2) An employer shall award one day's paid leave, in addition to the leave mentioned in the foregoing paragraph, for each consecutive year employed to these workers who have worked more than two consecutive years. Provided, however, that if the total number of days of leave exceeds 20 days, the employer may either pay the ordinary wage or grant the paid leave for each day in excess of 20 days.

(3) The employer shall allow holiday with pay under paragraph 1 and 2 at the time when the employee requests, and ordinary wage under rules of employment or any other rules or the average wage shall be given during the paid period provided that the period may be altered, if there may arise therefrom a great impendiment to carrying out the enterprise.

(4) The period of temporary interruption of work resulting from an occupational injury or disease, or the period before and after childbirth for a female employee under Article 60, shall be regarded as equivalent to performance of work without interruption in the case of application of paragraph 1.

ARTICLE 49. (Exception to Application) Provisions related to working hours,

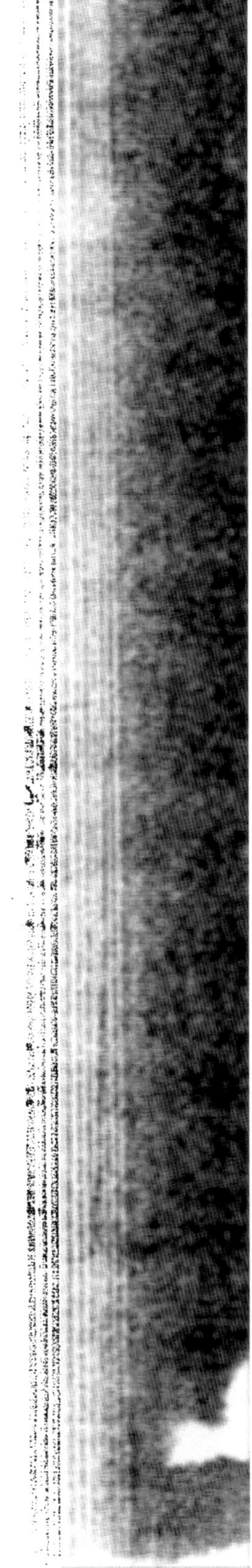

reccss and off-day or holidays as set forth in this chapter and in chapter 5 shall not be applicable to any of the following employees:

1. Cultivation of arable land, reclamation works, seeding and planting of plant, picking work or any other agricultural and forestry work.
2. Live-stock breeding, collection of marine animals and plants, regeneration of marine products, cattle-breeding, sericulture, and fishery business.
3. Employees engaged in supervisory work or intermittently assigned work the employer there of have obtained the approval of the Director General of the Office of Labor.
4. Employee engaged in such work as may be prescribed by a Presidential decree.

CHAPTER V. Female and Child

ARTICLE 50. (Minimum Age) (1) No child under thirteen full years shall be employed in any work, except for those who have obtained an emplyment authorization certificate from the Director General of the Office of Labor.

(2) An employment authorization certificate under paragraph 1 shall be issued at the request of a desiring person, by designating each classified occupation, inasmuch as there may be no impediment to the compulsory education.

ARTICLE 51. (Ban on Employment) No female nor child under eighteen full years shall be authorize to engage in any work detrimental to morality or harmful to maintenance of health. The prohibited kinds of work shall be decided by a Presidential decree.

ARTICLE 52. (Certifying Documents) As regards child employee under eighteen years, the employer shall keep at each workshop a copy of census register testifying its age and a written approval of its parent or guardian.

ARTICLE 53. (Labor Contract) (1) No parent nor guardian shall have authority to make a labor contract on behalf of a minor employee.

(2) When it may be deemed as disadvantageous to a minor employee, the parent, guardian or the Director General of the Office of Labor may terminate said labor contract.

ARTICLE 54. (Claim for Wage) A minor employee may claim his wages in his own right.

ARTICLE 55. (Working Hours) The working hours of a child between thirteen years and eighteen full years shall be limited to seven hours per day and forty two hours per week, provided, however, that the daily working hours may be extended within the limit of two hours by authorization of the Director General of the Office of Labor.

ARTICLE 56. (Ban on Night Work) No female, nor child under eighteen full years shall be authorized to work between 22:00 hours and 06:00 hours or on any off-day, unless otherwise authorized by the Director General of the Officeof Labor.

ARTICLE 57. (Overtime Work) Employers shall be forbidden to place any female not younger than eighteen full years to overtime work for a period exceeding two hours per day, six hours per week, and one hundred and fifty hours per year.

ARTICLE 58. (Work Inside Pit) Employers shall be forbidden to place a female or child under eighteen full years to any work inside a pit.

ARTICLE 59. (Menstruation Leave) Employers shall allow one monthly day off with pay for menstruation upon request from a female employee.

ARTICLE 60. (
ployee, who are p
before and after c
granted for not le
(2) Female emplc
work, whenever d
ARTICLE 61. (
baby shall be all
minutes each.
ARTICLE 62. (
necessary for hom
desires to return
ation; except whe
circumstance and
this connection.
ARTICLE 63. (
who are under eig
however, that edu
with the approva
(2) Provisions n
be prescribed by

ARTICLE 64.
for prevention of
in connection wit
(2) Employee sh
(3) The standar
wed by employee
ARTICLE 65.
work shall not b
uate standard an
(2) Classificatior
stall ations to be
decree.
ARTICLE 66.
in particularly d
unless the Direct
(2) Classificatio
by a Presidential
(3) If machines
of the Director (
Presidential decr
efficiency inspect
ARTICLE 67.
prejudicial to pul
for the purpose (

114

ARTICLE 60. (Recuperation Holiday) (1) Employers shall allow for a female employee, who are pregnant, a recuperation holiday with pay for a period of sixty days before and after childbirth; provided, however, that paid, protective leave shall be granted for not less than 30 days after birth.

(2) Female employee who are pregnant, shall be transferred to more comfortable work, whenever desired and shall never be assigned to overtime work.

ARTICLE 61. (Nursing Period) A female employee with a less than one year old baby shall be allowed twice daily a nursing period for not shorter than thirty minutes each.

ARTICLE 62. (Travel Expenses) Employers shall be liable to bear the expenses necessary for homeward travelling, when a female or minor under eighteen years desires to return within fourteen days from the declared date of contractual termination; except when the reason of discharge should be ascribed to the employee's circumstance and the employer has obtained confirmation of the Labor Committee in this connection.

ARTICLE 63. (Educational Facilities) (1) An employer using more than 30 persons who are under eighteen 18 years shall set up educational facilities for them, provided, however, that educational facilities maybe dispensed with by awarding scholarships, with the approval of the Minister of Health and Social Affairs.

(2) Provisions necessary to the educational facilities provided in paragraph 1 shall be prescribed by a Presidential decree.

CHAPTER VI. Safety and Health

ARTICLE 64. (Prevention of Danger) (1) Employers shall devise necessary measures for prevention of danger or maintenance of health, morality and protection of life in connection with installations dangerous to work or harmful to health.

(2) Employee shall comply with necessary matters for pervention of danger.

(3) The standard of measures to be taken by employer and the matters to be followed by employee under paragraph 1 and 2 shall be established by a Presidential decree.

ARTICLE 65. (Safety Installations) (1) Machines or apparatus required dangerous work shall not be transferred or lent or set up unless they are furnished with adequate standard and safety installations.

(2) Classification of the machines and apparatus, adeguate standard, and safety install ations to be furnished under paragraph 1 shall be established by a Presidential decree.

ARTICLE 66. (Particularly Dangerous Work) (1) Machines and apparatus required in particularly dangerous work shall not be manufactured, transferred, or installed unless the Director General of the Office of Labor has given prior authorization.

(2) Classification of machines and apparatus under paragraph 1 shall be established by a Presidential decree.

(3) If machines and apparatus under paragraph 1 and 2 have obtained authorization of the Director General of the Office of Labor and the term as stipulated by the Presidential decree has expired, they shall not be used before successfully passing the efficiency inspection conducted by the Director General of the Office of Labor.

ARTICLE 67. (Harmful Objects) (1) Sulphur, matches, and other harmful objects prejudicial to public health shall not be manufactured, sold, imported, or possessed for the purpose of selling.

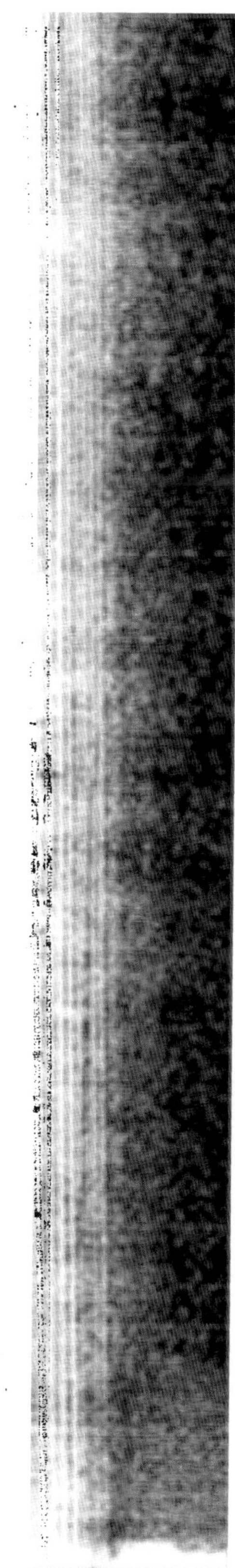

115

(2) Classification of harmful objects under paragraph 1 shall be set out by a Presidential decree.

ARTICLE 68. (Ristriction on Dangerous Work) (1) No employee shall be assigned to any dangerous work if inexperienced or technically incapable.

(2) The extent of such a work as may be mentioned in paragraph 1, the experience and technical skill shall be established by a Presidential decree.

ARTICLE 69. (Safety and Sanitary Training) Upon being employed, the employee shall be given training for necessary safety and health required in the carrying out of said work, by the employee.

ARTICLE 70. (Ban on Work by Patients) (1) Employer shall prohibit an employee from working when he has an infectious disease, mental disorder, or other disease which may easily become worse by continuance of work.

(2) The classification and degree of discontinuance of work under paragraph 1 shall be prescribed by a Presidential decree.

ARTICLE 71. (Physical Examination) (1) Employees shall be requested by employers at the time of employment and thereafter at regular interval to undergo physical examination by a physician as regards a certain work.

(2) If employee has no desire to ask physician who has been designated by the employer, the said employee may submit a certificate of another physician evidencing the result of his physical examination.

(3) In compliance with the result of physial examination as mentioned in paragraph 1 and 2, the employer shall be liable to devise necessary measures for maintenance of employee's health.

(4) The classification and standard of works and frequency of physical examination under the first paragraph shall be established by a Presidential decree.

ARTICLE 72. (Safety Manager and Health Administrator) (1) Employers shall assign a safety manager and a health administrator as regards certain kinds of work.

(2) The classification, standard, qualification, and assignment of safety manager and health administrator under paragraph 1 shall be prescribed by a Presidential decree.

(3) If necessary, the Director General of the Office of Labor shall have authority to instruct employer to increase or remove the of staff member, safety manager, or health admini strator..

ARTICLE 73. (Administrative Measures on Supervision) (1) When an employer desires to establish or reorganize an enterprise, having a constant number of ten or more employees, hes hall submit to the Director General of the Office of Labor a plan of construction in accordance with the standards under this Act and those of ordinance pursuant ther eto, no later than fourteen days prior to commencement of said construction work.

(2) The Director General of the Office of Labor may order postponement of commencement or alteration of the original plan whereever may be deemed necessary for safety and maintenance of health of employees.

(3) If buildings, where employees work, dormitory, annexed establishments, or raw materials are contrary to the standard fixed for safety and health, the Director General of the Office of Labor may order the employer to discontinue reconstruction of the said ones in whole or in part or any other necessary actions.

(4) In case of paragraph 3, the Director General of the Office of Labor may order employees to take necessary action in coordination with the matters required of

employer.

ARTICLE 74. (
loyee or apprentic
title, shall be put
business not relate
ARTICLE 75. (
technicians for lo
probational traini
wages shall be pre
(2) If an employe
under paragraph
Labor as regards
standard of wage
(3) If an employ
graph 2, he shall
testifying to the
site of workshop.
ARTICLE 76.
be given twelve
paragraph 1.
ARTICLE 77.
are subject to th
in contravention
shall exercise au

CH

ARTICLE 78.
necessary medica
employee who is
(2) The extent
shall be prescril
ARTICLE 79.
care under Arti
60% of average
ARTICLE 80.
even after com
shall give him
multiplied by t
table.
ARTICLE 81.
sation) If an e
negligence, and
provide a rest
ARTICLE 82.
result of the p

employer.

CHAPTER VII. Apprenticeship

ARTICLE 74. (Ban on Work by Apprentice) No employee who is a training employee or apprentice or any other employee intending to apprentice in whatever job title, shall be put to severe labor or requested to engage in employer's own household business not related to probational works.

ARTICLE 75. (Training of Technicians) (1) If there is necessity to foster special technicians for long period training in the course of regular employment, method of probational training, qualification of employer, term of contract, working hours, and wages shall be prescribed by a Presidential decree by consulting the Labor Committee.

(2) If an employer wishes to use an employee in accordance with Presidential decree under paragraph 1, he shall obtain approval of the Director General of the Office of Labor as regards the number of employee, method of training, term of contract, standard of wage, and means of its payment.

(3) If an employer uses an employee in accordance with the approval under paragraph 2, he shall get a certificate from the Director General of the Office of Labor testifying to the probational training on technical skill and keep it constantly at the site of workshop.

ARTICLE 76. (Minor) Minors who are subject to the provisions of Article 75 shall be given twelve holidays per year with pay under the provisions of Article 48, paragraph 1.

ARTICLE 77. (Revocation of Authorization) If an employer using employees who are subject to the provisions of Article 75 has forfeited his qualification or has acted in contravention of the terms as approved, the Director General of the Office of Labor shall exercise authority to rescind the authorization under Article 75, paragraph 2.

CHAPTER VIII. Worker's Accident Compensation

ARTICLE 78. (Medical Care Compensation) (1) Employers shall be bound to provide necessary medical care at their own expense or give the corresponding expenses for an employee who is hurt or deseased during the performance of contractual duty.

(2) The extent of occupational disease or medical care as mentioned in paragraph 1 shall be prescribed by a Presidential decree.

ARTICLE 79. (Rest Compensation) When an employee is in the course of medical care under Article 78, the employer shall make a rest compensation equivalent of 60% of average wage during the period of medical care.

ARTICLE 80. (Disability Compensation) If an employee has a physical disability even after complete recovery from an occupational wound or disease, the employer shall give him disability compensation equivalent to the sum of average wage multiplied by the number of days provided in the first tabulation of the annexed table.

ARTICLE 81. (Exception to Rest Compensation and Physical Handicap Compensation) If an employee is wounded or diseased through his own the employer need not negligence, and the employer has obtained the permission of the Labor Committee, provide a rest compensation or a physical handicap compensation.

ARTICLE 82. (Survivor Compensation) If an employee is killed during or as a result of the performance of contractual duty, the employer shall allow survivor

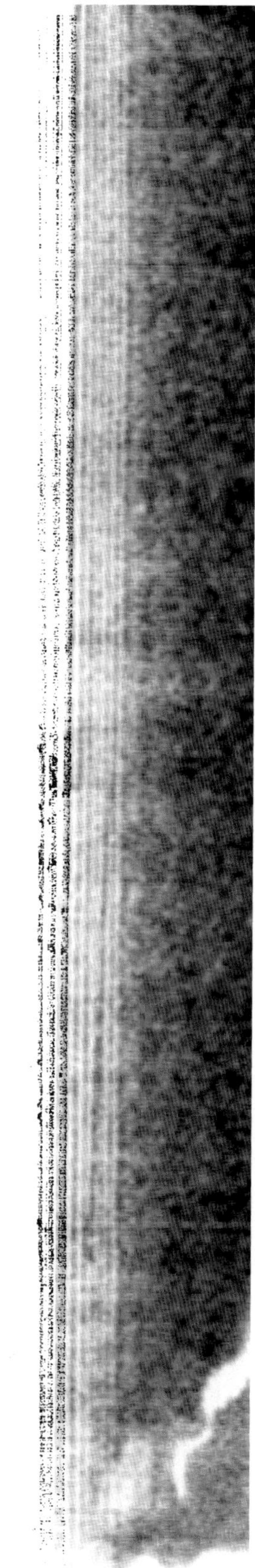

117

compensation equivalent to one thousand days average wage for the surviving family.

ARTICLE 83. (Funeral Expenses) If an employee is killed during or as a result of the performance of contractual duty, the employer shall allow funeral expenses equivalent to ninety days average wage.

ARTICLE 84. (Lump Sum Compensation) If an employee receiving medical care compensation under Article 78 has not completely recovered from said occupational wound or disease even after lapse of two year since the medical care started, the employer shall be exonerated from all further liability of compensation under this Act after providing a lump sum compensation in an amount equivalent to 1, 340 days average wage.

ARTICLE 85. (Instalment Payment) If an employer has testified concerning his ability to pay, and has the consent of the employee, he may pay the compensation by instalments for one year in accordance with the provisions of Articles 80, 82 or 84.

ARTICLE 86. (Claim for Compensation) No claim for workmen's compensation shall be forfeited form retirement, transferred, or confiscated.

ARTICLE 87. (Relations with Other Claims) If an employee entitled to compensation is to receive another source of money or goods for the same reason by operation of the Civil Code or other legal provisions in an equal value to a workmen's accident compensation, the comployer shall be exonerated from liability to the extent of the said value.

ARTICLE 88. (Review and Arbitration of the Director General of the Office of Labor) (1) When a person has an objection with respect to affirmation of occupational injury, disease, method of medical care, determination of compensation, or any other compensational actions, the said person shall request the Director General of the Office of Labor for a review or an arbitration of the dispute.

(2) A review or an arbitration shall be made no later than one month from acceptance, if a request under paragraph 1 has been filed with the Director General of the Office of Labor.

(3) The Director General of the Office of Labor has authority to conduct a review or an arbitration of dispute *ex officio*, whenever it may be necessary.

(4) The Director General of the Office of Labor has authority to request a physician to conduct physical examination or an autopsy, if it is deemed necessary for the purpose of a review or an arbitration.

(5) With regard to the interruption of prescription, the request for review or arbitrtaion under paragraph 1, and commencemnet of review or arbitration under paragraph 2, shall be regarded as a judicial claim.

ARTICLE 89. (Review and Arbitration of Labor Committee) (1) When a review or arbitration has failed to be conduct within the period specified in paragraph 2 of Article 88, or when a person is dissatisfied with the result of a review or arbitration already made, a request may be filed to the Labor Committee for review or arbitration.

(2) The Labor Committee shall execute a review or an arbitration no later than one month from acceptance, when a request as mentioned in paragraph 1 has been filed.

ARTICLE 90. (Civil Action) No civil action shall be instituted with regard to matters relative to the workmen's accident compensation under this Act before going through review or arbitration of the Labor Committee; except for the case where a review or an arbitration has not been completed before the expiration of said term in Article 89.

ARTICLE 91. (E
rmed by means of
regarded the empl
(2) A sub-contrac
ractor under parag
compensation with
more sub-contracto
(3) When a prima
compensation, dem
furnish said compe
bankrupt or missin
ARTICLE 92. (F
men's accident com
ARTICLE 93. (F
of this Act shall h

ARTICLE 94. (F
having a constant
regulation with re
the Office of Labo
1. Matters perta
holiday, and sl
2. Matters perta
and terminatio
3. Matters perta
allowance.
4. Matters perta
5. Matters perta
6. Matters perta
and others.
7. Matters perta
8. Matters perta
9. Matters perta
labor service.
10. Matters perta
11. All other mat
ARTICLE 95. (I
the formulation an
required to comply
composed of the n
or the expressed d
said employees in
the majority of e
(2) When an emp
with the provisio
opinion as mentio

118

ARTICLE 91. (Exception to Sub-Contract) (1) When an enterprise is to be performed by means of several different sub-contractors, the primary contractor shall be regarded the employer with regard to the accident compensation.

(2) A sub-contractor shall equally be regarded as an employer, if the primary contractor under paragraph 1 has made an agreement in writing for providing accident compensation with a sub-contractor; however, it shall be impossible to request two or more sub-contractors to undertake compensation with regard to the same enterprise.

(3) When a primary contractor under paragraph 2 has been requested to provide compensation, demand may be made of a sub-contractor liable to compensation to furnish said compensation; except when the said sub-contractor has been adjudged bankrupt or missing

ARTICLE 92. (Preservation of Documents) Essential documents relative to workmen's accident compensation shall be kept on file by employer for two years.

ARTICLE 93. (Prescription) Claim for accident compensation under the provisions of this Act shall be extinguished by prescription, if not exercised for three years.

CHAPTER IX. Employment Regulations

ARTICLE 94. (Formulation and Report of Employment Regulations) An employer having a constant number of ten or more employees shall formulate an employment regulation with regard to the following matters and notify the Director General of the Office of Labor The same shall be complied with when amended:

1. Matters pertaining to opening and closing and closing hours, recess, off-days, holiday, and shift turn.
2. Matters pertaining to determination, calculation and means of payment of wages and termination thereof, and promotion.
3. Matters pertaining to computation and means of payments of family maintenance allowance.
4. Matters pertaining to voluntary retirement from work.
5. Matters pertaining to retirement allowance, bonus and minimum wage.
6. Matters pertaining to employee's expense for boarding operational necessaries, and others.
7. Matters pertaining to education facilities for employees.
8. Matters pertaining to safety and health.
9. Matters pertaining to accident relief arising from or outside of performance of labor service.
10. Matters pertaining to commendation and penalty.
11. All other matters applicable to the group employees of each workshop concerned.

ARTICLE 95. (Procedures for Formulation and Amendment of Regulation) (1) Upon the formulation and amendment of employment regulation, an An employer shall be required to comply with the intention of a labor union, if there is a labor union composed of the majority members of employees attached to each workshop concerned or the expressed desire of the representative, who may represent the majority of said employees in matters of labor relations, if there is no labor union composed of the majority of employees.

(2) When an employer needs to notify the employment regulation in compliance with the provision of Article 94, a written document describing the expressed opinion as mentioned in paragraph 1 shall be attached to the written notification.

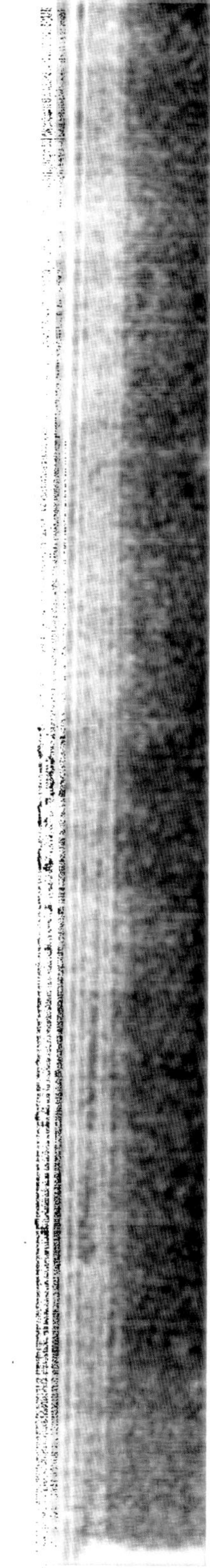

11P

ARTICLE 96. (Limit on Penalty) In case of establishing the penalty of demotion in the employment regulation, the amount of wage reduction shall be limited to half the amount of one day average wage for each time, and its total amount may not exceed one-tenth of the total wage amount at the time of wage payment.

ARTICLE 97. (Collective Agreement) (1) No employment regulation shall conflict with any collective agreement applicable to the workshop concerned.

(2) The Direcor General of the Office of Labor has authority to order the alteration agreement.
or amendment of any employment regulation, which may conflict with a collective

ARTICLE 98. (Effect of Violation) A labor contract setting forth labor conditions below the standard of the employment regulations shall be regarded as void to the extent of such portion. In such a case, such portion as has been invalidated shall follow the standard as established in the employment regulation.

CHAPTER X. Dormitory

ARTICLE 99. (Guarantee of Dormitory Life) (1) Employer shall not be allowed to interfere with the private life of any employee lodging in the annex dormitory.

(2) The employer shall not be allowed to intervene in the election of necessary staff members who deal with autonomous management of dormitory.

ARTICLE 100. (Formation and Amendment of Regulations) (1) The employer who wishes to board his employees in the annex dormitory shall formulate dormitory rules with regard to following matters and report them to the Director General of the Office of Labor. The same shall be followed when amended:

1. Matters pertaining to rising, bedtime, absence, and outside lodging.
2. Matters pertaining to observances of routing matters.
3. Matters pertaining to meals.
4. Matters pertaining to safety and health.
5. Mattars pertaining to maintenance of buildings and installations.
6. All other matters applicable to all boarding members.

(2) An employer shall have to obtain the consent of the representative of the majority of boarding members in order to formulate or amend the provisions of the regulations rules under paragraph 1.

(3) When employer needs to report the employment regulation in compliance with the provision of paragraph 1, a wrtten document describing the consent as mentioned in paragraph 2 shall be attached to.

(4) Both the employer and the boarding members shall comply with dormitory regulation.

ARTICLE 101. (Safety and Sanitation of Facilities) (1) Employers shall be required to take necessary measures for health, public morals, and maintenance of life of the members of annex dormitory.

(2) The standard of the necessary measures to be taken under the provision of paragraph 1 shall be prescribed by a Presidential decree.

CHAPTER XI. Labor Inspector

ARTICLE 102. (Labor Inspector) (1) The Office of Labor and its sub-ordinate agencies shall designate labor inspectors for the maintenance of the standard of labor conditions.

(2) Matters pertai
ment of service of
ARTICLE 103. (1
to inspect the worl
cuments and questi
(2) The labor insp
a medical examina
as may preclude hi
(3) Before perforn
or a physician desi
and order of med
respectively.
(4) The written
area under the pa
(5) The labor ins
police as provided
of this Act and of
(6) The labor in
Director General
immediately, upo
health under thi
employees.
ARTICLE 104.
to disclose confid
offical duty; the
ARTICLE 105.
violation or cont
decree pursuant
port on the said
inspector.
(2) The report
or any other ad
ARTICLE 106.
pector shall exc
ogation and any
tutes; an except
to an offence o

ARTICLE 107
punished by ha
ARTICLE 108
to a fact of co
three years or
ARTICLE 10
67, shall be pu
ding 5 million

(2) Matters pertaining to the qualification, appointment and dismissal and deployment of service of labor inspector shall be prescribed by a presidential decree

ARTICLE 103. (Power of Labor Inspector) (1) The labor inspector has authority to inspect the workshop, dormitory, and annex buildings, require presentation of documents and question both the employer and the employee.

(2) The labor inspector or a physician designated by him has authority to conduct a medical examination of an employee who appears to be easily liable to such a disease as may preclude his continuation of service.

(3) Before performing the duty mentioned in paragraph 1 and 2, the labor inspector or a physician designated by him shall be required to show his personal identification and order of medical examination of the Director General of the Office of Labor, respectively.

(4) The written inspection or examination order shall bear distinctly its date and area under the paragraph 3.

(5) The labor inspector shall have authority to perform the function of judiciary police as provided for in the Code of Criminal Procedure with regard to the violation of this Act and other laws and decree of labor affairs.

(6) The labor inspectors shall have authority to exercise the executive order of the Director General of the Office of Labor under Article 73, paragraph 2 and 3, immediately, upon recognition of violation of the standards relative to safety and health under this Act and consequently, appearance of imminent danger to the employees.

ARTICLE 104. (Duties of Labor Inspector) No labor inspector shall be authorized to disclose confidential matters coming to knowledge in the course of performing his offical duty; the same shall be complied with even when he is retired.

ARTICLE 105. (Report to Inspect Organ) (1) Whenever there may be found any violation or contravention of any of the provisions under this Act or presidential decree pursuant thereto at a workshop, it shall be the privilege of employee to report on the said fact to the Director General of the Office of Labor or to the labor inspector.

(2) The reporting employee under paragraph 1 shall be protected from discharge or any other adverse treatment by reason of the reporting act.

ARTICLE 106. (Restriction on Exercise of Rights) The proscutor and labor inspector shall exclusively be in charge of inspection, presentasion of documents, interrogation and any other investigation by virtue of this Act and any other labor statutes; an exception, however, shall be found when an investigation be made in regard to an offence or crime of the labor inspector in the performance of offcial duty.

CHAPTER XII. Punitive Provisions

ARTICLE 107. Those who violate the provisions of Article 6, 7 and 8 shall be punished by hard labor not exceeding five years or a fine not exceeding 15million won.

ARTICLE 108. A labor inspector who has committed a wilful connivance in regard to a fact of contravention of this Act shall be punished by hard labor not exceeding three years or by disqualification for a period not exceeding five years.

ARTICLE 109. Those who violate the provisions of Article 51, Article 58 or Article 67, shall be punished by hard labor not exceeding three years, or a fine not exceeding 5 million won.

121

ARTICLE 110. Those who come under one of the following items shall be punished by hard labor not exceeding two years or a fine not exceeding 5 million won:

1. Who have violated Article 9, Article 26, paragraph 1, Article 27, paragraph 1 and 2, Article 27-2, Article 28, Article 35, Article 42, paragraphs 1 and 2, Articles 43, 44, 50, 55, 56, 57, 60, 61, 64 paragraph 1, 65, 66, 68, 76, 78, 79, 80, 82, 83, and Article 105, paragraph 2;
2. Who have not complied with the order as mentioned in Articles 42-paragraph 3, 73-paragraph 2 and 4; and
3. Who have not complied with the prescribed number of employees, method of training, term of contract, working hours, standard of wage and means of its payment as approved in accordance with the provision of Article 75, paragraph 2.

ARTICLE 110-2. Those who violate the provisions of Article 30, 36, 37 and 38 shall be punished by a fine not exceeding 5 million won.

ARTICLE 111. Those who come under one of the following items shall be punished by a fine not exceeding 2,500,000 won.

1. Who have violated the provisions of Articles 5, 13, 21, 22, 24, 25, 31-paragraphs 1, 2 and 3, 32, 33, 39, 40, 42-paragraph 2 proviso, 45, 46, 47, 48-paragraph 1 and 3, 52, 53, 59, 62, 63, 64-paragraph 2, 69, 70, 71-paragraphs 1 and 2, 72 -paragraph 1, 73-paragraph 1, 74, 75-paragraph 3, 92, 94, 95, 96, 99-paragraph 2, 100, 101 and 104.
2. Who have failed to comply with the ways and means of custody and repayment as approved in accordance with the provision of Article 26, paragraph 2.
3. Who have failed to comply with the Ministerial order as mentioned in Article 72, paragraph 3 and Article 97, paragraph 2.
4. Who have refused, obstructed or evaded the inspection of the labor inspector under the provision of Article 103 or an examination of the physician designated by him under the provision of Article 103, or have been reluctant to make any required statement in answer to official interrogation or have made false statement, or have neglected to present to the required labor documents or have presented the fraudulent one
5. Who have failed to make a proper report, or present a fraudulent report, or have failed to be present at a prescribed place, in compliance with the demand of the Director General of the Office of Labor, the Labor Committee or labor inspector in accordance with the provision of Article 12.

ARTICLE 112. (1) When a person who has committed an act in contravention of this Act is an agent or servant or an employee acting on behalf of the employer on matters relating to the employees of said enterprise or work, the manger of enterprise who is the employer shall likewise be punished by fine as provided in each corresponding article except when the manager (the representative in case of a juridical person, and the legal representative shall be regarded as manager, if the manger is an minor, or incompetent, lackng in the same legal capacity as of an adult person) has previously taken adequate measures for prevention of violation.

(2) The employer shall also be punished as an offender, if when the said employer has negleceted adequate measures for prevention of violation in spite of his knowledge, or when he has failed to provide corrective measures or incited such a violation to be performed in spite of knowledge about its illegality.

ADDENDA

ARTICLE
lgation
ARTICLE
Hours Act,
Korean Inte
ARTICLE
under the M

(1) This A
(2) Monthl
Article
the enfo

This Act

Cl
(C
Cl

ARTICLE 113. This Act shall become effective on 90 days from the date of promulgation

ARTICLE 114. Military Government Ordinance, No. 121, The Maximum Working Hours Act, and the Child Labor Protection Act, Public Law No. 4 of the South Korean Interim Government shall hereby be repealed.

ARTICLE 115. This Act shall not apply to an employee subject to military service under the Military Service Act during the period of military service.

ADDENDA (December 4, 1961)

(1) This Act shall become effective on and after the date of its promulgation.

(2) Monthly paid leave already accumulated in accordance with the provision of Article 47 before promulgation of this Act shall be used within one year after the enforcement of this Act.

ADDENDUM (December 24, 1974)

This Act shall become effective on and after January 1, 1975.

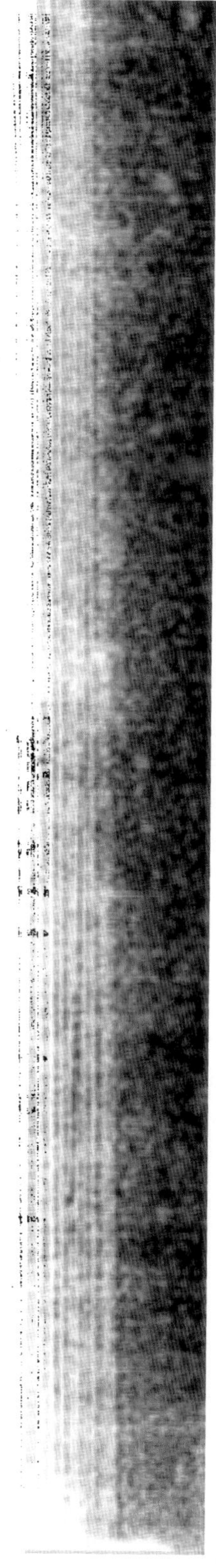

ANNEX TABLE

Classes of physical disability and accident compensation amount.

(Class)	(Compensation)		
Class 1.	1,340	days	wages
〃 2.	1,190	〃	〃
〃 3.	1,050	〃	〃
〃 4.	920	〃	〃
〃 5.	790	〃	〃
〃 6.	670	〃	〃
〃 7.	560	〃	〃
〃 8.	450	〃	〃
〃 9.	350	〃	〃
〃 10.	270	〃	〃
〃 11.	200	〃	〃
〃 12.	140	〃	〃
〃 13.	90	〃	〃
〃 14.	50	〃	〃

123

LABOR UNION ACT

Law No. 1329, Promulgated on April 17, 1963
Amended by Law No. 1481, December 7, 1963
Amended by Law No. 2610, March 13, 1973
Amended by Law No. 2705, December 24, 1974

CHAPTER I. General Provisions

ARTICLE 1. (Purpose). The purpose of this Act shall be to guarantee, on the basis of the Constitution, the autonomous right of laborers to enjoy freedom of association, collective bargaining and collective action, and to maintain and improve the working conditions of laborers, thereby making contribution to the enhancement of the economic and social status of the laborers and to the development of the national economy.

ARTICLE 2. (Legal Act) The provisions of Article 20 of the Criminal Code shall be applied to the collective bargaining and other legal acts of the labor unions, which have been done to attain the purposes enumerated in Article 1. However, an act of violence or any other destructive action shall not be considered as a legal act under any circumstances whatsoever.

ARTICLE 3. (Definition of Labor Union) "The labor union" in this Act means an organization or a federation of the organizations, which is formed at the initiative of laborers for the purpose of maintaining and improving labor conditions and seeking the enhancement of the economic and social status thereof, under voluntary association. However, in the case falling under the category of any of the following items, the definition made in this article shall not be applied:

1. When participation therein by the employer or the person who always acts for the benefit of the employer is allowed;
2. When it receives assistance mainly from the employer in the disbursement of the expenses thereof;
3. When the purpose thereof is only to promote mutual benefits, moral culture and welfare undertakings;
4. When membership thereof is granted to a person other than laborers; and
5. When the purpose of the organization is to hamper ordinary operation of the already existing labor unions.

ARTICLE 4. (Definition of Laborers) "A laborer" in this Act means the person who lives on wages, salaries, or any other income similar thereto regardless of the kind of his occupation.

ARTICLE 5. (Definition of Employers) "An employer" in this Act means the owner of enterprise, the person who is in charge of the operation of the enterprise, or the person who acts on behalf of the owner of the enterprise with regard to the matters concerning the laborers engaged in the enterprise.

ARTICLE 6. (Labor-Management Council) (1) Employers and labor unions shall establish labor-management councils to seek improvement of productivity through the mutual cooperation.

(2) The labor-management council shall consult production, education, training, working environments, disposition of grievances, prevention of labor-management dispute etc., within the scope of the collective agreements and employment regulations concerned.

(3) Matters necessar
dential decree.

ARTICLE 7. (Req
than the labor unior
labor dispute or to a
mentioned provision s
prescribed in item 1
(2) No one shall be
unions pursuant to th
ARTICLE 8. (Res
may organize, or join
shall be stipulated se
ARTICLE 9. (Acc
may become a juridi
(2) In case a labor
be made in accordanc
(3) To a labor unio
ning juridical persons
ARTICLE 10. (Ex
except for the busin
ARTICLE 11. (Pr
union shall not be su
to the difference of
ARTICLE 12. (Pr
allowed to conduct a
specific political par
(2) A labor union s
(3) Fund for a labo

ARTICLE 13. (R
union, a report whe
submitted together w
Labor by a labor org
of Seoul, mayor of
"the administrative
1. Name;
2. The site of its
3. Full names and
4. Name of the f
5. Name of labor
main office, an
(2) When changes
of paragraph 1, a
within seven days
(3) Deleted.

(3) Matters necessary for operation of the council shall be prescribed by a Presidential decree.

CHAPTER II. Labor Union

SECTION I. General Regulations

ARTICLE 7. (Requirements for the Protection of Labor Union) (1) No one other than the labor unions, as defined in this Act shall be entitled to request report of labor dispute or to apply for relief prescribed in Article 40. However, the above mentioned provision shall not be considered as denying the protection of laborers as prescribed in item 1 and item 2 of Article 39.

(2) No one shall be entitled to use the name of the labor union, except for the labor unions pursuant to this Act

ARTICLE 8. (Restriction on Formation and Membership of Labor Unions) Laborers may organize, or join, labor unions unrestrictedly. However, as for public officials, it shall be stipulated separately by Act.

ARTICLE 9. (Acquisition of the Status of a Juridical Person) (1) A labor union may become a juridical person by virtue of the charter thereof.

(2) In case a labor union plans to become a juridical person, registration shall have to be made in accordance with the stipulation of a Presidential decree.

(3) To a labor union which is a juridical person, provisions of the Civil Code concerning juridical persons shall be applied except as prescribed by this Act.

ARTICLE 10. (Exemption of Taxes) No taxes shall be imposed on labor unions except for the business enterprises thereof.

ARTICLE 11. (Prohibition of Discriminative Treatment) A member of the labor union shall not be subjected to discriminative treatment under any circumstances due to the difference of race, religion, sex, political affiliation, or personal status.

ARTICLE 12. (Prohibition of Political Activities) (1) A labor union shall not be allowed to conduct any act, in the election of any public office, in order to support a specific political party or have a specific person elected.

(2) A labor union shall not be able to collect political funds from its members.

(3) Fund for a labor union shall not be misappropriated as political funds.

SECTION II. Establishment of Labor Union

ARTICLE 13. (Report of Establishment) (1) When planning to establish a labor union, a report wherein the matters enumerated below are described, shall have to be submitted together with the charter thereof to the Director General of the Office of Labor by a labor organization of nation-wide scale and to the Mayor of the Special City of Seoul, mayor of Busan City or the Provincial Governor (hereinafter referred to as "the administrative office") by a labor organization of regional or enterprising scale.

1. Name;
2. The site of its main office;
3. Full names and addresses of executive members;
4. Name of the federate organization to which is belongs; and
5. Name of labor organization under its jurisdiction, number of its members, site of main office, and full names and addresses of executive members.

(2) When changes have taken place in the matters reported pursuant to the provision of paragraph 1, a report shall have to be made to the pertinent administrative office within seven days from the changes thereof.

(3) Deleted.

ARTICLE 14. (Charter) A labor union shall fill in the matters enumerated below in its charter.

1. Name;
2. Purpose and undertakings;
3. Site of main office;
4. Matters concerning union members;
5. In the case of a labor union which is a federate organization, matters concerning its constituent organizations;
6. Matters concerning conferences;
7. Matters concerning its representative and executive members;
8. Matters concerning union fees and accounting;
9. Matters concerning changes of charter;
10. Matters concerning dissolution;
11. Matters concerning the conclusion of collective agreement and labor dispute, in case a labor organization under a labor union on a nationwide scale is a concerned party thereof; and
12. Matters concerning representatives of labor-management joint council.

ARTICLE 15. (Certificate of Report) (1) After having accepted a report of establishment prescribed in paragraph 1, Article 13, the administrative office shall issue a certificate of report in accordance with the provisions of a Presidential decree.

(2) When the certificate of report as mentioned in paragraph 1, the labor union may request for reissuance of the certificate of report with a detailed explanation of the matter.

ARTICLE 16. (Cancellation or Change of Charter) When the charter of a labor union violates a law, an order, or is likely to harm public benefits, the administrative office may, through the resolution of the Labor Committee, order the cancellation or change thereof.

SECTION III. Management of Labor Union

ARTICLE 17. (Documents to be Prepared and Installed) A labor union shall, within 30 days from the date of establishment of the union, prepare and install at its main office the documents enumerated in the various items below.

1. List of union members (list of constituent organizations in case of a labor union which is a federate organization);
2. Charter;
3. Lists of addresses and full names of the executive members;
4. Proceedings of conference; and
5. Account books and documents concerning finance.

ARTICLE 18. (Holding of General Conference) (1) A labor union shall have to hold a general conference at least more than one every year.

(2) The representative of the labor union shall become the chairman of the general conference.

ARTICLE 19. (Matters Requiring Decision by the General Conference) (1) Matters enumerated below shall require decision by the general conference.

1. Matters concerning enactment and change of charter;
2. Matters concerning election of executive members;
3. Matters concerning collective agreement;
4. Matters concerning budget and settlement;
5. Matters concerning establishment, management or disposition of funds;

6. Matters con
or withdrawa
7. Matters con
8. Matters on
(2) A decision b
duly authorized u
present. However
Provided, howe
changes of the c
(3) Enactment
be made through
ARTICLE 20.
meeting which i
2. Deleted.
3. The delega
4. When the
shall apply t
5. Deleted.
ARTICLE 21.
union violates a
public benefits,
Labor Committe
ARTICLE 22.
the right to pa
However, the la
rights of those
ARTICLE 23.
shall have to be
ARTICLE 24.
pay every mon
ARTICLE 25.
let the account
every six mont
(2) An accou
of the labor un
ARTICLE 26.
tative of a la
extraordinary
(2) If more
is a federate
jurisdiction) h
matters to be
have to conve
delegates with
(3) In case t
the convocat
administrativ

6. Matters concerning establishment of a federate organization, and admission thereto or withdrawal therefrom;
7. Matters concerning merger, division or dissolution; and
8. Matters on labor disputes.

(2) A decision by the general conference shall require the presence of a majority of duly authorized union members and the consent of a majority of the union members present. However, in case of a tie vote, chairman shall have the right to break it.

Provided, however, when there exist specific provisions in the charter concernining changes of the charter and dismissal of executive members.

(3) Enactment and change of the charter, and election of executive members shall be made through the direct and secret vote of the union members.

ARTICLE 20. (Delegates' Meeting) (1) Labor unions may establish a delegates' meeting which is to be substitute for the general meeting by the charter.

2. Deleted.
3. The delegates shall be elected by the union members' direct and secret ballots.
4. When the delegates' meeting is established, the provisions on the general meeting shall apply to the delegates' meeting *mutatis mutandis.*
5. Deleted.

ARTICLE 21. (Cancellation or Change of Decisions) In case a decision of a labor union violates a law or an order concerning labor or is considered likely to harm public benefits, the pertinent administrative office may, through the decision of the Labor Committee, order the cancellation or change thereof.

ARTICLE 22. (Rights of Union Members) Members of a labor union shall have the right to participate in all the matters of the labor union in an equal capacity. However, the labor union may, by virtue of its charter, impose restrictions on the rights of those union members who do not pay membership fees.

ARTICLE 23. (Election of Executive Members) Executive members of a labor union shall have to be elected from among the union members thereof.

ARTICLE 24. (Membership Fee for Labor Union) A member of a labor union shall pay every month a membership fee that as less than two percent of the wage thereof.

ARTICLE 25. (Inspection of Account) (1) The representative of a labor union shall let the account inspector conduct inspection of account of the labor union at least once every six months.

(2) An accounting inspector of a labor union may conduct inspection of accounting of the labor union whenever it is considered necessary.

ARTICLE 26. (Convocation of Extraordinary General Conference) (1) The representative of a labor union may convoke an extraordinary general conference or an extraordinary council of delegates whenever it is considered necessary.

(2) If more than one third of the union members (in case of a labor union which is a federate organization, more than one third of the labor organizations under its jurisdiction) have requested convocation of a conference with the presentation of the matters to be discussed at the conference, the representative of the labor union shall have to convoke an extraordinary general conference or an extraordinary council of delegates without delay.

(3) In case the representative of a labor union has intentionally dodged or neglected the convocation of the conference prescribed in paragraph 2, the pertinent administrative office may, with the approval of the Labor Committee, nominate a

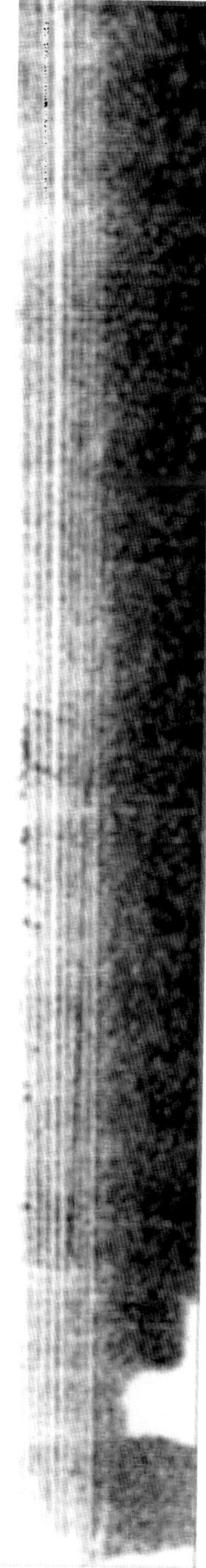

120

person who is to convoke the conference in order to have the conference convened.

ARTICLE 27. (Procedures for Convocation) A general conference or a council of delegates shall have to be convoked, with the matters to be discussed at the conference put on public notice 15 days ahead of the openi· · date of the conference at the latest, in accordance with the procedures as stipulat. by the charter. However, in case the labor union is composed of the laborers w· ing at a same workshop, the procedures as stipulated by the charter. However. in · : the labor union is composed of the laborers working at a same workshop, the p· ·d for public notice may be shortened by virtue of the charter thereof.

ARTICLE 28. (Exception Concerning the Right to \ :) In case the labor union is to make a decision in connection with specific me: ·s of the union, members of the union at issue shall not have the right to vote.

ARTICLE 29. (Opening the Status of Operation t. Public) When it has been requested by its union members, the representative o· labor union shall make the state of the operation of the union open to the publ:

ARTICLE 30. (Inspection by Administrative Offic: When it is considered necessary, the pertinent administrative office may k· public officials concerned investigate or examine the accounting status or other ·ry documents of the labor union.

(2) In the case mentioned in the foregoing paragraph, ·ublic officials concerned. shall have to present identification cards certifying the : ·rity thereof the persons concerned.

SECTION IV. Dissolution of Labor : n

ARTICLE 31. (Causes for Dissolution) (1) A labor uni· ·ll be dissolved due to causes falling under the category of any of the followin;

1. Occurrence of the causes for dissolution as stipulated the charter;
2. Extinction due to merger or division;
3. A resolution for dissolution adopted by a general · ·rence or a council of delegates, with the presence of two thirds or more the union members or delegates and with the consent of two thirds or mo: the union members or delegates present; and
4. An order of dissolution issued by the pertinent admi· :ive office as prescribed in Article 32.

(2) When a labor union has been dissolved the represen: thereof shall have to report to the pertinent administrative office within 15 d ·m the dissolution.

ARTICLE 32. (Order of Dissolution) When a labor u: ·s violated the law or an order concerning labor or is considered likely to harm ·enefits, the pertinent administrative office may, through the decision of the Committee, order the dissolution thereof or order re-election of its executive n

CHAPTER III. Collective Agree

ARTICLE 33. (Authority to Conduct Bargaining) (1) ·esentative of a labor union or a person entrusted by a labor union shall ha· ·uthority to conduct negotiations, for the benefit of the labor union or its n with regard to the matters concerning conclusion of a collective agreement : problems with the employer or the organization of employers.

(2) Deleted.

(3) "An organization of employers" mentioned in paragra; ·s the organization

of employers, which
the employers who

(4) Deleted.

(5) An employer o
justifiable reasons,
of labor unions.

ARTICLE 34. (D
shall be drawn up i
and affix seals the:

(2) The parties to
administrative offi
agreement.

ARTICLE 35. (V
ement, no valid pe

(2) When no vali
has been fixed for
one year.

(3) In case a new
expiration of the
the agreement con
agreement, the fo
after the expiratic

ARTICLE 36. (
or a labor contrac
the treatment of
become null an v

(2) In the case r
be handled in acc
The same shall a

ARTICLE 37. (
same kind perma
the binding force
applied to the ot
shop, or the offic

ARTICLE 38.
of the same kind
of a collective
decision of the L
to the collective
applied to the ot

(2) When an a
paragraph, a pu

ARTICLE 39.
under the categ
practice").:

1. An act dis

of employers, which has the authority to make adjustment or impose regulations on the employers who constitute the organization, concerning matters related to labor.

(4) Deleted.

(5) An employer or an organization of employers shall not refuse or neglect, without justifiable reasons, to conclude a *bona fide* collective agreement with representatives of labor unions.

ARTICLE 34. (Drawing up of a Collective Agreement) (1) A collective agreement shall be drawn up in a written form, and both parties concerned shall make signatures and affix seals thereto.

(2) The parties to a collective agreement shall have to report to the pertinent administrative office within 15 days from the date of conclusion of the collective agreement.

ARTICLE 35. (Valid Period of Collective Agreement) (1) For any collective agreement, no valid period exceeding one year shall be allowed.

(2) When no valid period has been fixed, or when a valid period exceeding one year has been fixed for a collective agreement, the valid period thereof shall be considered one year.

(3) In case a new collective agreement has not been concluded before or after the expiration of the valid period of a collective agreement, even though both parties to the agreement continued collective negotiations in order to conclude a new collective agreement, the former collective agreement shall remain valid until three months after the expiration thereof.

ARTICLE 36. (Validity of Fixed Standard) (1) When a part of a working regulation or a labor contract is in violation of the labor conditions or the standards concerning the treatment of laborers, prescribed in a collective agreement, the part thereof shall become null an void.

(2) In the case mentioned in paragraph 1, matters concerning the part nullified shall be handled in accordance with the standards stipulated by the collective agreement. The same shall apply to the matters not prescribed in the labor contract.

ARTICLE 37. (General Application) In cases a majority of the laborers of the same kind permanently employed by a factory, workshop, or an office come under the binding force of a collective agreement, the same collective agreement shall be applied to the other laborers of the same kind employed by the same factory, workshop, or the office.

ARTICLE 38. (Validity in Area) (1) In case two thirds or more of the laborers of the same kind, who are engaged in work in an area, come under the application of a collective agreement, the pertinent administrative office may, through the decision of the Labor Committee, make a decision, upon request of one or both parties to the collective agreement or *ex officio*, that the said collective agreement shall be applied to the other laborers of the same kind engaged in the same area.

(2) When an administrative office has made a decision prescribed in paragraph 1, paragraph, a public announcement thereof shall be made without delay.

CHAPTER IV. Uufair Labor Pratice

ARTICLE 39. (Unfair Labor Practice). An employer shall not commit an act falling under the category of any of the following items (hereinafter to as "unfair labor practice").:

1. An act dismissing a laborer or an act discriminating against a laborer on the

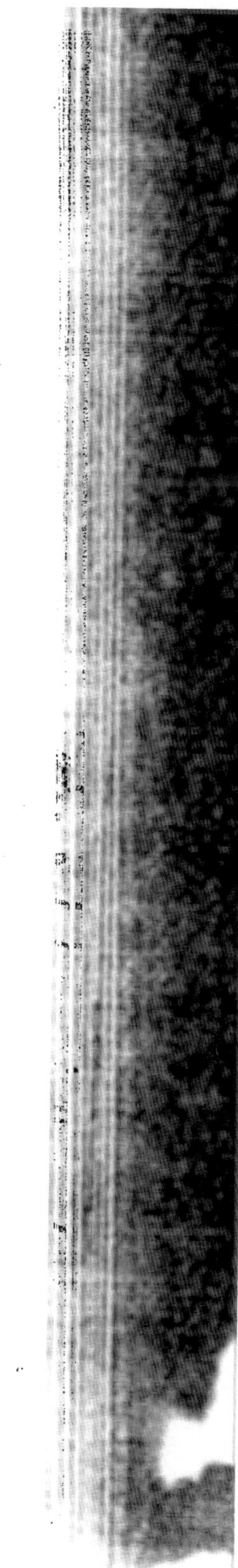

ground that the laborer has joined or tried to join a labor union, or has attempted to organize a labor union, or has done a justifiable act for the operation of a labor union;

2. An act fixing a condition for employment that a laborer does not join, or withdraws from, a specific labor union, or an act fixing a condition for employment that the laborer become a member of a specific labor union. However, the provision of this item shall not be applied to the conclusion of a collective agreement which makes it a condition for employment that the laborer become a member of a labor union, in case the labor union represents two thirds or more of the laborers engaged in the workshop.
3. An act rejecting or neglecting, without justifiable reasons, conclusion of a collective agreement or any other collective negotiations with the representative of a labor union or with the person entrusted by a labor union.
4. An act controlling, or interfering with the laborers in the formation or operation of a labor union, and an act subsidizing the expenses, for operation of a labor union. However, it shall be justifiable that the employer allow the laborer to conduct negotiations or bargaining with the employer during the labor hours, and that the employer donate welfare funds or fund for prevention or relief from economic troubles and other disasters, or that the employer offer an office building on the minimum scale for the labor union.
5. An act dismissing a laborer or an act discriminating a laborer on the ground that the laborer has joined a collective action which is justifiable, that the laborer has reported or made a testimony to the Labor Committee that the employer violate the provision of this article, or that the laborer has presented the evidence of violation to the administrative office.

ARTICLE 40. (Application for Relief) (1) A laborer or a labor union, whose right have been infringed upon because of an unfair labor practice on the part of the employer, may request for the relief thereof to the Labor Committee.

(2) The application for relief prescribed in paragraph 1 shall have to made within three (3) months from the date of unfair labor practice (in case of a continous act, from the date of the completion thereof).

ARTICLE 41. (Investigation, etc.) (1) When having received an application for relief as prescribed in Article 40, the Labor Committee shall conduct necessary investigation and query of the persons involved without delay.

(2) When conducting the query prescribed in paragraph 1, the Labor Committee may, upon the request of the persons involved or *ex officio*, have a witness present himself at the scene and question him on necessary matters.

(3) When conducting the query prescribed in paragraph 1, the Labor Committee shall have to give the persons involved and the witness enough opportunities to present evidence and to conduct a query thereagainst, respectively.

(4) Procedures concerning the investigation and the query by the Labor Committee as prescribed in paragraph 1 shall be in accordance with what is stipulated by the Central Labor Committee separately.

ARTICLE 42. (Order of Relief). (1) When having completed the query prescribed in Article 41 and having judged that there took place an unfair labor practice, the Labor Committee shall have to issue an order of relief to the employer, and, if having judged that an unjust act of labor did not exist, it shall have to make a decision turning down the application for relief.

(2) The judgement, o
a written form, and d
and the applicants, res
(3) When an order pr
shall have to follow t
ARTICLE 43. (Fina
an objection to the or
Committee or a specia
for review thereof to t
which he received the
(2) With regard to th
tral Labor Committee
rendered by the Centr
concerned may bring a
of the Administrative
letter of order, the let
to him.
(3) In case an applica
cedure has not been br
said order of relief, de
become final.
(4) When the decisio
finalized in accordanc
shall have to abide th
ARTICLE 44. (Vali
decision of turning do
shall not be suspended
or bringing up of an a

ARTICLE 45. (Enfo
Act shall be prescribed

ARTICLE 46. (Puni
prescribed in Article 4
by hard labor not exc
on won.
ARTICLE 46-2. (Di
up pursuant to the pr
in Article 38 shall be
ARTICLE 47. (Ditt
tigation or inspection
be punished by hard l
exceeding 100,000 wo
ARTICLE 48. (Dit
Article 7 shall be pun
ARTICLE 49. (Ditt

(2) The judgement, order or the decision prescribed in paragraph 1 shall be made in a written form, and document shall have to be delivered to the pertinent employer and the applicants, respectively.

(3) When an order prescribed in paragraph 1 has been issued, the persons involved shall have to follow the order.

ARTICLE 43. (Finalization of an Order of Relief). (1) A person involved, who has an objection to the order of relief or the decision of turning down by a local Labor Committee or a special Labor Committee as prescribed in Article 42, may request for review thereof to the Central Labor Committee within 10 days from the date on which he received the delivery of the letter of order or the letter of decision.

(2) With regard to the order of relief or decision of turning down given by the Central Labor Committee as prescribed in Article 42 or the adjudication after review rendered by the Central Labor Committee as prescribed in paragraph 1, the person concerned may bring an administrative procedure in accordance with the provisions of the Administrative Procedure Act within 15 days from the date on which the letter of order, the letter of decision or written adjudication after review was served to him.

(3) In case an application for review has not been made or an administrative procedure has not been brought within the period prescribed in paragraph 1 and 2, the said order of relief, decision of turning down or the adjudication after review shall become final.

(4) When the decision of turning down or the adjudication after review has been finalized in accordance with the provision of paragraph 3, the parties concerned shall have to abide thereby.

ARTICLE 44. (Validity of an Order of Relief) The validity of the order of relief, decision of turning down or the adjudication after review by the Labor Committee shall not be suspended by an application for review to the Central Labor Committee or bringing up of an administrative procedure.

CHAPTER V. Supplementary Rules

ARTICLE 45. (Enforcement Decree) Matters necessary for the enforcement of this Act shall be prescribed by a Presidetial decree.

CHAPTER VI. Punitive Provisions

ARTICLE 46. (Punitive Provisions) A person who has violated an order of relief prescribed in Article 42 or the provision of paragraph 4 of Article 43 shall be punished by hard labor not exceeding two years or a fine in an amount not exceeding 15milli on won.

ARTICLE 46-2. (Ditto) A person who has violated the collective agreement drawn up pursuant to the provision of Article 34, paragraph 1 and the decision as prescribed in Article 38 shall be punished by a fine not exceeding 5 million won.

ARTICLE 47. (Ditto) A person, who has rejected, disturbed, or dodged the investigation or inspection of public officials concerned as prescribed in Article 30, shall be punished by hard labor not exceeding three months or a fine in an amount not exceeding 100,000 won.

ARTICLE 48. (Ditto) A person who has violated the provision of paragraph 2 of Article 7 shall be punished by a fine in an amount not exceeding 100,000 won.

ARTICLE 49. (Ditto) When a labor union has fallen under the category of the

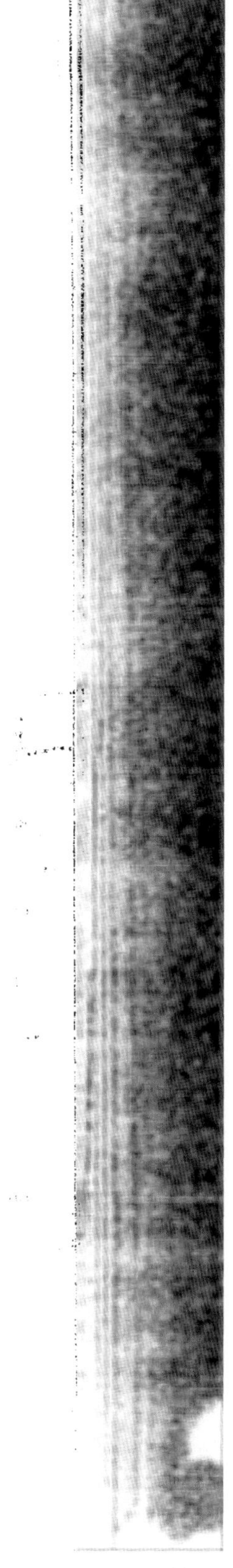

following items, the representative thereof shall be punished by a fine in an amount not exceeding 100,000 won.

1. When the labor union has violated an order of the pertinent administrative office, which was issued on the basis of this Act.
2. When it has failed to make a report as prescribed in paragraph 2 of Article 13, paragraph 2 of Article 31 or paragraph 2 of Article 34, or when having made a false report.
3. When having not prepared an installed documents prescriabed in Article 17.

ARTICLE 50. (Provision of Concurrent Punishment) (1) When a representative of a juridical person, or an agent, employee or any other person working for a juridical person or an individual has committed an act of violation prescribed in Article 46 Article 46-2 or Article 47 in connection with the business of the juridical person or the individual, a penalty or fine as prescribed in each of the pertinent articles shall be imposed on the juridical person or the individual, in addition to the punishment of the person who has committed the act.

(2) The provision of paragraph 1 shall be applied to the labor unions which are not juridical persons.

ADDENDA

(1) (Effective Date). This Act shall become effective from the date of its promulgation.

(2) (Law to be Abrogated) "The Temporary Measures Act on Collective Activities of Laborers" shall be abrogated upon the enforcement of this Act.

(3) (Interim Measures) Labor unions and collective agreements existing at the time of the inforcement of this Act shall be regarded as the labor unions and collective agreements pursuant to this Act.

(4) (Ditto) Cases concerning unfair labor practice, for which the period mentioned in paragraph 2 of Article 40 has not elapsed at the time of the enforcement of this Act, shall be disposed of in accordance with this Act.

ADDENDA (December 7, 1963)

(1) (Effective Date) This Act shall become effective on and after the date of its promulgation.

(2) (Interim Measures) Application for relief with regard to unfair labor practice effected before the enforcement of this Act shall be governed by the former Act.

ADDENDUM (March 3, 1973)

This Act shall become effective on and after the date of its promulgation.

ADDENDUM (December 24, 1974)

This Act shall become effective on and after January 1, 1975.

LABC

Law
Ame
Ame
Ame
Ame

ARTICLE 1. (Purpc
relations and to preve
maintained and contr
ARTICLE 2. (Defi
a controversy of clai
welfare, dismissal an
labor relations.
ARTICLE 3. (Defi
this Act means such
dispute tactics by wh
claims, and the acts
tion of business.
ARTICLE 4. (Def
the following enterp
"people":
1. Transportation
2. Water service,
of which is dire
3. Public health
4. Stock market
(2) This Act shall
bodies or State-run
will exert great inf
dential decree, mutc
(3) Deleted.
ARTICLE 5. (Du
shall prescribe the
council and ration
make every endea
ARTICLE 6. (D
concerned with lal
themselves if thei
every endeavor to
ARTICLE 7. (P
this Act, the part
pertinent agencies
ARTICLE 8. (F

LABOR DISPUTE SETTLEMENT ACT

Law No. 1327, Promulgated on April 17, 1963
Amended by Law No. 1483, December 7, 1963
Amended by Law No. 1606, December 16, 1963
Amended by Law No. 2608, March 13, 1973
Amended by Law No. 2707, December 24, 1974

CHAPTER I. General Provisions

ARTICLE 1. (Purpose) The purpose of this Act is to effect fair adjustment of labor relations and to prevent and settle labor disputes, so that peace in industry may be maintained and contribution may be made to the development of national economy.

ARTICLE 2. (Definition of Labor Disputes) The labor dispute in this Act means a controversy of claims concerning working conditions, such as wages, work hours, welfare, dismissal and treatment, etc. arising between the parties concerned with labor relations.

ARTICLE 3. (Definition of Acts of Labor Dispute) The act of labor dispute in this Act means such act as strike, sabotage, lockout ("workshop closing") and other dispute tactics by which the parties concerned with laborrelations accomplish their claims, and the acts against such tactices, both of which hamper the normal operation of business.

ARTICLE 4. (Definition of Public Utilty) (1) the Public utility in this Act means the following enterprises which are indispensable for daily life of the general public "people":

1. Transportation, communication, monoply and minting.
2. Water service, supply of electricity, and gas and oil supply the loss and profit of which is directly attributable to the State.
3. Public health and medical treatment.
4. Stock market and banking business.

(2) This Act shall apply to the businesses run by the State, local self-governing bodies or State-run enterprising bodies, or businesses or enterprising bodies which will exert great influences upon the national economy and are designated by a Presidential decree, *mutatis mutandis* to the public utilities under paragraph 1.

(3) Deleted.

ARTICLE 5. (Duty of the Parties) The parties concerned with labor relations shall prescribe the matters necessary for establishment of a labor and management council and rationalization of labor relations in the collective agreement, and shall make every endeavor so as to settle labor disputes independently, if they arise.

ARTICLE 6. (Duties of the Government) The Government shall assist the parties concerned with labor relations so as to adjust disputable labor relations by the parties themselves if their claims on labor relations conflict with each other, and shall make every endeavor to prevent occurance of labor disputes.

ARTICLE 7. (Prompt Settlement) In case of adjustment of labor relations under this Act, the parties concerned with labor relations, labor committees and any other pertinent agencies shall do their best to effect prompt settlement of labor disputes.

ARTICLE 8. (Restriction on Claim for Damages) An employer may not be allowed to claim damages which have been suffered from a labor dispute under this Act against a trade union or a worker.

ARTICLE 9. (Restriction on Personal Restraint of Workers) The workers shall not be placed under any restraint during the period of dispute under any pretext, except in the case of *flagrante delicto.*

ARTICLE 10. (Special Adjustment Commissioner) (1) The Central Labor Committee and a local labor committee may respectively assign special adjustment commissioners to each committee in order to make them participate in the mediation, conciliation or arbitration of a labor dispute to be conducted by the Central Labor Committee and a local labor committee.

(2) The special labor commissioners shall either represent an employer or workers or public interests, and the number of the representing commissioners shall be same as the other.

(3) The special adjustment commissioners representing an employer shall be commissioned from among the persons recommended by the employer's organization, the special adjustment commissioners representing the workers from among the persons recommended by a trade union, and the special adjustment commissioners representing public interests from among the persons for whom consent of the commissioners representing an employer and the commissioners representing workers in the labor committee concerned; and the special adjustment commissioners of the Central Labor Committee shall be commissioned by the Director General of the Office of Labor and the special adjustment commissioners of a local labor committee by the Mayor of Seoul Special City, mayor of Busan City or Provincial Governor, respectively.

ARTICLE 11. (Adjustment of Dispute of Public Interests on Preferential Basis) Adjustment of labor dispute related to public interests shall be handled on a preferential basis and such dispute shall be promptly settled.

CHAPTER II. Restriction on and Prohibition of Acts of Dispute

ARTICLE 12. (Restriction on Acts of Dispute) (1) The act of dispute of a trade union shall not be made unless a decision to do so has been made by an affirmative vote without entry cast directly by the majority of the union.

(2) Deleted.

ARTICLE 13. (Prohibition of Acts of of Violence, etc) (1) Any act of dispute employing violence or subversive activities (sabotage) shall not be allowed.

(2) Any act which suspends, discontinues or obstructs normal maintenance and operation of safety protection facilities of factories, work places or any other workshops shall not be regarded as an act of dispute.

(3) The Director General of the Office of Labor, the Mayor of Seoul Special City, mayor of Busan City or Provincial Governor (hereinafter referred to as "administrative agency") shall, if he considers that an act of dispute falls under one of the acts prescribed in the foregoing paragraph, order to suspend such act upon the decision of the labor committee. However, if there is no time to obtain a decision of the labor committee under an imminent situation, he may order to immediately suspend such act without obtaining a decision.

(4) In the case of the proviso of paragraph 3, the pertinent administrative agency shall obtain an *ex post facto* approval of the labor committee, and in case of failure of obtaining such approval, the pertinent order shall lose its effect thereafter.

ARTICLE 14. (Coc
elapse in the general
the report under Art
agency.

ARTICLE 15. (Rest
be allowed to employ,
the dispute or to repl

ARTICLE 16. (Rep
the parties concerned
agency and the labor

(2) When the compet
1, the agency shall ex
progress of collective
or not, within five da
that they are not lega
delay turn down the re

(3) Deleted.

(4) Deleted.

ARTICLE 17. (Repor
shop, he shall report i
tee concerned.

ARTICLE 18. (Mediati
agency received a report
agency shall designate w
public officials.

(2) A mediation official
ating between the partie
of issue of the claims of

ARTICLE 19. (Investi
cy, if it considers neces
of the dispute, may cause
ment of the parties conce
to enter the work place f

(2) In case of investigat
official shall show his ide
concerned.

ARTICLE 20. (Period
mediation within ten day
of public utilities from th
16, paragraph 1, the adm
ments concerning the case
opinion are written, attac

ARTICLE 21. (Effect of
ation official shall prepare
with the parties concerned

(2) The content of the me
collective agreement.

ARTICLE 14. (Cooling Period) The act of dispute shall not start unless 20 days elapse in the general business and 30 days in the public utilities from the date when the report under Article 16, paragraph 1 is received by the competent administrative agency.

ARTICLE 15. (Restiction on the Employer's Employment) An employer may not be allowed to employ, during the period of dispute, a person who is not related to the dispute or to replace an employee by such person.

ARTICLE 16. (Report on Labor Dispute) (1) In case a labor dispute has occured, the parties concerned shall report it thereof without delay to the administrative agency and the labor committee concerned.

(2) When the competent administrative agency receives the report under paragraph 1, the agency shall examine and determine whether the qualifications for the parties, progress of collective negotiations, procedures for filing of disputes, etc. are legal or not, within five days from the receipt of the report, and when the agency deems that they are not legal as a result of the examination, the agency shall without delay turn down the report.

(3) Deleted.

(4) Deleted.

ARTICLE 17. (Report on Lockout) In case an employer intends to close his workshop, he shall report it thereof to the administrative agency and the labor committee concerned.

CHAPTER III. Mediation

ARTICLE 18. (Mediation of Administrative Agency) (1) In case an administrative agency received a report pusuant to the provision of Article 16, paragraph 1, the agency shall designate without delay a mediation official from among its subordinate public officials.

(2) A mediation official shall make endeavor for the settlement of the case by mediating between the parties for the settlement of the dispute and confirming the point of issue of the claims of both parties.

ARTICLE 19. (Investigation of Adminstrative Agency) (1) An administrative agency, if it considers necessary for the mediation beween the parties for the settlement of the dispute, may cause the mediation official to request the appearance and statement of the parties concerned or references, to inspect the documents concerned or to enter the work place for investigation.

(2) In case of investigation pursuant to the provisions of paragraph 1, the mediation official shall show his identification card with his authority prescribed to the person concerned.

ARTICLE 20. (Period of Mediation) When the dispute is not settled through mediation within ten days in case of general business or within fifteen days in case of public utilities from the receipt of the report pursuant to the provision of Article 16, paragraph 1, the administrative agency shall send a labor Committee the documents concerning the case with the documents, in which mediation procedure and opinion are written, attached.

ARTICLE 21. (Effect of Mediation) (1) When a mediation is successful, the mediation official shall prepare a mediation record and affix his seal thereon together with the parties concerned.

(2) The content of the mediation record shall have the same effect as that of the collective agreement.

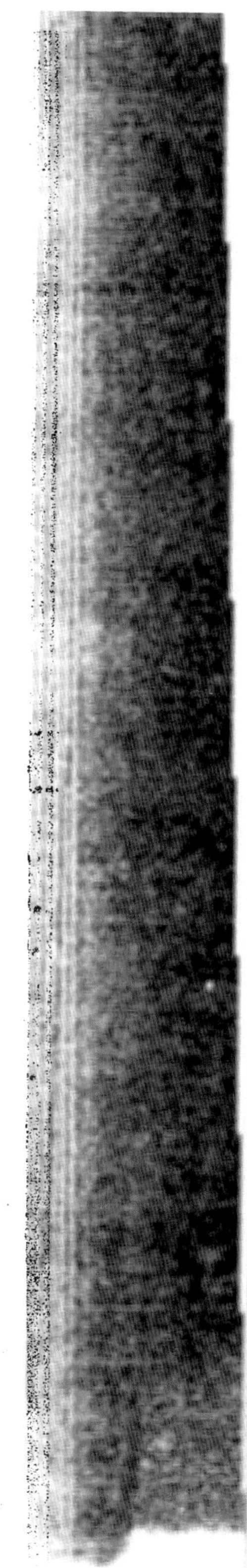

CHAPTER IV. Conciliation

ARTICLE 22. (Conciliation) When the Labor Committee receives the transfer of cases pursuant to Article 20, it shall without delay commence conciliation of the labor disputes concerned.

ARTICLE 23. (Formation of a Conciliation Committee) (1) A labor committee shall establish a conciliation committee in order to effect a conciliation of a labor dispute.

(2) The conciliation committee prescribed in paragraph 1 shall be composed of three (3) conciliation commissioners.

(3) One each of the persons representing the employer, the persons representing workers and the person representing public utilities from among the members of the labor committee concerned or the special conciliation commissioners shall bedesignated as the conciliation commissioner under paragraph 2.

ARTICLE 24. (Chairman of a Conciliation Committee) (1) There shall be one (1) chairman in a conciliation committee.

(2) A conciliation commissioner representing public interests shall be the chairman.

ARTICLE 25. (Meeting) (1) The chairman of a conciliation committee shall convoke a meeting of the conciliation committee and shall preside at the meeting.

(2) A conciliation committee shall open its meeting with the presence of all the members of its committee and shall make decision by an affirmative vote of the majority of the committee members.

(3) The chairman shall have a vote, and in case of a tie vote, he shall break the tie.

ARTICLE 26. (Hearing Opinions) A conciliation committee shall hear the opinions of the parties by fixing a date and requiring the parties to present themselves before the conciliation committee.

ARTICLE 27. (Prevention of Attendance) The chairman of a conciliation committee may prevent the attendance of those persons other than the parties concerned and references in a meeting and may order such persons as might disturb the fair proceeding of a meeting to leave the place of meeting.

ARTICLE 28. (Preparation of a Draft Conciliation) (1) The conciliation committee shall prepare a draft conciliation, present it to the parties concerned, advise the parties concerned to accept it, may simultaneously publicly announce it thereof attaching the reason thereto, and may request cooperation of the press or radio for such announcement, if necessary.

(2) If, after the draft conciliation under paragraph 1 has been acceptedby both parties concerned there occurs any disagreement between the parties concerning interpretation of or how to perform such draft conciliation, the parties con cerned shall request the conciliation committee concerned to give a clear opinion concerning how to interprete or perform such draft conciliation.

(3) The conciliation committee shall, if it receives a request under paragraph 2, give a clear opinion within 15 days from the date of receipt of such request.

ARTICLE 29. (Effect of Conciliation) (1) In case a draft conciliation under paragraph 1 of Article 28 has been accepted by the parties concerned, all the members of the conciliation committee shall prepare a text of conciliation and it shall be signed and sealed by them together with the parties concerned.

(2) The content of the text of conciliation shall have the same effect as that of

the collective agr
(3) The opinion
iation commitee
the same effect a

ARTICLE 30. (
for anyone of th
1. In case both
2. In case one
with provisic
3. In case ther
arbitration o
or *ex-officio*

ARTICLE 31.
are referred to a
the date of the

ARTICLE 32.
established an ar
ration committe
(2) The arbitra
arbitrators.
(3) Arbitrators
the Labor Comm
and the special
(4) If, in the c
assigned to a la
shall take the p

ARTICLE 33.
man in the arbi
(2) The chairm
representing pub

ARTICLE 34.
convoke a meet
(3) The meeti
all the members
a tie vote, he s

ARTICLE 35.
employers or re
nated by the pa
approval of the

ARTICLE 36.
committee may
cerned and ref
fair proceeding

ARTICLE 37.
prepared in wr

ARTICLE 38.

135

the collective agreement.

(3) The opinion concerning interpretation and how to perform, given by the conciliation commitee pursuant to the provision of paragraph 3 of Article 28, shall have the same effect as that of an award of arbitration.

CHAPTER V. Arbitration

ARTICLE 30. (Commencement of Arbitration) A labor committee shall arbitrate for anyone of the following disputes:

1. In case both parties concerned have requested an arbitration.
2. In case one of the parties concerned has requesed an arbitration in accordance with provisions of the collective agreement.
3. In case there is a decision to refer a dispute concerning public utility to the arbitration of a labor committee upon the demand of an administrative agency or *ex-officio* of a labor committee.

ARTICLE 31. (Ban of Acts of Dispute during Arbitration) When labor disputes are referred to arbitration, acts of disputes shall not take place for 20 days from the date of the reference, irrespetive of the provisions of Article 14.

ARTICLE 32. (Formation of Arbitration Committee) (1) A labor committee shall established an arbitration committee within the labor committee to make the arbitration committee conduct an arbitration or review of labor disputes.

(2) The arbitration committee under paragraph 1 shall be composed of three (3) arbitrators.

(3) Arbitrators mentioned in paragraph 2 shall be described by the Chairman of the Labor Committee concerned from among the members representing public interest and the special adjustment commissioners representing public interests.

(4) If, in the case of paragraph 3, no special adjustment commissioners have been assigned to a labor committee, the committee members representing public utility shall take the place of such commissioners.

ARTICLE 33. (Chairman of the Arbitration Committee) (1) There shall be a chairman in the arbitration committee.

(2) The chairman shall be elected from among the arbitrators who are the members representing public utility of the labor committee.

ARTICLE 34. (Meeting) (1) The chairman of the arbitration committee shall convoke a meeting of the committee and shall preside at the meeting.

(3) The meeting of the arbitration committee shall be opened by the presence of all the members, and decisions shall be made by an affirmative vote, and in case of a tie vote, he shall break the tie.

ARTICLE 35. (Stating Opinions) The member of the labor committee representing employers or representing workers, or the special adjustment commissioner, as designated by the parties concerned, may state his opinion before the meeting by obtaining approval of the arbitration committee.

ARTICLE 36. (Prevention of Attendance) The chairman of the arbitration committee may prevent the attendance of those persons other than the parties concerned and references in a meeting, and may order such persons as might disturb the fair proceedings of a meeting to leave the place of meeting.

ARTICLE 37. (Award of an Arbitration) An award of an arbitration shall be prepared in writing, and the date of effectuation shall be clearly stated on the paper.

ARTICLE 38. (Final Award of an Arbitration) (1) The party concerned may, if

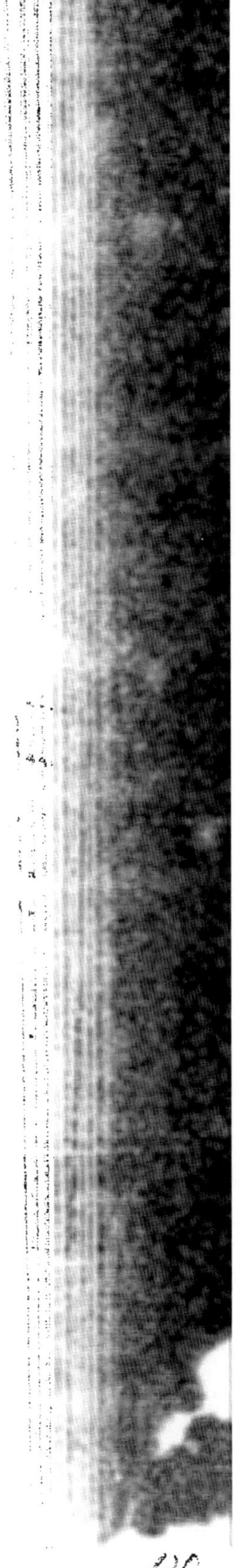

he considers that an award of an arbitration rendered by a local labor committee or a special labor committee pursuant to the provision of Article 37 is in violation of law or is an act going beyond its authority, demand the Central Labor Committee to review the case within 10 days from the date of service of the award of arbitration.

(2) The party concerned may, if he considers that an award of arbitration rendered by the Central Labor Committee pursuant to the provision of Article 37 or the decision for review rendered by the Central Labor Committee pursuant to the provision of paragraph 1 is in violation of law or is an act going beyond its authority, institute an administrative procedure within 15 days from the date of service of the award of arbitration or the decision for review, irrespective of the provisions of Article 15 of the Administrative Procedure Act.

(3) If the party concerned has failed to demand a review or to institute an administrative procedure within the period prescribed in paragraphs 1 and 2, such award of arbitration or decision for review shall become final.

(4) When an award of arbitration or a decision for review has become final in accordance with the provision of paragraph 3, the parties concerned shall accept it.

ARTICLE 39. (Effect of an Award) (1) The effect of an award rendered by a labor committee or the decision for review shall not be suspended by demanding a review to or instituting an administrative procedure against the Central Labor Committee pursuant to the provision of Article 38.

(2) The content of the award or decision for review which has become final in accordance with the provisions of the foregoing article shall have the same effect as that of the collective agreement.

CHAPTER VI. Emergency Adjustment

ARTICLE 40. (Decision of Emergency Adjustment) (1) The Minister of Health and Social Affairs may render a decision for an emergency adjustment, in case an act of dispute is related to public interests, or it is of large scale or of specific character, and that, because of such act of dispute there exists same danger which might impair the national economy or endanger the daily life of the general public.

(2) The Director General of the Office of Labor shall hear the opinion of the Central Labor Committee in advance, if he intends to make a decision for an emergency adjustment.

(3) In case the Minister of Health and Social Affairs has made a decision for an emergency adjustment in accordance with the provisions of paragraphs 1 and 2, he shall without delay announce thereof with the reasons therefor and shall simultaneously notify thereof to the Central Labor Committee and the parties concerned.

ARTICLE 41. (Suspension of Acts of Dispute at the Time of Emergency Adjustment) The parties concerned shall immediately suspend any act of dispute when a decision for an emergency adjustment under paragraph 3 of Article 40 is announced, and no act of dispute shall be commenced again unless 30 days has elapsed from the date of announcement.

ARTICLE 42. (Conciliation by the Central Labor Committee) The Central Labor Committee shall without delay undertake a conciliation, when the committee receives a notice under paragraph 3 of Article 40.

ARTICLE 43. (Central Labor Committee's Right to Decide Referring a Dispute to Arbitration) (1) The Central Labor Committee shall, if it considers that a conciliation

under Article 42
referred to an a
(2) A decision
receipt of the n
ARTICLE 44.
Committee shall
Committee is re
Committee has
Article 43.

ARTICLE 45.
of this Act shall

ARTICLE 46.
dispute or comm
visions of Articl
labor for not ex
ARTICLE 46-2.
38, paragraph 4
a fine of not ex
ARTICLE 46-3.
tion record presc
prescribed in Ar
shall be punishe
ARTICLE 47.
Article 13, para
paragraph 3, sha
fine of not exce
ARTICLE 48.
has failed to sub
report, he or th
or a fine of not
ARTICLE 49.
of a juridical per
person or an ind
48 concerning th
violator shall be
cerned shall be p
(2) The provisi
a juridical perso

(1) This Act sh
(2) The cases p
committee a
dance with t
(3) The provisi

138

under Article 42 is not likely to be attained, decide whether the case "dispute" be referred to an arbitration or not.

(2) A decision under paragraph 1 shall be made within 10 days from the date of receipt of the notice under paragraph 3 of Article 40.

ARTICLE 44. (Arbitration by the Central Labor Committee) The Central Labor Committee shall without delay conduct an arbitration, when an arbitration by the Committee is requested by both or one of the parties concerned or when the Committee has made a decision to refer a dispute to an arbitration mentioned in the Article 43.

CHAPTER VII. Supplementary Rules

ARTICLE 45. (Implementing Decree) Matters necessary for the implementation of this Act shall be prescribed by a Presidential decree.

CHAPTER VIII. Punitive Provisions

ARTICLE 46. (Punitive Provision) In case of failure in suspension of an act of dispute or commission of an act of dispute within 30 days, in violation of the provisions of Article 41, the ring leader of the act of violation shall be punished by hard labor for not exceeding two (2) years or a fine of not exceeding 1 million won.

ARTICLE 46-2. (Ditto) Any person who has violated the provisions of Article 38, paragraph 4 shall be punished by hard labor for not exceeding two (2) years or a fine of not exceeding 5 million won.

ARTICLE 46-3. (Ditto) Any person who has not follow the content of the mediation record prescribed in Aticle 21, paragraph 2, the content of the text of conciliation prescribed in Article 29, paragraph 2, and the content of an award of arbitration shall be punished by a fine of not exceeding 5 million won.

ARTICLE 47. (Ditto) Any person who has violated the provisions of Article 12, Article 13, paragraph 2, Article 14, 15 or 31 or the order prescribed in Article 13, paragraph 3, shall be punished by hard labor for not exceeding one (1) year or a fine of not exceeding 500,000 won.

ARTICLE 48. (Ditto) In case a party, or parties concerned with a labor dispute, has failed to submit a report prescribed in Article 16 or 17 or has submitted a false report, he or they shall be punished by hard labor for not exceeding six (6) months or a fine of not exceeding 200,000 won.

ARTICLE 49. (Provision of Concurrent Punishment) In case the representative of a juridical person, or the agent, employee or any other hired person of a juridical person or an individual person, has committed an act of violation of Article 46 to 48 concerning the business of such juridical person or individual person, not only the violator shall be punished, but also the juridical person or the individual person concerned shall be punished by a fine prescribed in the respective provision.

(2) The provision of paragraph 1 shall also apply to the trade union which is not a juridical person.

ADDENDA

(1) This Act shall become effective on and after the date of its promulgation.

(2) The cases pending in the examination of an administrative agency and a labor committee at the time of enforcement of this Act shall be disposed of in accordance with the provisions of this Act.

(3) The provision of paragraph 5 of the Military Revolutionary Committee Pro-

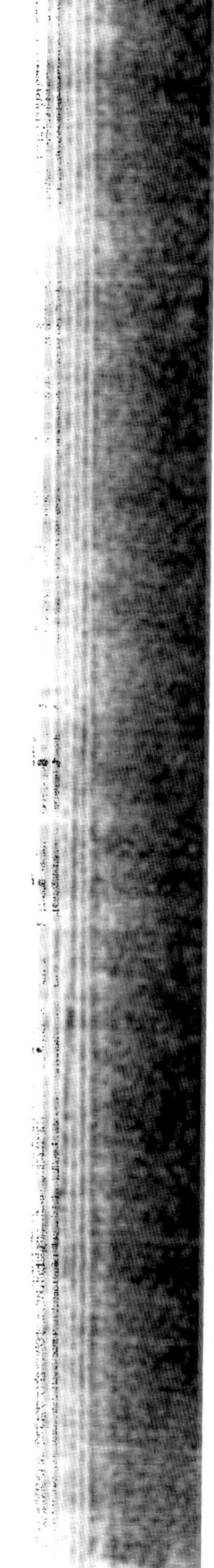

clamation No.1 shall not apply to the acts of dispute under this Act.

ADDENDUM (December 7, 1963)

This Act shall become effective on and after the date of its promulgation.

ADDENDUM (December 16, 1963)

This Act shall become effective on and after the enforcement day of the Amended Constitution promulgated on December 26, 1962.

ADDENDUM (March 13, 1973)

This Act shall become effective on and after the date of its promulgation.

ADDENDUM (December 24, 1974)

This Act shall become effective on and after January 1, 1975.

ARTICLE 1. (
policy and stabil
by encouraging
ARTICLE 2. (
persons who emi
their families, o
(including marri
permanent resid
relationship wit
(2) Families m
the same census
ARTICLE 3. (
following items
that exceptions
falling under ite
1. A person w
2. Persons wh
of such sent
undergo the
3. Incompeten
tated;
4. Mentally d
5. Alcoholics
6. Deaf, dumb
7. Persons wi
8. Persons wh
State or of
9. Persons wh
nance of th
ARTICLE 4.
fied into collec
matters concern
shall be prescri
ARTICLE 5.
ration shall no
the viewpoint o
emigrate overs
ARTICLE 6.
emigrate in acc
ration to the N

140

공 란

공 란

공 란

공 란

기 안 용 지

분류기호 문서번호	미안 723-	(전화번호 70-2324)	전결규정 조 항 장관전결사항
처리기간		차관	장관
시행일자	79. 5. 23.		
보존년한			

보조기관				협조	
	차관보				
	국 장		심의관		
	담당관				
기안책임자		유창현	안보문제담당관실		

경 유 수 신 참 조	내부결재	발신		통제	
제 목	주한미군 한국인 세출기관 종업원 퇴직금 가지급 합의각서 시행				

1. 주한미군 근로자 퇴직금 지급문제와 관련, 그간 동 퇴직금 지급(약 600억원)이 통화에 미치는 영향등을 관련부처와 협의한 바 동 합의각서 시행에 합의를 보았고, 외기노조측에서 동 합의각서 시행을 적극 희망하므로 동 합의각서의 시행을 건의합니다.

2. 동 각서의 시행에 관한 관계부처의 의견은 다음과 같읍니다.

경제기획원 : ◦ 동 합의각서 시행에 이견이 없음.
◦ 다만 동 퇴직금의 일시 인출시 통화에 미치는 영향을 고려, 장기은행 예치를 적극 권장하도록 해야 할 것임.

재 무 부 : ◦ 동 합의각서의 시행은 불가피함.
◦ 이에 부수하여 통화 정책면에서 참조, 저축 증대의 방법을 추진할 것임.

정서 / 관인 / 발송

0201-1-8A (갑)
1969. 11. 10 승인

190mm×268mm (2급인쇄용지60g/m²)
조 달 청(1,500,000매 인 쇄)

145

노 동 청 : 동 합의각서 시행 지연은 근로자들의 동요의 우려가 있으므로 조속 시행이 바람직함.

첨 부 : 1. 동 각서의 내용 및 교섭경위

2. 경기원 및 재무부 공문 사본

3. 동 각서 사본.

끝.

0201-1-43A(2-2)
1972. 12. 29. 승인

190mm×268mm(인쇄용지2급60g/m²)
조 달 청(4,000,000매 인쇄)

146

주한 미군 한국인 세출기관 종업원 퇴직금 가지급
합의각서 내용 및 교섭경위

1979. 5. 23.

안보문제담당관실

1. 동 합의각서의 내용

- 동 합의각서 적용대상 인원 : 16,400명
  (세출기관 근로자 : 12,500명, 한국노무단 : 3,300명,
  초청계약자 한국인 근로자 : 600명)

- 퇴직금 예상액 : 약 600억원 ($1.2억)

- 1979. 4. 30. 까지 퇴직금을 산출, 주한미군은 79. 6. 11. 까지 예금통장을 각 종업원이 수령할수 있도록 퇴직금의 은행예치를 완료하고, 각 종업원은 예치된 금액을 인출하거나 예치하거나 선택권을 갖음.

- 1979. 4. 30. 이후의 퇴직금은 1년 1개월분의 비율로 매년 각 종업원의 개인구좌에 예치함.

- 현존 퇴직금 규정은 효력이 소멸되고 이 합의각서의 규정으로 대체됨.

2. 교섭경위

78. 5. 22. 외기노조는 주한미군 당국에 퇴직금제도 개선을 요청함.

147

78. 9. 26.	SOFA 합동위 미측간사 Kinney 는 한국정부가 미국정부로 부터 퇴직금 전액을 인수할 것을 제의
79. 1. 24.	SOFA 합동위 퇴직금 지불문제를 노무분과위에 과제 위촉
79. 2. 13.	노무분과위 한.미 양위원장은 동 문제를 주한 미군과 외기노조가 협의할 것에 합의
79. 4. 3.	주한 미군과 외기노조는 동 각서에 합의를 봄.
79. 5. 4.	노무분과위 한.미 양위원장, 동합의각서에 서명.
79. 5. 10.	제 131차 SOFA 합동위에서 양측대표는 한.미 양국정부의 승인 즉시 동 각서에 서명할 것에 동의함.

끝.

148

경 제 기 획 원

투사 316-20   (70-4171)   1979. 5. 8.

수신 외무부장관

제목 주한미군 종업원 퇴직금 지급 합의각서에 대한 의견회시

미안 723-19184 (79. 5. 7)로 조회하신 주한 미군 한국인종업원 퇴직금 지급 합의각서 시행에 관한 당원의 의견을 다음과 같이 통보 합니다.

다 음

1. 동 퇴직금 문제는 당사자인 주한미군과 외기노조간에 합의가 된 것이므로 그 시행에는 이견이 없음

2. 다만 동퇴직금의 일시 인출시 통화에 미치는 영향을 고려하여 장기 은행예치를 적극 권장토록 하여야 할것임. 끝.

경 제 기 획 원 장 관

김재익

에너지는 국력이다 아껴써서 애국하자

149

저축은 국력

미주국

재 무 부

금정 1221 - 641 70-4705 1979. 5. 12.

수신 외무부 장관

제목 주한 미군 종업원퇴직금 가지급 합의각서 시행에 대한 의견

1. 미안 723 - 19184(79. 5. 7)과 관련입니다.

2. 동 합의각서가 시행될때 퇴직금 일시 지급에 따라 통화증대 가능성에 따른 통화 정책면에서 대책 강구가 요구되나, 동 자금이 근로자의 노임적 성격이라는 점을 감안할 때 합의 각서 내용대로 시행하는 것은 불가피 하다고 사료됩니다.

3. 이에 부수하여 통화 정책면에서 참조하여 저축증대등의 방법을 적극 추진할 것임. 끝.

재 무 부 장 관

영 주고받아 서로믿고 사고팔지

150

공 란

MEMORANDUM OF UNDERSTANDING

SUBJECT: Advance Severance Payment Procedures for Korean National Appropriated Fund Employees of the US Forces, Korea

1. In accordance with the ROK-US Joint Committee task assigned to the Labor Subcommittee on an exigent basis on 24 January 1979 and the agreement between the US and ROK Component Chairmen of the Labor Subcommittee on 13 February 1979 for carrying out the task, the US Forces, Korea and the Foreign Organizations Employees Union now agree as follows:

a. Payment will be made in advance of actual separation for all severance pay credit accumulated to employees as of 30 April 1979 and will be placed in individual employee bank accounts in a bank selected by the employee from all of those banks which have agreed to participate in the plan. The union may negotiate depositor services directly with those banks if they agree. The union may publicize the services agreed to by the banks to the employees for their consideration in bank selection; however, the individual employees selection remains optional. The USFK will complete the deposits at the earliest possible date so that the bank books are made available for pick up by the employees before 11 June 1979. In those few cases with advance severance pay computation difficulties, the bank book pick up date may be delayed but those delays should not exceed 10 days. Employees will have the option of withdrawing the money from the bank, in full or in part, or leaving the entire amount on deposit. Agreements with the banks on deposit procedures will be formulated in consultation with the union.

b. The advance severance pay for services up to the cut off date, 30 April 1979, will be calculated: (1) At the Schedule II (High Line) rate based on the average of the highest three consecutive months of normal wages received in the 24 months prior to the last day of the pay period ending before 20 March 1979; or (2) at the rate of one month's total wage for each one year of service based upon the average of total wages received for the highest three consecutive months during the 12 months prior to the last day of the pay period ending before 20 March 1979 with bonus payments prorated over the entire 12 months, whichever is greater.

c. Advance severance pay for services of less than one full credit period up to the cut off date, 30 April 1979, will be prorated to the last full month of service. The proration will be: (1) 1/12th of the increment between full-year credits, or 1/6th of the increment between half-year credits, for each full month of service; or (2) 1/12th of one month's total wage for each one full month of service based upon the average of total wages received for the highest three consecutive months during the 12 months prior to the last day of the pay period ending before 20 March 1979 with bonus payments prorated, if the basic advance severance pay computation is based upon 1b(2) above.

d. There will be no change in Service Computation Date (SCD) for leave accrual or Reduction-in-Force retention priority purposes.

e. The rate of severance pay for services after the cut off date, 30 April 1979, will be one month's average of the total wages received during the highest three consecutive months during the 12 months immediately preceding the last day of the pay period ending before 31 March of each successive year with bonus payments prorated over the entire 12 months. This amount will be placed in the employees' bank accounts annually. The deposits will be completed not later than 30 days after the annual cut off date.

f. Upon separation, the service period for which severance pay has not been deposited in the employees' accounts will be prorated to the last full month of service. The proration will be 1/12th of the average one month of total wages received during the period since the last cut off date immediately preceding the separation with bonus payments received during the previous 12 months prorated for each full month of service since the last annual cut off date.

g. In cases of separation due to Reduction-in-Force, one additional month's normal wage will be paid, provided 1 full year of service has been completed.

h. The service credit for severance pay purposes, at the time of separation by other than resignation or separation for cause, will be extended for a period equal to the total number of hours of unused sick leave accumulated by the employee.

i. A deposit of severance pay in an individual's bank as provided herein, and provision, where applicable, of the additional benefits contemplated herein shall fully discharge the entire US Forces, Korea severance pay obligation for the services for which the severance pay deposits have been made, and shall preclude any further claim for severance pay or related additional benefits by an employee or his representative based upon services for which the deposit has been made. Individual employees will execute an affidavit to this effect at the time of bank selection.

j. This revised plan will be applicable to all full-time Korean employees of Appropriated Fund activities, invited contractors, and members of the Korean Service Corps.

k. This Memorandum of Understanding, when approved in accordance with paragraph 2, below, shall supersede and replace all existing plans applicable to the employees specified in paragraph j above.

2. Implementation of this Memorandum of Understanding is subject to the prior approval of the US Department of Defense and the ROK-US Joint Committee.

FOR THE US FORCES, KOREA:

George A. Blakeslee

GEORGE A. BLAKESLEE
Civilian Personnel Director
Chairman
Joint Labor Affairs Committee

FOR THE FOREIGN ORGANIZATIONS EMPLOYEES UNION:

HWANG, KYU MU
President

4 May 1979
Date

154

합 의 각 서

제목: 주한 미군 한국인 세출 기관 종업원 퇴직금 가 지급

1. 1979년 1월 24일자 한—미 행협 합동 위원회가 노사 분과 위원회에 분임한 과제와 이 과제 이행에 관한 1979년 2월 13일 노사 분과 위원회 한—미 양 위원장의 합의에 따라, 주한 미군과 전국 외국 기관 노동 조합은 등 문제를 협의, 이제 다음과 같이 합의한다.

a. 1979년 4월 30일로 정하는 기산일 까지 축적된 각 종업원의 퇴직금은 가 지급 국내 모든 은행중 예금 접수에 동의하는 은행중에서 각 종업원이 선정한 은행 개인 구좌에 예치한다. 노동 조합은 예금 접수에 동의하는 은행과 써비스 관리 규정을 별도 교섭 약정하여 이를 각 종업원에게 주지 시켜 각자의 은행 선정에 참고가 되도록 할 수 있으나 은행 선정은 어디 까지나 각자 종업원의 의사에 맡긴다. 주한 미군은 1979년 6 월11일 까지 예금 통장을 각 종업원이 수령 할 수 있도록 가능한 한 빠른 시일내에 은행 예치를 완료한다. 퇴직금 가 지급액 산정상의 문제가 있는 소수의 경우 통장 수령 기한일을 10일간 연장 할 수 있다. 각 종업원은 예치된 금액을 전액 또는 일부를 인출하거나, 또는 예치를 계속하는 선택권을 갖는다. 은행과의 예치 절차는 외기 노조와 협의 작성한다.

b. 1979년 4월 30일 기산일 까지의 퇴직금 가 지급액 산출은 다음과 같이 한다. (1) 1979년 3월 20일 이전에 끝난 봉급 기간 최종일 이전 24개월 기간중 종업원이 받은 최고 계속 3개월 동안의 평상 임금 월 평균액을 산출 기초로하여 제 II 울표 (고용) 에의한 액수, 또는 (2) 1979년 3월 20일 이전에 끝난 봉급 기간 최종일 이전 12개월 기간중 종업원이 받은 최고 계속 3개월의 총 임금 월 평균액 (보나스는 년 총액을 월 균할) 을 산출 기초로한 1년 근무에 1개월분의 비율에 의한 액수중 높은액으로 한다.

c. 1979년 4월 30일 기산일을 기하여 퇴직금 가 지급액 수령 만기에 미달되는 근무 기간은 월할 지급한다. 월할은 다음과 같이한다. (1) 매 단 1개월의 근무 기간마다 년 누진액의 12분의 1, 또는 6개월 누진의 경우 그 누진액의 6분의 1, 에 해당되는 금액, 또는 (2) 위 제 1b(2) 항 규정에

155

따라 퇴직금 가 지급액이 산출 되었을때 매 만 1개월의 근무 기간마다 1979년 3월 20일 이전에 끝난 봉급기간 최종일 이전 12개월 동안에 종업원이 받은 최고 계속 3개월의 총 임금 (보나스는 년 총액을 월 균할) 월 평균액의 12분의 1에 해당하는 금액으로 월할한다.

d. 휴가 취득 및 감원 우선 순위에대한 근무 기간 기산 일자 (SCD) 는 현재와 동일하게 변동없이 계속한다.

e. 1979년 4월 30일 이후의 퇴직금율은 1년 근무에 대하여 1개월분의 급여율로하되 그 산출 기초는 매해 3월 31일 이전에 끝난 봉급 기간 최종일을 기하여 이날 직전 12개월 동안에 종업원이 받은 최고 계속 3개월의 총 임금 (보나스 는 년 총액을 월 균할) 월 평균액으로 한다. 앞으로 이 금액은 매년 각 종업원의 은행 구좌에 예치하되 산출 기산일인 4월 30일을 기하여 늦어도 30일 이내에 은행에 예치 완료한다.

f. 해직 당시 만 1년이 미달되어 은행에 미 예치된 부분에 대하여는 월할 지급한다. 월할은 매 만 1개월의 근무 기간으로하며 그 산출 기초는 마지막 은행 예치 기산일과 해직일 사이 기간에 받은 총 급여의 (보나스는 년 총액을 월 균할) 월 평균의 12분의 1에 해당되는 금액으로 한다.

g. 감원이 되었을때는 1개월분의 평상 임금을 추가 지급한다. 단 총 근무 기간이 1년이 미달되는 자는 제외 한다.

h. 자진 사직 및 귀책 사유로 인한 해직을 제외한 퇴직 경우, 퇴직 당시까지 종업원이 축적하여둔 병가에 대하여는 그 시간에 해당되는 기간 만큼 근무 기간으로 간주 연장하여 퇴직금 산출 근무 기간으로 한다.

i. 본 합의 각서에 정한 퇴직금은 각자의 은행에 예치와 본 합의 각서에 정한 해당 추가 혜택을 지급 완료 함으로서 주한 미군은 은행 예치 완료된 해당 기간의 근무에 대한 퇴직금 지급 의무를 전부 그리고 완전히 이행 완료 하며 종업원 또는 그의 대리인으로부터 은행 예치 완료된 해당 기간의 근무에대한 퇴직금및 해당 혜택에대한 추가 청구의 대상이 되지 않는다. 각 종업원은 이를 확인하는 서약서를 은행 선정 통고시 작성 제출한다.

156

j. 이 합의 각서에 명기된 퇴직금 제도는 전 세출 기관, 초청 정부 업자 한국인 종업원과 한국 근로단 단원에게 적용한다.

k. 본 합의 각서가 아래 제2항의 규정에 의하여 승인됨과 동시 위j 항에 명시된 신분의 종업원에게 적용되는 모든 현존 퇴직금 규정은 효력이 소멸되며 이 합의 각서의 규정으로 대체된다.

2. 본 합의 각서의 시행은 미 국방성 및 한 미 행협 합동 위원회의 승인을 조건으로 한다.

주한 미군을 위하여:	전국 외국 기관 노동 조합을 위하여:
George H Blakeslee	황규무
조지 에이. 브렉스리 인사 처장 주한 미군 합동 노무 위원회 의장	황 규 무 위원장

1979. 5. 4
일 자

159

주한 미군 근로자 퇴직금 지급 문제

1. 문제 제기

주한 미군과 전국 외기노조간에 합의된 주한 미군 한국인 세출기관 종업원 퇴직금 지불에 관한 양해각서(79. 4. 3.)는 주한 미군이 1979. 4. 30.까지의 퇴직금을 은행에 예치하고, 종업원은 동 퇴직금을 은행에 예치를 계속하거나 인출할 수 있으므로 약600억원($1.2억)이 일시에 풀릴 경우 물가 및 금융에 미치는 영향을 고려할 필요가 있음.

2. 동 각서의 교섭 경위 및 내용

1) 경 위

- 78. 9. 26. SOFA 합동위 미측간사 Kinney, 한국정부가 미국정부로 부터 퇴직금 전액을 인수할 것을 제의
- 79. 1. 24. SOFA 합동위는 퇴직금 지불문제를 노무분과위에 과제 위촉
- 79. 2. 13. 노무분과위 한.미 양위원장은 동 문제를 주한 미군과 외기노조가 협의할 것에 합의
- 79. 4. 3. 주한 미군과 외기노조는 동각서에 합의를 봄

참 고 : 비 세출기관 종업원(약6,000명)의 퇴직금 문제는 제123차 합동위원회(77. 12. 6.)

150

첨부물 제32호'비 세출자금 기관 근로자의 퇴직금 문제는 외기노조와 주한 미군간에 계속 협의하여 해결한다는 합의각서에 따라 78. 4. 1. 합의(인사규정 690-11) 로 해결됨.

2) 합의 각서 내용

- 1979. 4. 30. 까지의 퇴직금을 미측은 79. 5. 31. 까지 은행예치, 각 종업원은 인출하거나 예치하는 선택권을 갖음
- 79. 4. 30. 이후의 퇴직금율은 1 년 근무, 1 개월분의 급여율로 함.
- 동 합의 각서의퇴직금제도는 전 세출 기관, 초청청부업체 한국인 종업원과 근로단 단원에게 적용함
- 모든 현존 퇴직금 규정은 효력이 소멸되며 이 합의각서의 규정으로 대체됨
- 본 합의각서의 시행은 미 국방성 및 SOFA 합동위원회의 승인을 조건으로 함.

* 세출 기관 고용원	:	16,400명
근로단 단원	:	3,300명
초청계약자 한국인 고용원	:	600명

159

3. 동 문제에 대한 경기원.재무부 반응

경 기 원 : 동 금액이 동시에 시중으로 유출될 경우
(자금기획과) 문제가 있음.

재 무 부 : 이재국(금융정책과) : 통화정책에 영향을 줄 것 임.
외환국(외환정책과) : $1.2억의 유 입은
별 문제 없음

노 동 청 : 퇴직금 문제 지연은 근로자 동요의 우려가 있음.
(노정과) (4. 6. 노정과장 내방)

외기노조 : 동 퇴직금을 근로자들이 일시에 인출하지
않을것으로 보임 (동 퇴직금에 관한 근로자의
인출여부 및 사용용도에 관해 표본조사를 실시,
자료제출할 것임.) (4. 6. 외기노조 위원장,
사무국장 내방)

첨 부 : 1. 동합의각서
2. 인사규정 (별첨)
3. 비세출자금기관 근로자 퇴직금 지불에 관한
합의각서

160

4. 건 의

가. 동 퇴직금이 일시에 풀려도 국내 경제에 커다란 지장이 없는 경우 외기노조 - 주한 미군 과의 합의내용을 양해한다.

나. 국내 경제에 영향이 있는 경우 노무분과위에서의 서명 이전에 다음 조치를 취한다.

- 재무부와 노동청과 협의하에 외기노조를 설득한다.

  ㅇ 시차별 지급 (예 : 분기별)

  ㅇ 특별사유가 있는 경우에만 일시 지급

- 예치된 금액에 대하여는 법정 최고 이자를 지불한다.

- 외기노조 설득 기간중 국내 경제에 영향이 없는 범위에서 최대 금액을 우선 지급한다.

  ㅇ 적정 최고 금액은 재무부와 노동청과 협의 결정

- 외기노조의 설득이 용이하지 않는 경우 취급 은행을 설득하여 일시 지불을 위한 예치 요청에 응하지 않도록 한다.

- 만족할 만한 합의 또는 기간이 경과한후 노무분과위원회 절차를 취한다.

끝.

161

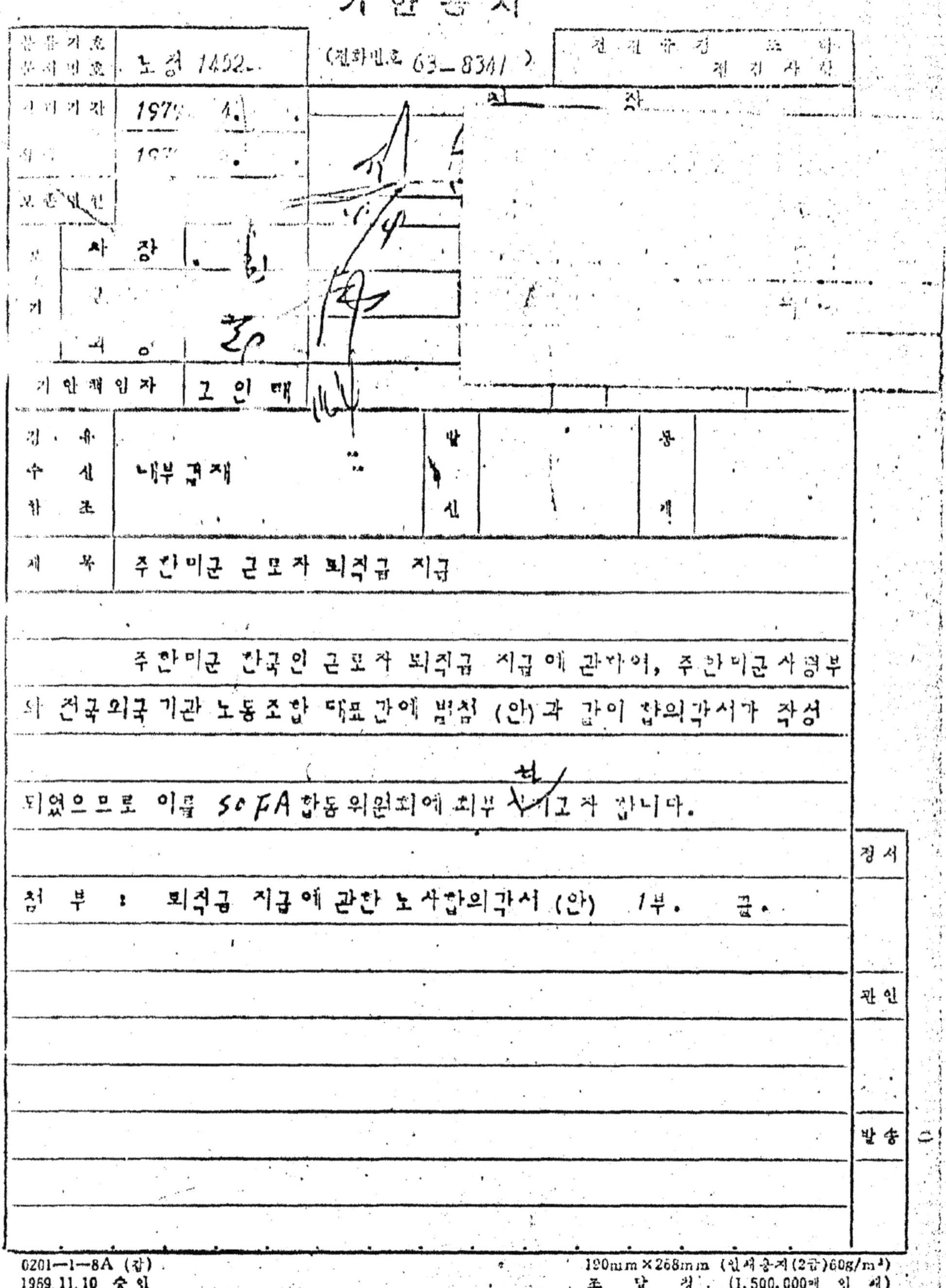

기안용지

분류기호 문서번호	노정 1452-	(전화번호 63-8341)	전결규정 조 항 전결사항
처리기간	197 . .		
시행일자	197 . .		
보존년한			
보조기관	차장 / 국장 / 과장		
기안책임자	고인배		

경유 수신 참조	내부결재	발신	통제

제목	주한미군 근로자 퇴직금 지급

주한미군 한국인 근로자 퇴직금 지급에 관하여, 주한미군 사령부와 전국외국기관 노동조합 대표간에 별첨 (안)과 같이 합의각서가 작성되었으므로 이를 SOFA 합동위원회에 회부하고자 합니다.

첨부 : 퇴직금 지급에 관한 노사합의각서 (안) 1부. 끝.

정서 / 관인 / 발송

0201-1-8A (갑) 1969.11.10 승인

190mm×268mm (인쇄용지(2급)60g/m²) 조달청 (1,500,000매 인쇄)

162

합 의 각 서

제 목: 주한 미군 한국인 세출 기관 종업원 퇴직금

1. 1979년 1월 24일자 한-미 행협 합동 위원회가 노사 분과 위원회에 분임한 과제와 이 과제 이행에 관한 1979년 2월 13일 노사 분과 위원회 한-미 양 위원장의 합의에 따라, 주한 미군과 전국 외국 기관 노동 조합은 동 문제를 협의, 이제 다음과 같이 합의한다.

a. 1979년 4월 30일로 정하는 기산일 까지의 각 종업원의 퇴직금은 국내 모든 은행중 예금 접수에 동의하는 은행중에서 각 종업원이 선정한 은행 개인 구좌에 예치한다. 노동 조합은 예금 접수에 동의하는 은행과 서비스관 리규정을 별도 교섭 약정하여, 이를 각 종업원에게 주지 시켜 각자의 은행 선정에 참고가되도록 할 수 있으나 은행 선정은 어디 까지나 각자 종업원의 의사에 맡긴다. 주한 미군은 1979년 5월 31일 까지 예금 통장을 각 종업원이 수령 할 수 있도록 가능한 한 빠른 시일내에 은행 예치를 완료 한다. 퇴직금 산정상의 문제가 있는 소수의경우 통장 수령 기한일을 10일간 연장 할 수있다. 각 종업원은 예치된 금액을 전액 또는 일부를 인출하거나, 또는 예치를 계속하는 선택권을 갖는다. 은행과의 예치 절차는 외기 노조와 협의 작성한다.

b. 1979년 4월 30일 기산일 까지의 퇴직금 산출은 다음과 같이 한다. (1) 1979년 3월 20일 이전에 끝난 봉급 기간 최종일 이전 24개월 기간중 종업원이 받은 최고 계속 3개월 동안의 평상 임금 월 평균액을 산출 기초로 하여 제II호표 (고용)에의한 액수, 또는 (2) 1979년 3월 20일 이전에 끝난 봉급 기간 최종일 이전 12개월 기간중 종업원이 받은 최고 계속 3개월의 총 임금 월 평균액 (보나스는 년 총액을 월 균분)을 산출 기초로한 1년 근무에 1개월분의 비율에 의한 액수중 높은액으로 한다.

c. 1979년 4월 30일 기산일을 기하여 퇴직금 수령 만기에 미달되는 근무 기간은 일할 지급한다. 일할은 다음과 같이한다. (1) 매 만 1개월의 근무기간마다 년 누진액의 12분의 1, 또는 6개월 누진의 경우 그 누진액의 6분의 1, 에 해당되는 금액, 또는 (2) 위 제1b(2)항 규정에 따라 퇴직금이

정과장 / 경찰 2 과장

163

산출 되었을때는 매 만 1개월의 근무 기간마다 1979년 3월 20일 이전에 끝난 봉급기간 최종일 이전 12개월 동안에 종업원이 받은 최고 계속 3개월의 총 임금 (보나스는 년총액을 월 균할) 월 평균액의 12분의 1에 해당하는 금액으로 월할한다.

d. 휴가 취득 및 감원 우선 순위에대한 근무 기간 기산 일자 (SCD)는 현재와 동일하게 변동없이 계속한다.

e. 1979년 4월 30일 이후의 퇴직금율은 1년 근무에 대하여 1개월분의 급여율로하되 그 산출 기초는 매해 3월 31일 이전에 끝난 봉급 기간 최종일을 기하여 이날 직전 12개월 동안에 종업원이 받은 최고 계속 3개월의 총 임금 (보나스는 년총액을 월 균할) 월 평균액으로 한다. 앞으로 이 금액은 매년 각 종업원의 은행 구좌에 예치하며 산출 기산일인 4월 30일을 기하여 늦어도 30일 이내에 은행에 예치 완료한다.

f. 해직 당시 만 1년이 미달되어 은행에 미 예치된 부분에 대하여는 월할 지급한다. 월할은 매 만 1개월의 근무 기간으로하며 그 산출 기초는 마지막 은행 예치 기산일과 해직일 사이 기간에받은 총 급여의 (보나스는 년 총액을 월 균할) 월 평균의 12분의 1에 해당되는 금액으로 한다.

g. 감원이 되었을때는 1개월분의 정상 임금을 추가 지급한다. 단 총 근무 기간이 1년이 미달되는자는 제외 한다.

h. 자진 사직 및 귀책 사유로 인한 해직을 제외한 퇴직 경우, 퇴직 당시 까지 종업원이 축적하여둔 병가에 대하여는 그 시간에 해당되는 기간만큼 근무 기간으로 간주 연장하여 퇴직금 산출 근무 기간으로 한다.

i. 본 합의 각서에 정한 퇴직금은 각자의 은행에 예치와 본 합의 각서에 정한 해당 추가 혜택을 지급 완료 함으로서 주한 미군은 은행 예치 완료된 해당 기간의 근무에 대한 퇴직금 지급 의무를 전부 그리고 완전히 이행 완료하며 종업원 또는 그의 대리인으로부터 은행 예치 완료된 해당 기간의 근무에대한 퇴직금및 해당 혜택에 대한 추가 청구의 대상이되지 않는다. 각 종업원은 이를 확인하는 서약서를 은행 선정 통고시 작성제출 한다.

j. 이 합의 각서에 명기된 퇴직금 제도는 전 세출 기관, 초청 청부 업체 한국인 종업원과 한국 근로단 단원에게 적용한다.

2

164

k. 본 합의 각서가 아래 제 2항의 규정에 의하여 승인됨과 동시 위 j 항에 명시된 신분의 종업원에게 적용되는 〈모든 현존 퇴직금 규정〉은 효력이 소멸되며 이 합의 각서의 규정으로 대체된다.

2. 본 합의 각서의 시행은 미 국방성 및 한 미 행협 합동 위원회의 승인을 조건으로 한다.

주한 미군을 위하여: 전국 외국 기관 노동 조합을 위하여:

조지 에이. 브랙스리
인사 처장
주한 미군 합동 노무 위원회
의장

황 규 무
위원장

1979. 4. 3
일 자

165

MEMORANDUM OF UNDERSTANDING

SUBJECT: Severance Pay Procedures for Korean National Appropriated Fund Employees of the US Forces, Korea

1. In accordance with the ROK-US Joint Committee task assigned to the Labor Subcommittee on an exigent basis on 24 January 1979 and the agreement between the US and ROK Component Chairmen of the Labor Subcommittee on 13 February 1979 for carrying out the task, the US Forces, Korea and the Foreign Organizations Employees Union now agree as follows:

a. Severance pay due to employees as of 30 April 1979 will be placed in individual employee bank accounts in a bank selected by the employee from all of those banks which have agreed to participate in the plan. The union may negotiate depositor services directly with those banks if they agree. The union may publicize the services agreed to by the banks to the employees for their consideration in bank selection; however, the individual employees selection remains optional. The USFK will complete the deposits at the earliest possible date so that the bank books are made available for pick up by the employees before 31 May 1979. In those few cases with computation difficulties, the bank book pick up date may be delayed but those delays should not exceed 10 days. Employees will have the option of withdrawing the money from the bank, in full or in part, or leaving the entire amount on deposit. Agreements with the banks on deposit procedures will be formulated in consultation with the union.

b. The severance pay for services up to the cut off date, 30 April 1979, will be calculated: (1) At the Schedule II (High Line) rate based on the average of the highest three consecutive months of normal wages received in the 24 months prior to the last day of the pay period ending before 20 March 1979; or (2) at the rate of one month's total wage for each one year of service based upon the average of total wages received for the highest three consecutive months during the 12 months prior to the last day of the pay period ending before 20 March 1979 with bonus payments prorated over the entire 12 months, whichever is greater.

c. Severance pay for services of less than one full credit period up to the cut off date, 30 April 1979, will be prorated to the last full month of service. The proration will be: (1) 1/12th of the increment between full-year credits, or 1/6th of the increment between half-year credits, for each full month of service; or (2) 1/12th of one month's total wage for each one full month of service based upon the average of total wages received for the highest three consecutive months during-

166

the 12 months prior to the last day of the pay period ending before 20 March 1979 with bonus payments prorated, if the basic computation is based upon 1b(2) above.

d. There will be no change in Service Computation Date (SCD) for leave accrual or Reduction-in-Force retention priority purposes.

e. The rate of severance pay for services after the cut off date, 30 April 1979, will be one month's average of the total wages received during the highest three consecutive months during the 12 months immediately preceding the last day of the pay period ending before 31 March of each successive year with bonus payments prorated over the entire 12 months. This amount will be placed in the employees' bank accounts annually. The deposits will be completed not later than 30 days after the annual cut off date.

f. Upon separation, the service period for which severance pay has not been deposited in the employees' accounts will be prorated to the last full month of service. The proration will be 1/12th of the average one month of total wages received during the period since the last cut off date immediately preceding the separation with bonus payments received during the previous 12 months prorated for each full month of service since the last annual cut off date.

g. In cases of separation due to Reduction-in-Force, one additional month's normal wage will be paid, provided 1 full year of service has been completed.

h. The service credit for severance pay purposes, at the time of separation by other than resignation or separation for cause, will be extended for a period equal to the total number of hours of unused sick leave accumulated by the employee.

i. A deposit of severance pay in an individual's bank as provided herein, and provision, where applicable, of the additional benefits contemplated herein shall fully discharge the entire US Forces, Korea severance pay obligation for the services for which the severance pay deposits have been made, and shall preclude any further claim for severance pay or related additional benefits by an employee or his representative based upon services for which the deposit has been made. Individual employees will execute an affidavit to this effect at the time of bank selection.

j. This revised plan will be applicable to all full-time Korean employees of Appropriated Fund activities, invited contractors, and members of the Korean Service Corps.

k. This Memorandum of Understanding, when approved in accordance with paragraph 2, below, shall supersede and replace all existing plans applicable to the employees specified in paragraph j above.

2. Implementation of this Memorandum of Understanding is subject to the prior approval of the US Department of Defense and the ROK-US Joint Committee.

FOR THE US FORCES, KOREA:

GEORGE A. BLAKESLEE
Civilian Personnel Director
Chairman
Joint Labor Affairs Committee

FOR THE FOREIGN ORGANIZATIONS EMPLOYEES UNION:

HWANG, KYU MU
President

30 Apr 1979
Date

168

d. Payment of per diem as distinct from wage is authorized, at rates prescribed in UNC/USFK/EA Reg 37-4, when an employee is required to travel or be absent from his normal place of employment or permanent duty station in connection with his official duties. Per diem is paid upon approval of a specific voucher supported by travel orders and not as part of a payroll.

e. The following procedures are applicable to employees who are paid by US Army Finance and Accounting Office, Korea:

(1) Service pay, prorated bonus and lump sum leave pay, if due, are payable with employee's final pay. Involuntarily separated employees will be paid as follows:

(a) Employees who separate during the first two weeks of their pay period will be paid on the 12th calendar day following the end of the second week of the pay period. The employee's supervisor must submit a request for accelerated payment to the Chief, KN Pay Branch, USA F&AO,K.

(b) Employees who separate during the last two weeks of their pay period will be paid on their regular payday.

(2) All other employees, except those involuntarily separated, will be paid their final pay on their normal payday. Time and attendance reports for all separated employees will be forwarded to USA F&AO,Korea, ATTN: KN Pay Branch, immediately after the last day of duty. Employees should report to the servicing finance office on payday to receive payment or provide the KN Pay Branch a proper mailing address.

8-10. Severance Pay and Social Security Benefits on Separation. Upon separation, eligible employees including employees of invited contractors, will be paid severance pay based on the amount of creditable service, type of separation, and an average of the highest basic wage earned for 3 consecutive months during the period of creditable service which will be used in computing the severance pay.

a. Eligibility.

(1) Severance pay is authorized for full time employees with 1 full year or more of continuous service who are separated (See paragraph 18-3n).

(2) The cost of stolen or damaged items, in whole or in part, when considered appropriate by the commander concerned, will be deducted from final pay of employees removed for theft of or damage to US Government property to cover the cost of stolen or damaged items. Collection will be accomplished IAW governing regulations.

(3) CPOs will check with their local military investigating authorities before determining severance pay entitlement. If the authorities indicate that the separating employee is the subject of an investigation, the CPO will obtain sufficient information on which to base his determination to authorize payment of total severance pay; or authorize the ROK legal minimum, low-line; or postpone determination, pending receipt of the interim or final investigative report. SF 50 will be annotated to include reasons for postponing severance pay determination or reducing the final pay in any amount less than employee would otherwise be authorized. In these cases, a memo for

record will be prepared by CPO technicians to support each SF 50. Information will include: Identification of CPO technician who checked with authorities; identification of the investigating authority contacted; resume of findings; and date contact was made. The memo for record will be made a permanent part of the employee's official personnel folder.

c. Creditable service.

(1) Credit is authorized for continuous service starting on or after the dates cited below, as verified in each case by the official employment records for the employee concerned, at rates specified in Appendix E to this regulation.

(a) For appropriated fund employees - 1 December 1954.

(b) Army NAF employees paid from Central or Post Welfare Funds - 30 April 1956.

(c) Invited contractor employees - 1 March 1957.

(2) Service under NTE (Temporary) appointments will be credited [illegible] such service constitutes a part of an employee's total continuous [illegible]ice. A break in service of 3 calendar days or less between NTE [illegible]ointment and indefinite appointment, or between successive NTE [illegible]intments, will not interrupt otherwise continuous service. [illegible]loyees with a break in service who received severance payment at the [illegible] of separation will start a new SCD for severance pay purposes, but [illegible]ll be treated as having continuous service for RIF purposes only.

(3) Service under part-time and intermittent appointment is not creditable.

(4) Time spent in management-approved nonpay status (LWOP) is creditable if it does not exceed 6 months in any calendar year. However, any period in LWOP status is creditable if due to job-related disability; i.e., compensation cases under Federal Employee's Compensation Act or under workmen's compensation insurance plans.

(5) Employment prior to Separation-Military and following completion of military duty - if reemployment rights have been exercised and if severance pay was not collected at time of separation - will be treated as continuous service; although the period of military service is not creditable, 1 credit month will be added to the employee's severance pay account if his military service was 2 years or more in duration. In case the employee exercises his option to collect severance pay at time of Separation-Military, his service for severance pay purposes will begin anew when he is reemployed after military service and he will not be eligible for the extra month's credit for military service.
NOTE: In cases, however, where an employee received severance payment at the time of Separation-Military under earlier severance pay plans (prior to 16 May 1966), although he will not be eligible for the 1 month credit for his military service, his creditable civilian service will not be considered to have started anew when he exercised his reemployment rights; and, on a subsequent separation, the number of months of

110

severance pay he received at time of Separation-Military will be deducted from the total months of severance pay for which he would otherwise be eligible.

(6) Creditable service is not transferable between appropriated fund and NAF, to any organization that is not covered by a servicing agreement, or between direct-hire and invited contractor employment. Severance payment will be made at time of change from one type of employment to another.

c. Severance pay schedules set forth in Appendix E are applicable to all appropriated fund, NAF, invited contractor hire and USA Recreation Services Agency, Korea employees. Schedule I applies to voluntary separation effected at employee's choice and to certain separations for cause; schedule II applies to involuntary separation, effected for reasons outside the employee's control. The legal minimum of 1 month's average wage for each year of continuous service, as specified in the ROK Labor Standard Act, will apply to separation for abandonment of position, separation for violation of the ROK national security act, and separations as outlined in subparagraph (3), below.

(1) Schedule I (Low line). This schedule applies to the following separation actions:

(a) Resignation except resignations to avoid adverse actions.

(b) Separation - Declined assignment.

(c) Separation - Disqualification.

(d) Separation - Inefficiency.

(e) Separation - Security (except violation of the ROK national Security act).

(f) Optional Retirement (see para 8-10e(1), below).

(g) Removal for administrative type offenses; e.g., sleeping on duty, traffic violations, intoxicated or drinking alcholic beverages on the job, AWOL, insubordination, violation of security or administrative regulations, separation for falsifying official document, disqualification.

(2) Schedule II (High line). This schedule applies to the following separation actions.

(a) Retirement at management's discretion (see para 8-10e(2), below).

(b) Separation - Disability (except those in paragraph 10-4(h)(5), below).

(c) Death.

(d) RIF.

(e) Resignation - RIF.

(f) Separation - Military service.

(g) Separation - Declined relocation. (See paragraph 10-4m, below.)

(3) ROK legal minimum. One month's pay for each full year of continuous service. This type of severance pay will apply on: Separation for abandonment of position, separation for violation of the ROK national security act, and removal or resignation to avoid removal for offenses which could be construed as felonies or misdemeanors; e.g., theft, bribery, collusion, assault, black marketing, violation of US-ROK currency regulations. These are the type of offenses which could involve court action although removal action wouldn't be dependent thereon.

d. Computation. Effective on an after 1 January 1972, payment will be either the amount computed in subparagraphs (1) or (2) below, whichever is the greater.

(1) Divide by three the employee's total normal wage for (a) the 3-month period immediately preceding the date of separation or (b) any three consecutive full-month periods which represent the highest wages earned during the period of creditable service on which severance pay is based; multiply the result of (a) or (b) whichever provides the greater base by the number of credit-months applicable to the type of separation and amount of creditable service as provided in Appendix E.

(2) Divide by three the employee's total wages (including premium pay, allowances, and prorated bonuses) for the 3-month period immediately preceding the date of separation; multiply the result by the number of full years of continuous service.

(3) The following guidance pertains: The 3-month period immediately prior to effective date of separation is 3 calendar months; e.g., from 15 July through 14 October if separation is effective 15 October, and any 3 consecutive full months are in terms of full months; e.g., from 1 January through 31 March or 1 February through 30 April. Normal wage includes extended workweek but is exclusive of all overtime, holiday pay, night differential, allowances and bonuses; nonpay status during the 3-month period is included as if the employee had received his normal basic pay for the period of nonpay status. Total wage includes overtime pay, night differential, holiday pay, remote area allowance, subsistence allowance, allowance for PIK, CAP, and the prorated bonuses received by the employee during this 3-month period. Remote area allowance will be calculated based on number of full weeks (7 days) during the period multiplied by 700 Won. Subsistence allowance of 600 won daily will be credited for each workday to those employees who are provided meals during the 3-month period. Allowance for PIK will be 36 won multiplied by the number of straight time hours paid. Prorated bonuses will be 37.5 percent of the normal wage earned during the period.

Thus, the format for deriving monthly base for severance pay computation is:

$$\frac{\text{NW + OT + ND + HW + Remote Area All + Sub All + All for PIK + CAP + Bonuses (Normal Wage x 37.5\%)}}{3}$$

(NW - Normal Wage, OT - Overtime, ND - Night Differential, HW - Holiday Work, PIK - Payment-In-Kind, CAP - Consolidated Allowance Payment).

(4) As indicated in paragraph 4-4d, above, employees receiving or due to receive RIF notice after 1 November but NLT 10 January may, with management approval, resign in lieu of RIF with effective date no later than the date RIF notice will be issued. Management, at its option, may also accept resignation in lieu of RIF from an employee not scheduled to be separated by RIF if such action will result in retention of an employee who would otherwise be separated by RIF. In all such cases, employees will receive the involuntary severance pay and will have their entire severance pay computed at the hourly rate received as of their last workday.

e. Special provisions for optional retirement.

(1) An employee whose application for optional retirement is approved will receive severance pay according to his age and creditable service, as follows:

(a) Age 50-54 with 15 or more years of creditable service - the appropriate rate (credit-months) in Schedule I plus 90 percent of the difference between Schedules I and II.

(b) Age 55-59 with 10 or more years service - the appropriate rate (credit-months) in Schedule I plus 100 percent of the difference between the rates in Schedules I and II.

(2) An employee who is separated by retirement at management initiative will receive severance pay according to his age and creditable service as follows:

(a) Age 50-54 with 15 or more years of creditable service - 100 percent of the high line (Schedule II) severance pay.

(b) Age 55-59 with 10 or more years of creditable service - 100 percent of the high line (Schedule II) severance pay.

(c) Age 60 regardless of years of service - 100 percent of the high line (Schedule II) severance pay for his period of creditable service.

f. As announced when the USFK severance pay plan with social security benefits was authorized in 1966, the plan is subject to review

173

and revision in the event ROKG social insurance becomes applicable at some future date.

8-11. Bonuses. a. Eligible employees will be paid the following bonuses:

(1) Summer bonus. A summer bonus will be paid to eligible employees on the rolls as of 1 May who have 3 months continuous service; i.e., 1 Feb through 30 Apr. Payment will be made in June.

(2) Chu-Suk bonus. A Chu-Suk bonus will be paid to eligible employees on the rolls as of 1 Aug who have 3 months continuous service; i.e., 1 May through 31 July. Payment will be made before the Chu-Suk holiday.

(3) Year-end Bonus. A year-end bonus will be paid to eligible employees on the rolls as of 1 November who have 3 months continuous service; i.e., 1 Aug through 31 Oct. Payment will be made in December prior to Christmas.

(4) Spring bonus. A spring bonus will be paid to eligible employees on the rolls as of 1 Feb who have 3 months continuous service; i.e., 1 Nov through 31 Jan. Payment will be made in March.

b. Eligibility:

(1) Employees will be paid the full bonus (equivalent to 1 month's pay) for spring, summer, Chu-Suk and one and one-half month's pay for year-end bonus if they are on the rolls on appropriate eligibility date and have had 3 calendar months continuous service immediately prior to that date.

(2) Part-time and intermittent employees are eligible and computation will be as indicated in subparagraph c, below.

(3) New employees with at least 1 month (30 days) of continuous service during the 3 months immediately prior to the eligibility date will be paid 1/3 of the bonus payment, as appropriate, for each 30 days of service to their credit. (Employees on the rolls during the entire month of February, however, will be considered to have met the minimum requirement for 1 month eligibility).

(4) An employee who is separated for reasons other than resignation or removal for cause will be paid the prorated value of the appropriate bonus, based on his pay status as of date of separation. The following separation actions do not carry eligibility for prorated bonus payment: Resignation, Removal, Separation-Security, and Separation-Abandoned Position.

(5) Employees with a total of more than 2 workweeks in nonpay status during the 3-month period will have their creditable service reduced by

174

Recommended Severance Pay Schedules

건의된 퇴직금율

Years of Service 근무년수	Schedule I 제 I 율	Schedule II 제 II 율	Years of Service 근무년수	Schedule I 제 I 율	Schedule II 제 II 율
[illegible]	1	1	11	17½	23
[illegible]	2	2	11½	18½	25
[illegible]	2	2	12	19½	26
[illegible]	3	3	12½	20½	28
3	3	4	13	21½	29
3½	4	5	13½	22½	31
4	4	5	14	24	32
4½	5	6	14½	25	34
[illegible]	5½	7½	15	26½	35
[illegible]	6½	9	16	29	37
[illegible]	7½	10	17	31½	38½
[illegible]	8½	11½	18	34	41
7	9½	12½	19	37	42½
[illegible]	10½	14	20	40	43½
[illegible]	11½	15	21	42	45
8½	12½	16½	22	44	46
9	13½	17½	23	46	47½
9½	14½	19	24	48	48½
10	15½	20	25	50	50
10½	16½	22			

Length of Service for Severance Pay Purposes will be computed from 1 December 1954, for appropriated fund employees and for nonappropriated fund employees of Special Services, Korea Regional Exchange and Army-Air Force Motion Picture Service, subject to verification in each employee's case by official employment records.

퇴직금 계산을 위한 근무 년수는 1954년 12월 1일로부터 계산하되 영달자금 종업원 및 특별관계과 교역처와 육공군 영화사업 관계의 비영달자금 종업원이 해당되며 해당 종업원의 고용사실을 입증할수있는 자료가 있어야한다.

43rd JC (Incl 2 to Incl 20)
23 Oct 69

41

195

These minutes are considered as official documents pertaining to both Governments and will not be released without mutual agreement

합 의 각 서

1. 전국외국기관노동조합은 주한미군이 제의한 1978년 7월 1일부 시행 임금인상 안을 다음과 같이 수락한다.

가. 조정된 각급시간 급여액과 종합수당(CAP) 외는 별표 1과 같다.

나. 보나스를 0.5 개월분 추가하되 주한미군의 선택에 따라 추석 또는 연말 보나스에 추가 지급한다.

다. 언어수당(PIN)을 사무직 및 기능직은 36원에서 48원으로 그리고 해상직은 5원에서 7원으로 인상한다.

라. 해상 급식 수당을 1,100원에서 1,170원으로 인상한다.

2. 주한미군과 외국기관노동조합은 의료보험제도를 조속한 시일내에 시행할 수 있도록 계속 연구한다.

3. 주한미군과 외국기관노동조합은 근무시간 감축 또는 감동자가 원할때 퇴직금을 지급하는 문제를 조속한 시일내에 시행할 수 있도록 계속 연구 한다.

4. 주한미군의 차기 임금조사 승인 요청시 임금조사에 관련된 전국외국기관노동조합의 의견과 요청사항은 즉시에 제출되면 태평양지구 사령부 합동 노사정책위원회에 회부 적절한 검토와 고려를 받도록한다.

5. 한국 노동청에 계류중인 외국기관노동조합의 쟁의는 이로소 철회한다.

1978. 7. 1.

주한미군사령부를 대표하여	전국외국기관노동조합을 대표하여
조오지 에이.블렉스리	황 규 무
합동노무위원회 의장	위 원 장

한국노동청을 대표하여

한 진 희

노 정 국 장

8250

126th JC (Incl 24)
20 Jul 78

REPUBL
MANUAL
LOCALI

KMB
GRADE

1
2
3
4
5
6
7
8
9
10
11
12
13

Eff

D.
For
US

116

These minutes are considered as official documents pertaining to both Governments and will not be released without mutual agreement

US FORCES WAGE SCHEDULE

REPUBLIC OF KOREA
KWB (KWB) WAGE SCHEDULE
LOCALLY HIRED, NON-US CITIZEN EMPLOYEES

HOURLY RATES (KOREAN WON)

KWB GRADE	STEP A	STEP B	STEP C	STEP D	STEP E	STEP F	STEP G	STEP H	STEP I	STEP J	CONSOLIDA ALLOWANC PAYMENT
1	255	268	280	292	304	316	328	340	353	365	36
2	312	327	342	357	372	387	402	417	432	446	43
3	370	387	405	422	440	458	475	493	510	528	50
4	427	447	467	488	508	528	549	569	589	610	57
5	483	506	529	552	575	598	621	644	667	690	64
6	610	639	668	697	726	755	784	813	842	871	80
7	703	737	770	804	837	870	904	937	971	1004	92
8	797	835	873	911	949	987	1025	1063	1101	1139	104
9	891	934	976	1019	1061	1103	1146	1188	1231	1273	115
10	984	1031	1078	1125	1172	1219	1266	1313	1360	1406	127
11	1078	1129	1180	1232	1283	1334	1386	1437	1488	1540	139
12	1236	1294	1353	1412	1471	1530	1589	1648	1706	1765	158
13	1394	1460	1526	1593	1659	1725	1792	1858	1924	1991	178

Effective date: 1 July 1978

D. G. HASENYAGER
Foreign Labor Officer
US Army CINCPAC Support Group

JACK V. COMPTON
Director of Civilian Personnel
US Pacific Air Forces

HERBERT DAUBER
Fleet Civilian Personn
Director,
US Pacific Fleet

8251

126th JC (Incl 24)
20 Jul 78

177

These minutes are considered as official documents pertaining to both Governments and will not be released without mutual agreement

US FORCES WAGE SCHEDULE

REPUBLIC OF KOREA
NON-MANUAL (KGS) WAGE SCHEDULE
LOCALLY HIRED, NON-US CITIZEN EMPLOYEES

HOURLY RATES (KOREAN WON)

KGS GRADE	STEP A	STEP B	STEP C	STEP D	STEP E	STEP F	STEP G	STEP H	STEP I	STEP J	CONSOLIDATED ALLOWANCE PAYMENT
1	269	282	294	307	320	333	346	358	371	384	38
2	358	375	392	409	426	443	460	477	494	511	49
3	449	470	491	513	534	555	577	598	619	641	60
4	538	564	590	615	641	667	692	718	744	769	71
5	628	658	688	718	748	778	808	838	868	898	83
6	717	752	786	820	854	888	922	956	991	1025	94
7	807	846	884	923	961	999	1038	1076	1115	1153	105
8	898	941	983	1026	1069	1112	1155	1197	1240	1283	116
9	1102	1155	1207	1260	1312	1365	1417	1469	1522	1574	142
10	1308	1370	1432	1495	1557	1619	1682	1744	1806	1868	168
11	1513	1585	1657	1729	1801	1873	1945	2017	2089	2161	193
12	1782	1866	1951	2036	2121	2206	2291	2376	2460	2545	227
13	2046	2144	2241	2339	2436	2533	2631	2728	2826	2923	260

Effective Date: 1 July 1978

D. G. HASENYAGER Foreign Labor Officer US Army CINCPAC Support Group	JACK V. COMPTON Director of Civilian Personnel US Pacific Air Forces	HERBERT DAUBER Fleet Civilian Personnel Director US Pacific Fleet

8252

126th JC (Incl 24)
20 Jul 78

198

These minutes are considered as official documents pertaining to both Governments and will not be released without mutual agreement

US FORCES WAGE SCHEDULE

EPUBLIC OF KOREA
A[illegible] (NM) WAGE SCHEDULE
[illegible]CALLY HIRED, NON-US CITIZEN EMPLOYEES

HOURLY RATES (KOREAN WON)

KN GRADE	STEP A	STEP B	STEP C	STEP D	STEP E	STEP F	STEP G	STEP H	STEP I	STEP J	CONSOLIDATED ALLOWANCE PAYMENT
1	303	318	332	347	361	375	390	404	419	433	91
2	360	378	395	412	429	446	463	480	498	515	108
3	417	436	456	476	496	516	536	556	575	595	125
4	475	497	520	542	565	588	610	633	655	678	141
5	531	556	581	607	632	657	683	708	733	758	158
6	588	616	644	672	700	728	756	784	812	840	175
7	660	692	723	755	786	817	849	880	912	943	196
8	884	926	968	1010	1052	1094	1136	1178	1220	1262	262
9	1186	1243	1299	1356	1412	1469	1525	1581	1638	1694	351
10	1262	1322	1382	1442	1502	1562	1622	1682	1742	1802	374

Effective Date: 1 July 1978

D. G. HASENYAGER
Foreign Labor Officer
US Army CINCPAC Support Group

JACK V. COMPTON
Director of Civilian Personnel
US Pacific Air Forces

HERBERT DAUBER
Fleet Civilian Personnel Director
US Pacific Fleet

8253

126th JC (Incl 24)
20 Jul 78

199

These minutes are considered as official documents pertaining to both Governments and will not be released without mutual agreement

MEMORANDUM OF UNDERSTANDING

SUBJECT: Severance Pay Plan for Nonappropriated Fund Employees of United States Forces Korea

1. Further consultation on the matter of NAF severance pay has taken place as agreed to by USFK, FOEU, and ALA in the Memorandum of Understanding which resolved the 1977 wage dispute. This consultation has resulted in USFK and FOEU agreement to establish a uniform Korea-wide severance pay plan for USFK nonappropriated fund Korean employees as prescribed by UNC/USFK/EA CPR 690-11 (Incl 1).

2. Provisions of UNC/USFK/EA CPR 690-11 will become effective as specified by paragraph 2 of that regulation, upon endorsement of this memorandum of understanding by the Administrator of Labor Affairs, ROKG, and acceptance of this Memorandum of Understanding and its inclosure as agreed to SOFA minutes by the ROK US SOFA Joint Committee.

3. This Memorandum of Understanding, less its inclosure will be published as an appendix to UNC/USFK/EA CPR 690-11.

FOR THE UNITED STATES FORCES KOREA:

George A Blakeslee
GEORGE A. BLAKESLEE
Civilian Personnel Director
Chairman, Joint Labor Affairs Committee

FOR THE FOREIGN ORGANIZATIONS EMPLOYEES UNION:

황규무
HWANG, KYU MU
President

FOR THE ADMINISTRATOR OF LABOR AFFAIRS:

Tun, Young Bae

8140

125th JC (Incl 19)
4 May 78

180

These minutes are considered as official documents pertaining to both Governments and will not be released without mutual agreement

*UNC/USFK/EA CPR 690-11

HEADQUARTERS
UNITED NATIONS COMMAND
UNITED STATES FORCES KOREA
EIGHTH UNITED STATES ARMY
APO SAN FRANCISCO 96301

CIVILIAN PERSONNEL REGULATION
NUMBER 690-11 — 1 April 1978

CIVILIAN PERSONNEL
Nonappropriated Fund Severance Pay

Supplements to this regulation require prior approval of HQ, UNC/USFK/EUSA, ATTN: CPJ, unless the content of such supplements only spells out operating procedures.

1. Purpose. This regulation provides policies and procedures for the severance pay plan for full-time Korean civilian nonappropriated fund (NAF) employees of United States Forces Korea (USFK) NAF activities in accordance with Appendix A of this regulation.

2. Scope. Provisions of this regulation apply to full-time NAF Korean civilian employees of USFK. They apply as of 1 April 1979 for US Air Force (AF) NAF employees and are effective 1 April 1978 for other USFK NAF employees, to include those of the Korea Area Exchange (KOAX).

3. Responsibilities. a. USFK NAF activity commanders/directors will implement provisions of this regulation.

b. The Civilian Personnel Director, UNC/USFK/EUSA, will provide final interpretation of provisions of this regulation and serve as the principal point of contact for liaison with Republic of Korea Government (ROKG) officials, employee organizations, and others concerning NAF severance pay matters.

c. Civilian personnel officers will document personnel actions to comply with provisons of this regulation, provide employee counseling and staff assistance to commanders/directors as needed to interpret and administer provisions of this regulation.

d. Employees will familiarize themselves with contents of this regulation, and sign a bilingual statement (Appendix B) to show that they understand and agree to such contents as a condition of employment.

4. Definitions. a. Total average monthly wage. The monthly average of 3-months pay including base pay, premium pay, allowances, and prorated bonuses earned during the most recent 3-month period for which severance pay is being computed.

---

*This regulation supersedes Section 6, UNC/USFK/EA CPR 690-2, 2 Apr 74, and KOAX Bulletin 362 (15-28), 29 Mar 77, effective 1 Apr 78. It also supersedes 314AD Reg 40-8, 5 Nov 76, effective 1 Apr 79.

8141

125th JC (Incl 19)
4 May 78

181

b. Normal pay. The monthly average of 3 months of base pay including pay for extended workweek but excluding overtime, premium pay, allowances, and bonuses earned during the most recent 3-month period for which severance pay is being computed.

c. Twenty-four month variable installment account. An account covering a period of 24 months with eight quarterly deposits of unpredetermined amounts.

d. Twenty-four month special term account. An account covering 24 months with one deposit of a specific amount at the beginning of the 24-month term.

5. Policies. a. Upon conversion to this plan, eligible employees are to be paid all severance pay accrued prior to such conversion.

b. Severance pay is to be paid quarterly following conversion to this plan by means of deposits to employees' Korean bank accounts.

c. Severance pay accrued subsequent to conversion to this plan and deposited in the bank may be withdrawn, transferred, or used as collateral by employees only under emergency conditions requiring large expenditures of funds, and/or maturity of 24-month special term accounts. Withdrawal or transfer except under these provisions shall constitute resignation by the employee.

d. This severance pay plan is applicable to all full-time USFK NAF employees and activities, to include full-time employees of the KOAX.

e. Employees involuntarily separated through no fault of their own will receive an additional month of normal pay in addition to severance pay otherwise authorized under terms of this regulation, provided 1 full year of service has been completed at the time of separation.

f. Employees/applicants must sign a statement (Appendix B) acknowledging that they understand and agree to the provisions of this regulation as a condition of employment or continued employment.

g. Except for that specified in subparagraph e, above, severance pay shall be computed based on 1 month of severance pay for each full year of continuous full-time service and the employee's total average monthly wage which is based on the most recent 3-month period. Prorated computations shall be at 1/12 of a month of severance pay for each full month of service.

h. Service computation dates for severance pay purposes will be changed quarterly to the date immediately following the last day of the most recent quarter for which severance pay has been paid.

These minutes are considered as official documents pertaining to both Governments and will not be released without mutual agreement

i. Interest on employees' Korean bank accounts shall be paid by banks at their prevailing rates for those types of accounts specified by this regulation.

j. Severance pay accrued after conversion to this plan shall initially be deposited in employee's 24-month variable installment savings account and upon maturity of this account, the proceeds will be redeposited to 24-month special term accounts. At maturity of this latter account, the proceeds of such account may be withdrawn or redeposited at the employee's option. This cycle is to be repeated continuously.

k. Employees removed for cause involving theft or misappropriation of employing activity assets will forfeit that amount of final wages, bonuses earned, lump sum payment for accrued leave, and undeposited severance pay if needed to satisfy any financial liability to the employing activity.

l. Employees must complete 1 year of full-time continuous service to be eligible for severance pay.

6. Procedures. a. On and after 1 April 1978, EUSA and Navy employees may withdraw bank deposited severance pay for service performed prior to 1 July 1977. Severance pay earned prior to 1 April 1978 by EUSA and Navy employees and retained by employing activities will be paid direct to employees NLT 31 May 1978. Such payment to EUSA Morale Support Fund employees will be at the high line rate specified by UNC/USFK/EA CPR 690-1. Severance pay earned by KOAX employees prior to 1 April 1978 and retained by KOAX will be paid direct to employees NLT 31 May 1978. Upon completion of the current AF severance pay bank deposit cycle in November 1978, employees of AF NAF activities may withdraw bank deposited severance pay. Severance pay accrued by AF employees for service subsequent to completion of the current bank deposit cycle, and prior to 1 April 1979, will be paid direct to employees NLT 31 May 1979, prorated as provided for by paragraph 5g, above.

b. Severance pay earned for Army, Navy, and KOAX employees for service subsequent to 31 March 1978, and that earned by AF employees subsequent to 31 March 1979, will be paid quarterly to eligible employees by deposit to their 24-month variable installment bank accounts. Such pay will be computed based on guidance provided by paragraph 5g, above, and will be forwarded by employing activities to reach banks prior to the end of the second month following close of the quarter. Letters of transmittal will accompany remittances listing employees by name, designated bank, Korean identification number, employing activity, the amount of severance pay forwarded for each employee, and each employee's bank account number if an account has been established at that time.

c. Upon receipt of direct payments of severance pay mentioned in paragraph 6a, above, employees will be required to sign a statement

8143

125th JC (Incl 19)
4 May 78

183

(Appendix B) indicating that they understand and agree to terms of this regulation as a condition of continued employment. Employees will also designate their bank of choice from one of those listed at Appendix C and approved by the employing activity to serve as a depository for their severance pay when completing this statement. The statement will be prepared and signed in three copies, one each for the employee, the employing activity, and the personnel folder. Applicants tentatively selected for appointment will be required to complete and sign the statement prior to appointment. Refusal to do so will indicate an unwillingness to conform to conditions of employment and justifies nonselection. If a current employee refuses to sign the statement, the requesting official will annotate all copies of the statement accordingly showing the date of refusal, and prepare a request for personnel action in triplicate showing the nature of action as Separation - Failure to Accept Employment Conditions. A copy will be given to the employee to serve as a 30-day advance notice of separation, and the employee will be asked to acknowledge receipt of the copy. The original copy will be forwarded to the civilian personnel officer for use in preparing the notice of personnel action to effect the separation to be effective 30 calendar days following the date of employee's receipt of advance notice. The remaining copy may be retained by the employing activity. A review of personnel folders will be made annually to insure that the statement prescribed by Appendix B is on file.

d. Employing activities should enter into agreements with appropriate banks listed at Appendix C to serve as depositories for their employee's severance pay. Consideration will be given to the geographical dispersal of the workforce in determining which bank(s) are appropriate for a specific employing activity. A standardized agreement designed to comply with terms of this regulation and which each bank has indicated as being acceptable is at Appendix D.

e. One month of severance pay for employees who complete 1 continuous year of full-time service subsequent to conversion to this plan will be paid as of the end of the quarter in which the year of service is completed, and deposited into employees' 24-month variable installment accounts NLT the end of the second month following close of that quarter. Payment will be prorated for each full month of service with no credit given for periods of less than 1 month. The service computation date for severance pay purposes will then become the day immediately following the end of the quarter for which severance pay is paid.

f. Severance pay accrued subsequent to conversion to this plan and deposited in banks or retained by the employing activity may be withdrawn, transferred, or used as collateral only under conditions specified elsewhere in this regulation. Withdrawal, transfer, or use as collateral under other conditions will constitute the employee's resignation, and the employing activity will take action to separate the employee on the basis of said resignation upon being notified by the bank or learning of the unauthorized use of the severance pay monies. Approval to withdraw, transfer, or use as collateral in case of an emergency requiring a large expenditure must be requested in writing by the employee and approved in writing by the civilian personnel officer of the employing activity prior to any such transaction. Determination as to what constitutes a genuine emergency will be made by employing activities.

The proponent agency of this regulation is the Office of the Civilian Personnel Director. Users are invited to send comments and suggested improvements on DA Form 2028 (Recommended Changes to Publications and Blank Forms) to the CINC, UNC/USFK/EUSA, ATTN: CPJ-PM, APO 96301.

FOR THE COMMANDER IN CHIEF:

OFFICIAL:

BEN OWENS, JR.
CPT, USA
Asst AG

ROBERT C. KINGSTON
Major General, USA
Chief of Staff

4 Appendixes
A. Memorandum of Understanding
B. Severance Pay Statement
C. List of Banks
D. Memorandum of Understanding

DISTRIBUTION:
R
200 - HQ, 51st Combat Spt Gp (PACAF), APO 96570
50 - Seoul ACPO, APO 96301
30 - Taegu ACPO, APO 96218
20 - Pusan ACPO, APO 96259
20 - Ascom ACPO, APO 96483
20 - I Corps ACPO, APO 96358
30 - Camp Casey ACPO, APO 96224
20 - Camp Page ACPO, APO 96208
25 - Camp Humphreys ACPO, APO 96271
20 - CPO, KOAX, APO 96301
2 - HQDA, DAPE-CPR, WASH DC 20310
2 - USA CINCPAC SPT GP, FT SHAFTER HI 96858
100 - CPJ-PM
5 - AJ-PMB-P
6 - ACJ-AP
100 - PPCK

8145

125th JC (Incl 19)
4 May 78

135

These minutes are considered as official documents pertaining to both Governments and will not be released without mutual agreement

SEVERANCE PAY STATEMENT

I, the undersigned, understand and agree:

1. To terms and conditions of UNC/USFK/EA CPR 690-11 and any supplementing directives as conditions of employment or continued employment with ____________, a nonappropriated fund activity of the
(name of employing activity)
United States Forces Korea. Paragraphs 2,3 and 4 of this statement apply to employees on the rolls at the time UNC/USFK/EA CPR 690-11 becomes effective. Other provisions of this statement applies to all employees.

2. That, as a condition of my continued employment with ____________
(name of employing
________, the severance pay plan as identified in UNC/USFK/EA CPR 690-2,
activity)
Section 6, and supplementing directives will be cancelled as of ________
(date)
and that beginning ________, I will be under a different severance pay
(date)
plan as explained below.

3. That, in connection with the change of the severance pay plan, the severance pay due me as of ________ has been computed and paid in full
(date)
according to the procedures in UNC/USFK/EA CPR 690-2, Section 6, and supplementing directives.

4. That I have no further claim for severance pay for the service prior to ________.
(date)

5. That severance pay paid to me quarterly under terms of UNC/USFK/EA CPR 690-11 and supplementing directives constitute my sole severance entitlement for service rendered to my employer named above. I will not submit any claim for additional severance pay, permit/authorize any individual, organization, or firm to do so in my behalf.

6. That, effective ________, severance pay is to be paid to me
(date)
quarterly by deposit to my individual account with the ____________
(name of bank and
________ under terms specified by UNC/USFK/EA CPR 690-11 and any
location)
supplementing directives.

7. That bank deposited severance pay may be withdrawn, used as collateral, or transferred only under terms of UNC/USFK/EA CPR 690-11 and any supplementing directives, and that withdrawal or transfer on my part except under such terms will constitute my resignation from employment with my employer named above.

8146

Appendix B

125th JC (Incl 19)
4 May 78

186

8. That my service computation date for severance pay purposes will be adjusted and verified quarterly to coincide with the quarterly severance payment cycle and will be fixed as the day immediately following the most recent cycle. That for severance pay purposes only, I will be separated from employment with my employer named above on the last day of each quarterly severance pay cycle and be reemployed the following day without a break in service, and this separation will not change other conditions of my employment. The foregoing quarterly separation/reemployment actions will be an internal administrative procedures and will not necessitate the issuing of personnel action documents.

퇴직금 진술서

본인은 다음 사항을 이해하고 동의한다.

1. 주한미군 비충당 자금기관 ____________________ (근무 직장명) 과의 고용조건및 계속 고용으로서 주한미군 인사규정 690-11의 규정및 약정과 보충 지시서에 따른다. 본 진술서의 2,3및 4조는 주한미군 인사규정 690-11이 효력을 발생할 당시의 종업원에게만 해당되고, 다른 조항은 모든 종업원에게 해당된다.

2. 본인의 ____________________ (근무 직장명) 과의 고용 조건으로 주한미군 인사규정 690-2, 6조와 보충 지시서에 명시된 퇴직금 제도를 ______________ (일자) 부로 취소하고 ______________ (일자) 부로 아래 설명한 다른 퇴직금 제도를 갖게된다.

3. 이 퇴직금 제도 변화에 따라 ______________ (일자) 현재까지의 본인의 퇴직금은 주한미군 인사규정 690-2, 6조와 보충한 지시서에 의거 '계산되고 지불하게 된다.

4. 본인은 ______________ (일자) 이전 근무에 대한 퇴직금 청구권이 없다.

5. 주한미군 인사규정 690-11및 보충 지시서에 의거하여 본인에게 기분(3 개월)으로 지불되는 퇴직금은 본인의 근무에 대하여 지불되는 것이며, 그 이상의 퇴직금은 요구하지 않을 것이며, 또 본인을 대신하여 다른사람이나 단체및 회사로 하여금 청구행위를 허용하지 않는다.

8147

125th JC (Incl 19)
4 May 78

Appendix B

187

These minutes are considered as official documents pertaining to both Governments and will not be released without mutual agreement

6. 주한미군 인사규정 690-11 및 보충지시서에 의거하여 ________ (일자) 부로 본인의 퇴직금은 ________ (은행명 및 소재지) 에 본인 명의로 기본 (3 개월) 마다 예치된다.

7. 주한미군 인사규정 690-11 및 보충지시서에 의거 은행에 예치한 퇴직금을 인출할수있고, 담보로 할수있고 또 대체할수 있다. 상기규정에 의거하지않고 인출 또는 대체했을 경우에는 본인이 주한미군에서 자원 사직하는 것으로 간주된다.

8. 본인의 퇴직금 기산일은 기본 지불로 인하여 새로 조정될 것이며, 새 기산일은 기본 지불 다음날로 된다. 퇴직금 은행 예치로 인하여 기본 마지막날로 퇴직되고 연속해서 다음날로 재 고용된다. 그러나 이 퇴직은 본인의 고용조건에 아무런 변화가 없다. 위에 언급한 기본마다 퇴직및 재고용 조치는 내부적인 행정조치이며 정식인사 조치서를 발급하지 않는다.

____
Employing Organization
근무처명

____
Typed or Printed Name
직원성명

____
KN ID Number
주민증 번호

____
Signature of Employee
직원서명

____
Date
일자

____
Signature, Title, and Grade of Witness
인서인의 서명, 직위및 급수

____
Date
일자

8148

125th JC (Incl 19)
4 May 78

Appendix B

188

유

법 무 부

법무 810- (70-2778) 79. 5. 29.

수신 외무부장관

제목 주한미군 종업원 퇴직금 가지급 합의각서 시행

미안 723-19184 (79. 5. 10) 주한 미군 종업원 퇴직금 가지급 합의각서 시행과 관련하여 근로기준법에 저촉되는 사항이 없음을 회신합니다. 끝.

법 무 부 장 관

189

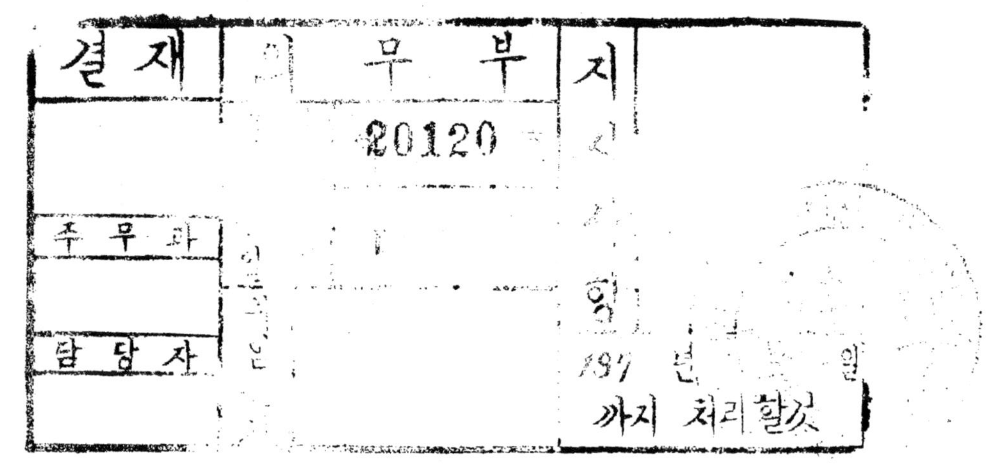

결재 | 외 무 부 | 지
20120
주무과
담당자
197 년 월 일
까지 처리할것

190

미 주 국

1979 . 6 . 19 .

안보과	담 당	과 장	심의관	국 장	차관보	차 관	장 관
	煥						

제 목 쟁의 발생 보고 및 조정의뢰서 통고

요 약 전국외기노조는 79.6.11.자로 노동청 및 중앙노동위원회에 하청 전환을 반대하는 노동쟁의를 조정하여 줄것을 의뢰하였음을 미 8군측에 통보하였음.

* 참 고 : SOFA 17조 (노무조항)에 따른 노동쟁의 조정 절차

1. 1차로 쟁의는 조정을 위하여 대한민국 노동청에 회부되어야 함.

2. 1항에 의해 해결되지 않은경우 그 문제는 합동위원회에 회부됨. 합동위원회는 이의 해결을 특별위원회에 회부할수 있음.

3. 쟁의가 상기절차에 의해 해결되지 않은경우, 합동위원회는 신속한 절차가 뒤따를 것이라는 확증하에 쟁의를 해결함. 합동위 결정은 구속력을 가짐.

조치사항

191

전 국 외 국 기 관 노 동 조 합

노 전79-126호 793-1407 1979. 6. 11

신 : 주한미군 사령관

조 : 인사국장

목 : 쟁의발생보고및 조정의뢰서(통고)

조합 제9차 중앙위원회(79. 5. 31) 결의에 의거 임금인상관련 "쟁의 보고및 조정의뢰서"를 별첨과같이 정부당국에 제출하였기 통고하오니 간 불미스러운일이 야기되지 않도록 임금인상계획(부산항만하역)을 하여 주시기 바랍니다.

첨 : "쟁의 발생보고및 조정의뢰서" 사본1부. 끝

위 원 장 강 영 구

192

전 국 외 국 기 관 노 동 조 합

전외노 제79-119호 79-1407 1979. 6. 6

수 신 노동청장, 중앙노동위원회 위원장

제 목 노동쟁의 발생보고 조정의뢰서

당사자

1. 노동단체

전국외국기관노동조합

위원장 강 구 무

서울특별시 용산구 갈월동 17-1

2. 사용자

주한미군 사령부

사령관 육군대장 존 다불유 베시

서울특별시 용산구 한강로 1가

위 당사자간에 노동쟁의가 발생하였기 한미 행정협정 제17조 제1항 4의 가 및 노동쟁의 조정법 제16조 1항의 규정에 의하여 다음과같이 보고 하오니 소정의 절차에 의하여 조정하여 주시기 바랍니다.

1. 노동쟁의 발생 사업장명과 소재지

주한미군 사령부

서울특별시 용산구 한강로 1가

193

2. 사업의 종류

주한미군 지원업무

3. 노동쟁의 참가 인원수

남 18,006명 여 2,318명 계 20,324

4. 안전보호 시설유무

(일부 있음)

5. 노동쟁의 발생년월일

1979. 5. 31

6. 요구조건 기타 쟁의 목적

(1) 주한미군 종업원 하청전환 기획을 철회할것.

(2) 현지 발생된 부산 항만하역 하청전환을 즉각 철회할것.

7. 노동쟁의에 관한 결의내용

조합은 79. 5. 31. 중앙위원회의를 개최하고 다음과같이 쟁의하기로 결의하다

(1) 하청전환 적극반대 쟁의결의

투쟁위원회 구성은 중앙위원및 상집으로 한다.

(2) 지역 투쟁위원회 구성은 지부 운영위원및 상집으로 한다.

(3) 행동대원을 아래와같이 구성한다.

당사지부 100명, 기타지부 50명

서울, 케이에스씨지부 100명

(4) 쟁의 발생보고를 노동청, 주한미군 당국에 제출한다.

194

8. 기타사항

1) 주한미군 당국에 지난 78년 5월 실시코저하던 미부산 항만하역 직속업무를 전반적으로 하청으로 운영하려는 계획을 조합측의 강력한 반대로 일단보류 되었으나 현재 조합측과 아무런 협의없이 또다시 79. 7. 1일자로 하청 수의 계약을 체결하여 동년 10월 1일부로 하청 기획을 수립함은 노사간에 신의를 저버린 부당한 처사이므로 이를 즉각 철회하여 줄것을 수차 노사회의에서 요청한바 있으나 고용주측은 이를 철회하지 않고있음.

2) 고용주측은 상기지역은 물론 전국적으로 하청전환을 시도하려는 기획을 하고 있으므로 조합은 부득히 쟁의신고에 이른것입니다.

유첨 : 1. 하청기획 검위 1부

2. 조합원 현황표 1부 끝

위 원 장 정 규 무

195

하 청 계 획 경 위

1. 현대상지역 : 부산지역(미항만 하역업무 종업원)
2. 대상인원 : 약250명
3. 하청기간 : 79. 7. 1 수위기능, 동년 12. 1 하역
4. 수위계약 예상업체
   (1) 한진
   (2) 일진
   (3) 대한통운
   (4) 국제실업
5. 경위
   (1) 79. 4. 9 부산지부 하청철회요청공문 접수 (별첨)
   (2) 79. 4. 27 노사회의에서 철회요청
   (3) 79. 5. 25 "

유첨 : "부산지부 하청철회요청" 사본1부

196

2. 지부조직현황

1979. 4. 30 현재

지부명	대표자	분회수	조합원수		
			계	남	여
계		[illegible]	20,324	18,006	2,318
서울	권영소	41	4,691	3,765	926
의정부	장수덕	11	830	761	69
동두천	유용우	14	1,617	1,428	189
파주	박성목	16	980	861	119
부평	조명구	12	753	692	66
오산	홍준의	29	1,332	1,161	171
부산	고형건	17	1,156	1,035	[illegible]
강원	김진협	7	454	448	6
평택	김칠수	18	1,576	1,460	116
대구	신상훈	21	1,277	1,035	242
	김규호	23	3,318	3,311	7
군산	고석현	12	738	562	176
왜관	하점석	23	[illegible]	1,047	96
전남	배진기	10	313	291	22
제2직할분회	송영복	4	[illegible]	[illegible]	[illegible]

197

전국 외기노조 부산지부장 귀하

79. 7. 10. 자로 보내주신 탄원서는 잘 받았읍니다. 당부에서는 이미 전국 외기노조를 통하여 귀지부에서 발생하고 있는 노무 문제에 관한 소식을 들은바 있어 ~~이미~~ 본 문제에 관심을 가지고 있던 터 입니다.

당부에서는 ~~이미~~ ~~SOFA 합동위 미국측 관사에게~~ 그간 비공식으로 미국측에 대하여 본 문제의 원만한 해결을 촉구한 바 있읍니다.

~~이미~~ 귀하께서도 잘 알고 계시겠지만, 현행 ~~SOFA 조약~~ 주둔군지위협정 제17조 노무 조항은 주한 미군과 전국 외기노조 사이에 발생된 노무문제는 1차로 ~~조정을 위하여~~ 노동청에 회부되어야 하고 노동청의 중재에 의해서도 해결되지 아니 한때에는 ~~SOFA~~ 한미 합동위원회를 통하여 해결을 한다고 규정하고 있읍니다.

따라서 당부에서는 노동청에 대하여 본 문제의 원만한 해결을 위한 협조를 요구하였으며, 노동청에서도 현재 이에 필요한 조치를 강구하고 있는 것으로 알고 있읍니다.

~~SOFA~~ 한미 합동위에 안건이 상정되는 경우 당부에서는 물론 본 문제의 해결에 최선을 다할 것임을 약속드리며 귀지부 조합원들의 건승을 기원합니다.

79. 7. 26
11:00 발송.

양 고 재	안보담당관	79년 7월 20일	담당	과장	심의관	국장
			煥	(서명)	(서명)	(서명)

198

탄 원 서

전국외국기관노동조합
부 산 지 부
부산시 동구 범일2동 124-4번지
(전화 : 부산 68-3406)

199

탄 원 서

전국민의 숙원인 민주적인 국토통일을 이룩하고 자립경제확립으로 번영된 조국건설과 국민복지 향상을 위하여 불철주야 몰두하시는 **외무부 장관 님** 께 진심으로 경의를 표하는 바입니다. 우리들은 30년동안 주한미군 부산 항만수송업무에 종사하면서 국가적으로는 인력제공으로 막대한 외화획득의 역군으로서 총력안보에 투철한 이념으로 거족적인 대 약진운동인 새마을운동에 선봉적으로 참여하여 내일의 영광된 조국건설에 온갖 노력을 다 하고 있읍니다. 그러나 근래에와서 미군들은 예산절약 계획으로 부산 부두지역 미군직속업무를 하청으로 전환 운영코저 함으로서 30년동안 종사해온 우리들 257명의 해당 종업원들은 직장을 잃고 부양가족과 함께 거리를 헤매는 처지에 놓이게 될뿐아니라 국가적으로도 막대한 외화획득에 손실을 가지게 되는 것입니다.

이와 같은 실정을 구체적으로 말씀드리자면 25년 전부터 현재까지 미군수 화물을 본선에서 하역하고 화차 또는 자동차에 실어주는 부두하역작업만을 하청업자인 국제실업주식회사가 작업하던 것을 미군의 직속선박작업을 비롯하여 부두지역 하역수송에 관한 전반적인 업무 일체를 하청업자인 국제실업주식회사 또는 대한통운주식회사가 이를 추가로 청부받을 계획을 1979년 10월 1일부로 실시함으로 다음과 같이 국가적으로나 개인적으로 막대한 손실을 보게될것이 확실한 것입니다.

1. 현재 미군이 직접운영하고 있는 선박 및 해상장비에 종사하고 있는 103명의 종업원들이 실직케되며 103명이 벌어들이는 월 $100,857 년 $1,210,289 의 외화수입이 손실될것이 확실합니다. 그 이유로서는 하청업자가 미군당국이 작업에 필요할시만 지역사회에서 선박(예인선) 또는 해상중장비를 빌려서 사용토록 하고 그 사용된 시간당 요금을 지급받는 제도를 추진중에 있으며 미군당국은 이러한 운영방법을 강구하여 운영비 및 인건비를 절약하고 또한 실지로 한국군에서 전혀 사용도

200

가 없는 이러한 해상장비등을 한국군 군사원조로서 이양케할 계획을 추진하고 있는 실정입니다.

2. 부두지역 미군 하역작업에 종사하는 감독, 검수, 행정직 및 장비등 기타 작업에 종사하고 있는 미군 직속종업원 82명이 실직케될것이 예상되며 이에 대한 월 $56,233 년 $674,800 의 외화수입이 줄어들 것입니다.

3. 육상수송(육상기중기 또는 중차량)에 종사하고 있는 미군직속 종업원 23명이 실직케 될것이 확실하며 이들이 벌어들이는 월 $16,320 년 $195,838 의 외화수입의 손실을 보게됩니다.

4. 추가된 하청계약 내역에 의하면 하청업자가 본선에서 화물하역시부터 미군영내에서 반출할시까지 화물의 파손 또는 분실물자까지 변상조치하는 책임 제도로서 현재 부두지역에 종사하고 있는 직속경비직원 49명이 또한 실직케 될것이 예상되며 이에 대한 월 $35,923 년 $431,074 의 외화확득에 손실을 보게되는 것입니다.

이상과 같이 총인원 257명의 종업원이 직장을 잃게됨은 물론 국가적으로도 막대한 외화수입 손실에 비하여 하청업자가 추가로 벌어드리는 외화수입은 이에 비교도 할 수 없는 년간 $199,000 이며 앞으로 물동량이 줄어들것이 확실함으로 이보다 훨신 미달될 것이라 하겠읍니다. 이러한 사실로서 국가적으로 막대한 손실은 감안하지도 않고 또한 30여년동안 종사해온 해당 257명의 종업원들의 생계문제도 아랑곳 없이 사리사욕에만 혈안이되어 덮어놓고 미군 작업을 청부받으려는 기업주들의 천만부당한 처사야 말로 마땅히 사회적으로 규탄받아야 할것이며 관계 기관으로 부터 응분의 처벌이 내려져야 할것입니다.

우리들은 30여년동안 이 업무에 종사하여 간신히 생계를 유지해 왔으며 지금은 평균 연령이 50세로서 타직에 전직조차 불가능한 처지에 있으며 이와같은 사례가 앞으로 미군 직속업무의 공병, 통신, 보급, 수송등 전국적으로 확대실시될 가능성이 충분함으

201

로 외기노조 부산지부산하 1.300여명 종합원은 물론이며 전국 외기노조 20.000여 종합원이 일치단결로서 우리들의 직장을 사수하고 악덕 기업주들의 횡포가 완전히 철회될때까지 극한투쟁으로 실력행사도 불사할 것이며 여하한 희생도 각오하고 미군 직속업무 하청전환을 반대하는 강력한 투쟁을 전개할 것을 굳게 다짐하고 있읍니다.

이와같은 사항으로 현명하신 외무부 장관 님 께서 근로자가 오로지 기득 작업권을 사수하여 생계를 유지하려는 우리들의 심정을 십분 이해 해주시고 이러한 문제가 사회적인 물의로 야기되지 않고 평화적으로 해결이 이루어 지도록 하루속히 원만히 제지해 주실것을 간절히 호소하는 바입니다.

1979년 7월

전국외국기관노동조합 부산지부

지부장 고 형 건

별첨 : 미군직속 종업원들의 년간소득 내역과 하청업자가 추가계약으로 수입되는 외화소득내역을 첨부합니다.

202

부두지역 부서별 임금 및 년간소득 내역서

분　회	인원	월급여액	년간급여액	보너스 500%	년간총액
선박부	103	$77,986	$935,832	$274,457	$1,210,289
수송부	23	12,343	148,116	47,722	195,838
경비부	49	27,864	334,368	96,706	431,074
항만연합부	82	41,913	502,956	171,844	674,800
계	257	$160,106	$1.921,272	$590,729	$2,512,001
		₩77,491,300	₩929,895,600	₩285,912,800	₩1,215,808,400

추가된 하청계획의 내역을 요약해서 말씀드린다면,

가. 미군작업에 필요한 선박(예인선) 또는 해상중장비 및 육상중장비를 미군당국이 작업에 필요할시 하청업자는 일반 지역사회에 있는 것을 대여받아 작업하도록 하고 그의 사용비용을 계산하여 미군당국은 하청업자에게 지불한다.

나. 하청업자는 본선에서 화물하역시 부터 미군영내에서 반출할시 까지 화물의 분실 또는 파손에 대하여 하청업자가 이를 변상 조치한다.

이러한 하청계약추가로 인하여 다음과 같은 결과가 발생 됩니다.

1. 현재의 미군직속 종업원수 257명이 벌어들이는 년간소득은 $2,512,001입니다.
2. 지금까지 순 하역업무만의 하청업자의 년간계약고는 $1,420,000입니다.
3. 새로 계약내용을 추가시켜서 앞으로 직속종업원들의 업무를 포함한 새회계년도 하청업자의 년간계약고는 $1,619,000입니다.
4. 즉 하청업자가 계약내용을 추가함으로서 벌어들이는 외화수입은 $199,000입니다.
5. 이상과 같이 많은 실직자가 발생되며 국가적으로 손실되는 년간 외화액은 $2,313,001입니다.

203

주한 미군 근로자 집단 해고

1. 주한 미군 당국은 부산항만 하역 작업에 종사하는 근로자 137명과 통신여단 소속 근로자 133명에 대하여 79. 8. 해고 예고서를 발부하였음.

2. 상기 해고 대상 근로자는 이에 대해 이미 농성, 시위등을 한 바 있고, 전국외기노조는 미군측의 집단 해고가 철회되지 않는 경우 극한적인 투쟁을 불사한다고 결의한 바 있음.

3. 노동청의 대책

- 부산 항만 하역 작업 근로자에 대해서는 집단 해고가 아닌 합리적인인원의 감축을 행하도록 함.
- 통신여단 근로자는 집단 해고가 아닌 시설이 폐쇄되는 지역에 국한된 해고를 행하도록 계획을 조정토록 함.
- 외교채널을 통하여 미측과 상기 문제를 해결토록 해줄 것을 요청함.

공람	안보과 관	79년 9월 6일	담당	담당관	심의관	국장	차관보	차관	장관
			煥	[signature]		[signature]	[signature]	[signature]	

204

노 동 청

노정 1454- 2193 63-8341 1979. 9. 6.

수신 외무부장관

참조 미주국장

제목 주한미군 근로자 집단 해고

1. 주한미군 당국은 정원 감축과 경비 절감을 이유로 부산항만 하역 작업에 종사하는 근로자 137명과 통신여단 소속 근로자 133명에 대하여 79. 8. 해고 예고서를 발부한 바 있으므로 79. 9월말에는 총 270명이 직장을 잃고 생계 위협에 직면하게 됩니다.

2. 이와 같은 심각한 상황하에서 전국 외국기관 노동조합 (위원장 황규무)에서는 큰 반발을 보이고 있는 바,

가. 79. 8. 22. 통신여단 소속 조합원 약 80명이 통신여단 본부에서 해고 철회를 요구하면서 농성, 시위를 한 사실이 있으며,

나. 79. 8. 30.-31 부산항만 하역 조합원 약 90명은 작업을 거부하고 미항만사령부에 집결하여 해고 반대 시위를 전개하였고,

다. 79. 9. 5. 외기노조 상무집행위원회에서는 미군측의 집단 해고 철회를 요구하기로 의하고 이 요구가 관철되지 않는 경우에는 극한적인 투쟁도 불사한다고 결의하였읍니다.

3. 당청은 집단해고로 인한 근로자의 농성, 시위등 단체행동을 예방하기 위하여 부산시 등 관계기관과 긴밀히 협조하여 사태가 악화하지 않도록 진력하고 있으나, 최근 Y.H 무역 사건과 관련한 근로자의 동태를 특별히 우려하고 이 문제에 대한 당청의 의견을 다음과 같이

205

노정 1454-　　　　　　　　　　　　　　　　　　　　　　1979. 9. 6.

알리며, 귀부의 적극적인 협조를 요청하오니 외교 경로를 통하여 원만히 해결되도록 조치하여 주시기 바랍니다.

가. 부산항만 하역 작업은 미군이 직영하고 있는 선박 및 해상 장비 작업을 경비 절감등의 이유로 하청을 계획하고 있고, 동 직종에 종사하고 있는 근로자에게 해고 예고서를 발부 한것이나 현 여건하에서는 물동량이 감소되지 않는 한, 종래의 직영에서 선박의 임대 또는 하청으로 전환하여 동 하역 업무를 수행하여야 하는 바, 따라서 해고로 인한 경비 절감에 못지 않게 비용이 가중될 것으로 예상되며, 인원 감축 방법으로는 인력감사를 실시하여 현원의 상당수를 줄일 수 있다고 판단되므로 집단 해고가 아닌 인원의 합리적 감축이 타당하다고 사료됨.

나. 통신여단 근로자 해고는 정원 조정과 기계 자동화에 의한 조치라고 주장하고 있으나 현재 가동중인 통신시설은 현원 감축으로는 유지가 곤란하다는 사실을 미측도 인정하고 있으므로 집단해고는 중지하고 다만, 현재 시설이 완전 폐쇄되는 지역의 해고에 국한 하도록 이 계획의 조정이 요청됨.

4. 주한미군에서 종사하는 근로자는 약 2만명이며, 평균 근속년수는 약 16년에 달하고 있으며, 해고후에는 새로운 직장에 취업하기는 연령상으로도 어려운 형편인 바, 앞으로의 근로자의 해고는 면밀한 계획하에 실시하여 가급적 다른 부서로의 전직 조치가 필요하고 부득이 해고할 경우에는 사전에 직업훈련등을 시행하여 해고로 인한 근로자의 충격과 노사 분규가 일어나지 않도록 미측과 협의하여 주시기 바랍니다. 끝.

노　동　청　장

206

駐韓美軍勤労者解雇反對紛糾

労 動 庁

207

1. 當事者

- 駐韓 美軍 司令部
- 全國 外國機関 勞動組合

2. 紛糾內容

駐韓 美軍司令部의 釜山港湾荷役및 通信旅団 勤労者 270名 解雇計劃에 対한 反対

所 属	現 員	解雇豫定人員	解雇豫定日
計	976名	270 名	
釜山港湾 通信旅団	199名 777 〃	137 名 133 〃	79. 9. 30 79. 9. 23

- 釜山港湾荷役은 荷役量및 豫算減少로 因한 下請試図
- 通信旅団은 定員減縮및 通信裝備 自動化에 依한 人力

3. 勤労者 動向

- 79.8.30~31 外機労組 釜山支部 勤労者 約 90名이 缺勤, 解雇豫告撤回를 要求하고 籠城
- 79.8.30 外機労組 委員長은 駐韓美軍司令官과 面談한바 美側은 解雇要求撤回 不可 通報
- 79.9.1 美軍釜山港湾 司令官이 上部에 解雇撤回 推進키로 約束하여 作業再開

208

4. 措置事項

가. 釜山港灣荷役

- 79.6.15 駐韓美軍에 下請中止要請
- 79.8.27 応札業体인 國際実業 下請抛棄通報
- 79.8.29 釜山市長및 労動庁 釜山中部所長에게 勤労者 動態 把握및 対策講究 指示
- 79.8.31 SOFA 美側 労務分科委員長, 人事處長과 当庁 労政局長 対策 協議
  - 作業量및 豫算減少로 解雇不可避
  - 解雇豫告者中 約15名은 転職可能

나. 通信旅団

- 79.8.22 人力減縮計劃 再考要請
- 駐韓美軍 人事處長과 會議를 開催 減縮計劃 撤回要請

209

5. 對 策

- ○ 駐韓美軍側과 協議를 繼續하여 解雇撤回. 轉職 · 職業訓練등 方案 模索
  (79. 9.6 SOFA 美側 労務分科委員長과 会議 豫定)

- ○ 外務部와 外交経路를 通하여 政治的 折衝을 取하도록 協議

- ○ 解雇경우에는 我國業体 就業斡旋

- ○ 集団行動 防止를 為하여 関係机関과 協助 対策 樹立

6. 展 望

韓·美间 政治的 折衝에 依하여 解決을 模索하여야 할것으로 判断되며 解決이 不可能 하면 勤労者 및 家族의 集団行動이 憂慮됨.

210

통신 여단 소속 근로자 해고문제

(79. 9. 14. 국장님 통화)

ㅇ 미측은 임시직 38명과 영구직 75명에 대해 해고 통고 (총 113 명)

ㅇ 영구직 52명은 재고용 될 것 임.

ㅇ 임시직 31-32명도 재고용될 것임.

ㅇ 내년 봄 신장비가 도입되면 추가 고용이 있을것임.

211

부산부두 노동자 해고 문제

(79. 9. 17. 국장님과 Fedak 면담)

1. 79. 9. 18. 현상태에 대한 대안을 찾기위해 미군측 내부의 회의가 열릴것 임.

2. 현재 미군은 기존 고용원이나 하청업자가 아닌 미군 기술자를 데려다가 쓰는 방안을 강구중이라함.

3. 하청계약을 체결할 수 있도록 노동청에 협조 요청

4. 재교육후 재고용을 위해 그 조건에 찬성하는 근로자의 서명을 받고 있는 바, 현재까지 34명이 서명하였음.

212

통 화 록

1. 통화시간 : 79. 10. 10. 11:00

2. 통 화 자 : 송화자 : 안보문제담당관실 김성환 사무관
   수화자 : 노동청 노정과 국제계장 김상남 사무관

3. 통화내용 :

외무부 : 부산 부두의 외기노조 노동자 해고에 대한 최근의 현황을 알려주기 바람.

노동청 : 미군 선박이 10. 8. 부산에 입항했음. 외기노조는 해운항만청의 예인선지원을 반대했으나 10. 4. 개최된 중앙노동대책위에서 미군선박에 대해 지원을 하기로 결정하고 이에대해 외기노조를 설득하기로 하였음.
현재 노동청은 노동자해고에 대한 근본대책을 수립키로 방침을 세웠으며 외기노조, 미8군측등은 노동청의 대책을 주시하면서 정관하고 있는 상태임.

79
10
10 煥 영

213

STATUS OF EUSA WATERCRAFT TRANSFER TO ROK

Type	1 Jan 79 Assigned EUSA	Given to ROK Army & Navy 26 Feb 79	To be Given ROK Army and Navy Upon Conversion of USA Port to Contract Opns	To Be Held By EUSA	Remarks Cost Price
Barge, Cargo	8	1		7	$77,800 per unit
Barge, Liquid Cargo	2		2		1 @ $72,000; 1 @ $126,3b…
Floating Crane, (89T)	1		1		$1,222,024
LCM-S	2	1	1		$174,650 per unit
LCU	2		1	1	$688,712 per unit
TUG, 65'	3	3			$316,988 per unit
TUG, 100'	3		3		$561,389 per unit
TUG	1				Retrograde to CONUS
J-Boat	1		1		$41,951 per unit
T-Boat	1	1			$134,647 per unit
Pontoon Barge	1		1		$543
Total	25	6*	10	8	Cost of water craft to be tr… ferred exceeds $5,000,000.

*In Feb 79, six watercraft transferred through JUSMAG channels; 3 to ROK Navy and 3 to ROK Army.

지14

외교문서 비밀해제: 주한미군지위협정(SOFA) 30
주한미군지위협정(SOFA) 노무 · 시설 분과위원회 1

초판인쇄 2024년 03월 15일
초판발행 2024년 03월 15일

지은이 한국학술정보(주)
펴낸이 채종준
펴낸곳 한국학술정보(주)
주 소 경기도 파주시 회동길 230(문발동)
전 화 031-908-3181(대표)
팩 스 031-908-3189
홈페이지 http://ebook.kstudy.com
E-mail 출판사업부 publish@kstudy.com
등 록 제일산-115호(2000. 6. 19)

ISBN 979-11-7217-041-7 94340
979-11-7217-011-0 94340 (set)

책에 대한 더 나은 생각, 끊임없는 고민, 독자를 생각하는 마음으로 보다 좋은 책을 만들어갑니다.